IAN STEPHEN is a writer, artist and storyteller from the Isle of Lewis. After graduating from Aberdeen University, he worked for fifteen years in the coastguard service, based in Stornoway, where he still lives. In 1995 he won the inaugural Robert Louis Stevenson award, and his poetry and fiction have been published widely. His first non-fiction book, *Waypoints*, was published to critical acclaim in 2017.

PRAISE FOR *BOATLINES*

'A writer uniquely attuned to the water, and to the relationships each boat shares with the places it shaped . . . Ian Stephen's stories restore past sea roads and river routes to life.'
David Gange, author of *The Frayed Atlantic Edge*

'This tour of Scotland's boats is rich in yarns and anecdotes, as much about those who built and sailed the boats as the vessels themselves . . . a deeply and authoritatively researched yet passionate passage around our sea-lanes and harbours.'
Mandy Haggith, author and poet

'A rich compendium of the Scottish engagement with the sea . . . Full of deep and real experience of boats and sailing them. A kind of love letter written by a man who has lived his life on and with the sea.'
Adam Nicolson, author of *Life Between the Tides*

'A remarkable book. A synthesis of history, heritage, nostalgia, traditions and all-round appreciation of the sea, and the multifarious small craft that were, and are, built to live in harmony with it.'
Iain Oughtred, boat designer

BOAT LINES

SCOTTISH CRAFT OF SEA, COAST AND CANAL

IAN STEPHEN

BIRLINN

First published in 2023 by
Birlinn Limited
West Newington House
10 Newington Road
Edinburgh
EH9 1QS

www.birlinn.co.uk

ISBN: 978 1 78027 790 5

British Library Cataloguing-in-Publication Data

A catalogue record for this book is available from the British Library

Designed and typeset by James Hutcheson
using Arno Pro and Futura

Printed and bound by Clays Ltd, Elcograf S.p.A.

Papers used by Birlinn are from well-managed forests
and other responsible sources.

CONTENTS

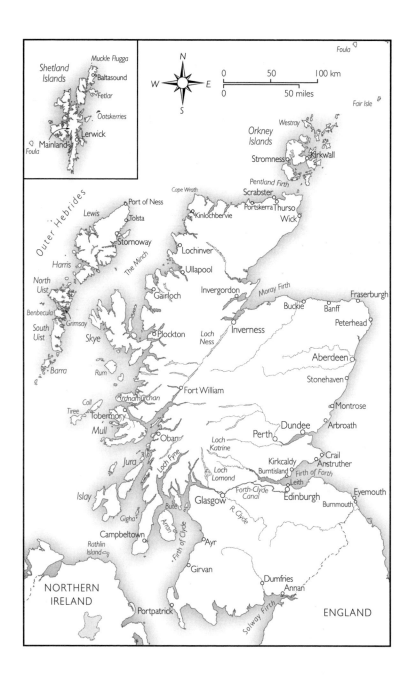

1
THE MAGNETISM
OF BOATS

PEOPLE ARE DRAWN TO HARBOURS. The space within a safe haven is now usually divided between working boats and pleasure boats, but this distinction is not a clear line. Sometimes a fishing vessel will shine with a 'yacht finish' and sometimes a sailing or rowing craft will be weathered and scarred from years of active use. As someone who lived for a dozen years in a slim townhouse, sectioned from the old sail loft in Stornoway, I can say for sure that the comings and goings of vessels still pull locals and visitors alike.

This strange magnetism is a property of wooden and fibreglass (GRP, or glass reinforced polyester) craft as well as those of welded steel or riveted iron. If you wander into the annual open art exhibitions held in The Pier, Stromness, or Taigh Chearsabhagh, Lochmaddy, the shapes of vessels will be recurring motifs, year to year. The islands council of my home territory displays a galley or *birlinn* as its banner, on paper and on cloth. The permanent collection in the City Arts Centre, Edinburgh, has strong maritime themes. The superyachts of the rich are no longer constructed at Fairlie on the Clyde, but the essential shape of William Fife's *Latifa* swings over the town as a windvane.

Vessels continue to navigate in Scotland's spoken stories and in our literature. Our first Makar, Edwin Morgan, translated the verse of

Creel boat, Fife, similar to those built by Millers of St Monans

Colmcille (St Columba),[1] who must have landed on Iona from a *curach* which had won its way through sweeping tides. Professor Alan Riach has returned to that great work of Gaelic literature, *The Birlinn of Clan Ranald*, to make a new translation for our own times.[2] Stevenson's *Kidnapped* takes us from the Forth, 'round the top' to shipwreck at the boiling waters around the Torren Rocks, off Mull. Neil Gunn also voyages from Scotland's east coast to its west in *The Silver Darlings*, an affirmation of survival, enabled by the craft that can take part in a great sea-harvest of herrings. The very different poets Norman MacCaig and W.S. Graham have both expressed the mood and tone of the night fishing of that industry in their day. And, in spoken word, the selkie tales and the myth of the woman who can harness the winds for sailors in three particular knots live on.

Over the centuries, the study of vessels has resulted in paintings and drawings, photography – still and moving – and contemporary arts projects. Many of these come to people's minds and enter conversations. The response to a vast Scottish culture of the construction and use of vessels has become a thing in itself. It is something that Scots share between themselves and with those who have crossed to visit us. The images range over the centuries.

If you enter St Clement's Church in Rodel, Harris, you will still see the lines of a *birlinn* chiselled in stone. There may be sculptor's licence, but the representation includes the technical details of rudder and rigging. Arguably, the Kintyre-born William McTaggart was an Impressionist before the movement got going. His lugsails are daubs above the colours of big waters and people are huddled into the seascape that provides for them or kills them. Will Maclean dismantles ring netters with the knowledge that comes from spending many nights aboard them and the care that suggests he is still in love with these craft. The former customs officer George Wylie hit on the idea of floating a huge paper boat to comment on the loss of the construction of more durable vessels on the Clyde. Ian Hamilton Finlay made his own models, to inhabit the sheltered waterways created in the cultivation and mining of culture that is the garden of Little Sparta. It is a vessel that provides the shape of his *Coble*, which now hangs in the Scottish Parliament building – though I'm not sure why he chose the lines of a Northumberland craft rather than one native to a section of Scotland's vast and wandering coastline.

And that bring us to the scope and limits of this summary, which I hope amounts to a celebration of the boats of Scotland, in word and image. The huge variations in forms of vessels, as we journey Scotland's coasts, speak to us of geography but are also a history of large sections of our work and our leisure. Why restrict the area of study to something we can call 'Scottish'? This is partly because the aim is to convey something more than the contrasting design of each vessel. There needs to be space to sketch some of the lore linked to that craft. Another reason is to make this book manageable. Many existing studies trace lines and construction of craft along the coastlines of an area usually termed Great Britain and Ireland. Like all who compare craft as they follow a coastline, I am indebted to the study of Eric McKee, who worked at the National Maritime Museum. (His plank-lines of a coble are the source of the Finlay work. The artist playfully added the colours of a finished vessel.) McKee proposed that vessels take the form they do for two main reasons. One is geography – the coastline, sea and weather conditions they are likely to meet. The other is function. A trawler must be able to take the strains of dragging gear, and a beach-launched boat has to 'take the ground'.

Several other excellent studies follow this line to trace working craft around the coasts. Others limit their range to provide detail and depth in their studies, say of the family of vessels which navigated between Fair Isle and Muckle Flugga. Detailed studies of the vessels of the Royal Navy and of the RNLI and of ferry operators such as David MacBrayne, now CalMac, are available. For that reason I have not attempted to outline these. There are also detailed studies of particular types of fishing craft or those from a single yard, often written by those with first-hand knowledge of the industry. My own experience is mainly of navigating and walking Scotland's coasts, mainland and islands. I have given more space to the variants of small craft, often overlooked, because they seem to me to link back to tell a story of learning, borrowing and adapting.

Arguably the kayak is the most efficient craft of all and the one best suited to exploring such an intricate coastline. These explorations have already been well served in a literature of their own. That ranges from a form of pilot book such as Sullivan, Emmott and Pickering's definitive guide to the Outer Hebrides,[3] to John MacAulay's argument ('Sliochd Nan Ron') that a history of Inuit sea-paddlers can illuminate the selkie story.[4] Brian Wilson's *Blazing Paddles*[5] remains in print and more recently David Gange's *The Frayed Atlantic Edge*[6] combines adventure, thought and analysis from a humane historian who is also an athlete of the sea.

Returning to larger craft, it seems to me that most of us don't

see 'working boats' as separate from 'pleasure craft'. We also think of
the flocks of sails sighted at regattas. We imagine the craft composed
of stretched skins which carried voyaging monks over oceans as well
as tideways. We laugh at the wry comments of the puffer captain who
didn't come up the Clyde on a two-masted toothbrush. The range, in
time and coastal geography, is vast.

This book can only speak of a biased selection of Scotland's vessels.
My hope is that the images and stories give some sense of the soul of
these boats as well as their appearance. I have been fortunate in being
able to navigate some of the countless searoads from Rathlin to Unst.
In 2007 I had the honour of skippering a traditional Lewis craft on a
voyage to join the Moray Firth Flottila. I hope that these experiences
have given a sense of kinship with the hardy folk who built, launched
and worked these craft. This was never only a man's world. The herring
industry could not have happened without the women who gutted
one per second, and mended the torn dark cotton miles of nets.
Thankfully, women now also take command of our ferries and supply
ships as well as our racing yachts.

There have been several specialised studies of the working,
sailing craft of the British Isles. Other publications have focused in
great detail on one particular type of power-driven vessel, such as
J. Reid's *Steam Drifters Recalled*,[7] which is the most diligent listing of
research on these ships. This book aims to describe and picture only
a biased sampling of vessels which have somehow become secular
icons. Their very shapes speak out. The approach will take the form of
a different kind of circumnavigation. Scotland is not an island, but it is
possible to transit from the south-east to the south-west coasts by the
reopened Forth and Clyde Canal. It is also usually possible to transit
from mainland to islands, weather and machinery permitting. Let's
respect tradition and tour Scotland sunwise, boat by boat.

NOTES

(1) St Columba, The Maker on High, *trans. Edwin Morgan (Edinburgh, Mariscat Press, 1997).*

(2) Alasdair Mac Mhaighstir Alasdair (Alexander MacDonald), The Birlinn of Clanranald, *trans. Alan Riach (Newtyle, Angus, Kettilonia, 2015).*

(3) Mike Sullivan, Robert Emmott and Tim Pickering, The Outer Hebrides – Sea Kayaking Around the Isles and St Kilda *(Gwynedd, Pesda Press, 2010).*

(4) John M. MacAulay, Seal-folk and Ocean Paddlers: Sliochd Nan Ron *(Cambridge and Strond, White Horse Press, 1998).*

(5) Brian Wilson, Blazing Paddles – a Scottish Coastal Odyssey *(Edinburgh, Birlinn, 2019).*

(6) David Gange, The Frayed Atlantic Edge: A Historian's Journey from Shetland to the Channel *(London, William Collins, 2019).*

(7) J. Reid, Steam Drifters Recalled: Spey to Shetland and Stornoway *(Moray, 2002).*

2
THE STEAM DRIFTER

IN THE YEAR 1903, A fishing vessel was making her way from Stromness to Wick harbour, then the largest herring port in Europe. She might have had the lines of a gentleman's yacht but she was a working boat, powered by steam. That was why she had been up and round the corner to Orkney with only three souls aboard. With repairs to her compound engine of 15 horsepower completed, she set out to rejoin the fleet. The forecast was not that great, but this was a vessel of nearly 78 feet, drawing close to 8 feet and less than three years old. The repairs held good and she cleared Duncansby Head. From the chart, she was nearly home, but even a routine trip on the sea never is. Rounding the corner, she faced the immense waves which rise quickly there, in a south-easterly wind. The tide sets very strongly at that point and runs for a longer period to the north.

Even today, Wick and many other ports on the north-east coastline of Scotland are often closed in easterly gales. Standing on the long breakwater will give some sense of what it must be like to be out from a haven in rising wind. You will need to wedge yourself in somewhere secure. Even the creativity of the Stevenson family of engineers could not devise coastal works that would be completely effective against the heavyweight punches of the North Sea. *Violet*, WK157, was at last gaining a grip on the waters of Wick Bay when her

Steam drifter (circa 1900–30)

steering gear failed. She was driven back round Noss Head.

Keiss Sands could not have been a soft landing. Many of the steam drifters were built in steel, but this was a ship of timber construction. She was built by Chambers and Colby of Lowestoft, a town joined to the Scottish ports by the searoad and by the trade that followed the migration of herring. Her skipper would have known that no vessel of any build could withstand the pounding she'd get in the rising south-easterly. He set with his two crew to lash hatches together to form a raft. They did that with him, but neither would trust to it. Any decision was taken out of their hands as the raft, with that one man clinging on, was swept off the flooded deck.

The wreck was sighted. A shore station for a 'pulling' lifeboat had been developed in Ackergill, some 5 nautical miles to the south of the grounding. She was launched into a huge surf but one which was shoving the double-ended craft in the right direction. Four of her oars were smashed as she approached *Violet*. The same breaking wave took away one of the wreck's crew, still clinging to the long drifter. The lifeboat herself was in imminent danger now but a rescue rocket, fired by the shore party, took a line out to the grounded vessel. The remaining man was rescued and the lifeboat herself gained the shore with all her crew. The skipper's improvised raft was also driven ashore further to the north. One life and one ship were lost.

This is a story which could, sadly, be repeated with variations, all around the world's coasts. It is as well to remember the losses when we admire the forms of past or present vessels. Even so, the work of shipwrights, engineers, navigators and crews must be recognised. Some of these vessels, such as *Violet*, were built to a designer's plans, but others took their shape from inherited experience.

The distances between Scottish ports are often considerable. As an example, once I sailed non-stop from my home port of Stornoway to Lerwick harbour. The plot showed that the distance covered was the same as if I'd gone direct to the harbour in the most southern of the Faroe Islands. Herring drifters under sail or steam would take such passages in their stride, following the seasonal fishing round the coasts. Catches and business were good. This permitted the building of a great fleet at a cost which was a huge investment for the day. Running costs were also high. Wind was free but more fickle than coal. The comparative reliability of steam propulsion allowed the fleet to range from Lowestoft to Baltasound. The vessels had to be longer than the sailing drifters, to give space to bulky boilers, but this also gave them a longer waterline. That is the secret of speed in a displacement craft. It applied to working boats as well as the steam yachts of the rich.

We should not forget that they were dirty, most of the time. I think of the witty yarns passed down from my mother's father, a Lewisman, telling of his days as a share-fisherman, often working for east-coast skippers. I had an image of tan sails and hemp ropes and imagined the sounds of creaking tackles and wind on flax. But my father spoke of his father, William, in Fraserburgh, wheeling barrow after barrow of coal down narrow planks to refuel the drifters. My Lewis grandfather, Murdo, probably worked on both wind-driven and power-driven drifters. The lines of smoking funnels earned them the nickname Woodbines. From a distance this is picturesque but there are first-hand accounts of the mucky reality, seen close-up.

Pleasure craft were not always that welcome in busy working harbours. W.E. Sinclair logged the visit of his yawl-rigged Falmouth quay punt, *Joan*, into a Moray Firth port when the herring season was in full swing:

> From Berwick we made Peterhead, a weary passage of three days. As we drew near we saw a number of steam drifters making for the harbour. We thought we should do well to let them get out of our way. But as we sailed and looked, their number did not seem to diminish. As fast as one dozen entered the harbour another dozen came up from the horizon and maintained a never-ending line.
>
> I don't like steamboats of any kind, speaking from a yacht-sailing point of view, but steam fishing-boats are the kind I like least. They are so dirty and tarry and fish-oily that a touch from one of them will slime a good-looking boat forever. We did not want to go near one in the *Joan* and yet judged that we should have to enter the harbour where they lay so that we might get ashore.[1]

Steam Drifters Recalled gives some sense of the sheer scale of the enterprise and the number of ships. Yet this was a type of vessel with a fairly short history. A few did survive two world wars, some seeing service as anti-submarine craft in both, and just a few examples remain afloat. But the creeks of the British Isles contain an industrial archaeology of ribs and boilers. One such wreck is outlined in the journal of a local history society in Heddon-on-the-Wall.[2] The Tyne's mud has preserved some features. The same article points to a late example, in steel, from 1930, now a floating museum in Great Yarmouth. Diesel engines proved more efficient and took up less space.

If we remain in the great bight of the Moray Firth for a while, we can gain a glimpse of the volume and quality of work which was generated in a period of 25 years or so. Another active local history society, at Hopeman, has gathered a collection of archive material that is both informative and emotive. It is difficult to imagine such a fleet between the bulwarks of a tidal harbour that now hosts lobster boats and pleasure vessels, all small craft. Along at Buckie, the archive of McIntosh Boat and Shipbuilders lists the firm's steam drifters with pride. The building of a steam liner of over 92 feet led to a commission for what was probably the first steam drifter to be launched in the district – the *Frigate Bird* BF398, launched in 1900. She was of composite construction with a hull of timber but deckhouses of iron. For engine buffs, the *Banffshire Advertiser* listed her vitals but also gives some clues to the running costs:

> . . . of the compound surface condensing type, 45hp with 20″ cylinders. The boiler is of the ordinary marine type, with two furnaces. There is a handy donkey engine for pumping etc., & forward is fitted a powerful Beccles winch which is supplied with steam from the same boiler, which works up to 130 lbs of steam pressure. In the bunkers there are 40 tons of coal, sufficient at 8 tons per week to carry the vessel for the next five weeks.[3]

The same firm built a further 18 steam drifters before that tide turned. Wherever they were built, the combination of the long hull and driving force of steam gave the steam drifter the range to migrate so that all the herring ports of Scotland would be packed gunnel to gunnel and funnel after funnel. I believe that the stories passed down, running parallel to the technical details, can give another slant to the picture we can now hold in our minds. This one is told on the west coast, Lewis in particular, but I'd bet there is a similar lore wherever these long vessels were berthed.

Did you hear about the man from Point who had a bit too much to drink in the port of Stornoway? You might know that the folk from out on the Eye Peninsula have a friendly way and so they use the word for 'dear' a lot. It was *a ghràidh* this and *a ghràidh* that. Anyway this fellow knew he wasn't going to make it home so he found himself somewhere down the harbour with a bit of warmth. That was fine but he wakes in the morning with a head being hammered and a thirst like no other. He looks up to see a sooty black figure with a couple of bright eyes. He's shovelling away, stoking a great fire. The piston is going and the screw is turning.

The stoker gets just as big a shock as he sees the stowaway rising from the coal-heap. 'Where the hell did you spring from?'

'Satan a ghràidh, when I was alive I was from Point.'[4]

NOTES

(1) 'Cruise of the Joan: Peterhead steam drifters, 1927', on Sailing By: Tales from our oceans, seas, coasts and inland waterways website: https://www.sailing-by.org. uk/cruise-of-the-joan-peterhead-steam-drifters-1927/. (W.E. Sinclair, Cruises of the 'Joan', *several editions, reprinted Lodestar Books.)*

(2) See online article by Andy Curtis, with additional material from Arthur Newton (checked August 2022): http://heddonhistory. weebly.com/blog/steam-drifter-2.

(3) 'The Frigate Bird BF398', on McIntosh Boat & Shipbuilders website: http://glennmci.brinkster.net/sds/sds.html.

(4) Heard from David Jardine after an exchange of stories, Ullapool Book Festival, 2011.

3
THE MORAY FIRTH SCAFFIE

MOST SCOTS WILL KNOW THE word, derived from 'scavenger', as a term for a bin-man, but this has nothing to do with the name given to generations of boats. 'Scaffie' is not so far from the word 'skiff', if that word is passed down over the years in a good Buchan voice. Most people would think of a 'skiff' as a small rowing craft, but that was not always so. It seems the Middle English word 'skif' has the same European root as the word we now say as 'ship'. At the height of their development, built to a length of over 40 feet and often two-masted, the scaffie could indeed be thought of as a ship. But they could never be heavy. These craft were clinker-built, of overlapping larch planks, partly because this was the proven Norse way and partly because the method results in a construction that is strong but light. Frames or ribs are placed after the shell of planking is complete.

There is no designer's name fixed to the form of vessel but the characteristic shape is distinct. She has a pronounced curve at her bow and a steep rake in her sternpost. Planks rise from a short keel before they round out to make a very buoyant shape, but taken in sharp at both ends. Everything is a trade-off. If her 'freeboard' from water-level to top plank were any higher she would have better protection from invading waves but be difficult to row. If her keel went to pretty well her full length overall, with vertical stem and stern, she would keep

A typical scaffie shape

on conceptual tracks like a train but be very difficult to turn. That might be an asset when crossing an ocean, but would be a danger if you were trying to turn into a doglegged breakwater or navigating a tight channel between reefs on either side. Many of the Moray Firth breakwaters and shores are exactly like that. Most of the home havens could only be accessed with a bit of tide under you, so your craft would need to be hauled up and down the shore to safety.

Decking might provide some protection to a crew out at night or in transit as the herring industry followed the shoals. But that would add weight and cost to an otherwise open vessel. In one night of 1848, 41 craft were lost off the port of Wick as they ran from a sudden storm. Wick had the largest number of registered craft at that time, followed by Fraserburgh. But between Stonehaven and Wick an estimated 148 vessels were lost. The herring industry was an immense international trade for the day and an inquiry was initiated to examine the causes of such tragic losses and any means of limiting them in future. The findings of Captain John Washington under the title 'Report on the Loss of Life, and Damage Caused to Fishing Boats on the East Coast of Scotland, in the Gale of 19th August 1848' made several recommendations, including consideration to decking the open scaffies. Drawings of existing craft and proposed safer designs were included. There was no suggestion that quality of build or shortage of skills to sail and work these vessels were factors. In fact, the most concise description of the scaffie, with a drawing and a comment on the skills of the Moray Firth boatbuilders, is included in the report:

> The typical herring lugger was the Buckie boat, variously called a scaffie, scaffa, or scaith. Length of keel was 32ft to 33ft, but a curved stem and a sternpost raking at 45deg increased the overall length to 41ft, beam was 13ft, and depth 4ft 9in. The clinker-built hull was lightly constructed of 1½in larch planking with oak ribs, keel, stem and sternpost, and the boat was coated with a crude varnish. As the hull only weighed 3 tons, it could easily be hauled up a beach. Draught light was, for'ard 2ft 6in, aft 2ft 9in, but with a loaded displacement of 16 tons, the boat drew 4ft 3in for'ard, and 4ft 9in aft, a ton of ballast being carried . . . Many of these scaffies were built by J. & W. McIntosh, of Portessie, a firm of high repute down to the last days of sail.[1]

Much has been written about how both purpose and geography combined with measures of tradition and innovation to shape working craft. These are gathered into a tight thesis in Eric McKee's *Working Boats of Britain: Their Shape and Purpose*.[2] The author worked at the National Maritime Museum. He includes such data as statistics on prevailing winds to propose their influence on the forms discovered for coastal fishing craft. Changes such as decking were resisted due to weight as well as cost. Another objection was that crew up on deck were more vulnerable to being washed overboard than if they were deep down within an open craft.

The excellent McIntosh Boatbuilders website describes how a bulkhead and a foredeck also created a cuddy or den, which made a hard life that bit more bearable.[3] Photographs of later scaffies often show 'three-quarter decking', which provided sheltered stowage space as well as shedding some of the water which came over the bow and beam. A canvas cover could give further protection when the scaffie was running for home, probably heavy with her catch. I have organised swamping tests on two different examples of a boat of proven seaworthy shape but completely undecked. One was 27 feet overall and one at 33 feet. Both were carried out in a sheltered harbour in calm conditions but with rig and sail up. Additional lead ballast was installed to simulate weight of additional crew and gear. The vessels remained very stable up until they were about two-thirds full. At that point the 'free-surface' effect, of water rolling back and fore, took over. Buoyancy was installed in the form of inflatable large fenders, with one litre for each kilo of ballast or other additional weight required. Without this, a fully ballasted vessel would sink. Distribution of the buoyancy was found to be crucial. The conclusion was that the rig had to be dropped as soon as possible if significant water came aboard. That had to be removed as quickly as possible by bailing or pumps before further water was taken. Of course, the vessel is more vulnerable to taking in more water, once a wave is shipped. The vessel would have a greater margin of safety if it were possible to work it at least part-decked. Covers over working hatches would also help.

As there is no extant example of the larger scaffie, the period photographs on sites such as McIntosh Boatbuilders and the Angus Macleod archive give us the best impression of these historic craft.[4] There are surviving examples of the smaller versions which also embody the essential shape. These can be seen in the courtyard of the Wick Heritage Centre and, way down the herring route, at Bridlington where the 1977 *Anne* is being preserved. Her lines were taken from the historic *Gratitude*, BF252. Many would say that this 1896 vessel, built at Portknockie by one George Innes, embodies the essentials of the craft even though she would be termed a 'scaffie yawl'. Just to add to confusion, the term 'yawl' or 'yole' here does not apply to the rig but to her size. At 25 feet (7.6 metres) with a beam of 8 feet 6 inches (2.6 metres) she would be at the upper end of a boat so described.

A full-scale replica of this legend was built for Portsoy Festival by Alex Slater and Sinclair Young and launched 100 years after the original. Another slightly scaled-down example but with that same stunning shape was built in Ardnamurchan by the farmer and boatbuilder Sandy Macdonald. I have seen both the Portsoy craft and Sandy's *Gratitude*, and I have had the pleasure of sailing with Sandy on his version. She is both fast and manoeuvrable. Sandy lets her heel a bit to increase her waterline length. Unlike the working boats, her ballast is now carried externally in weight bolted to her oak keel. This method is also applied to contemporary Orkney yoles as they prepare for their regattas. Traditional boats carried their ballast as round stones. As well as shape, the rig helps define the craft. The working scaffies carried the larger forward sail as a dipping lug. Sandy's smaller boat has a handy cutter rig (two triangular foresails) with a manageable standing lug as the main. The original rig can be studied in images of Alex Slater's replica, named *Obair-Na-Ghaol*.

Again we have a trade of risks and gains. This rig requires both skill and coordination from crew. The head (top edge) of the sail is secured to a long and heavy pole (yard) before that is hoisted up the mast. When you 'tack' to change course, so the wind is taken on the opposite side, the whole thing has to be 'dipped' or tilted and swung around the mast. Then the whole rig has to be dropped and unhooked so that the twist now introduced into the wire strop can be removed. Next, the tackle which raises yard and sail must be passed across the boat so it is secured on the new 'weather' side. On larger craft there may be an additional stay or 'burton' so that must be eased on one side and hardened on the other.

The bigger the boat, the bigger the sail and the heavier the gear. This single sail, tacked on the bow of the 25-footer, is plenty to handle. A 40-foot open boat, carrying such a rig, required immense skill and great physical strength to work it. Now imagine you are one of the crew seeking a narrow gap in the reefs, to regain shelter. The wind has gone north-easterly so the waves are building high behind you. Your skipper must make absolutely sure the wind is taken just off the stern lest it 'back' the sail and swing it violently to the other side. If that happens, the mast might come down, if you're lucky. Otherwise you will probably capsize. He might have one of the crew looking astern all the time, so he can keep his own eye and his instinct on a line to an entrance that is probably concealed in spray. There might be a commentary on these waters, spoken by the bowman, warning the skipper of what's coming. And the skipper might make a sign with a finger, off the tiller. That could well suggest lowering nearly all the sail to stop her from surfing out of control or powering up towards the wind, off that vital imaginary line. But the gale is tugging at the tanned flax. Cold fingers are gripping it, holding the forward and aft bottom parts down, so just a scrap of cloth is exposed.

At this point the skipper can see nothing ahead so he is completely dependent on the bowman, looking out under the cloth. If your speed is equal to that of the wave you will have no steerage. That skipper's finger might point to raising the sail another foot or so. And so, by negotiation and sensitivity and teamwork your scaffie comes in with enough depth under her so she can glide on to find shelter. At that point you might just breathe again.

I had the previous experience of sailing an even smaller scaffie yole. She was the *Sea Spray*, moored at Stonehaven, when I was a student at Aberdeen. I'd say she was no more than 19 feet, nose to tail, but she also carried a bowsprit and a single fair-sized jib. She had a standing lug too, probably because the smaller craft were often sailed 'short-handed'. Mike Aird and his wife Avril would sail her out to go handlining for cod. You could get caught out even with this handier rig. Once Mike took me out against his better judgement when a Force 6 or so seemed to ease. We were just clear of the breakwater when all sail had to come down sharpish as a squall hit. It's then you realise the shape of the vessel is not for style. It appears to the eye as beautiful because it is just right for its purpose. Mike had to know she would turn at that point. He had rigged 'brails' for the very purpose of taking power out of the cloth in a hurry. These lines gather in the sail from its leach, folding it in like a wing. The word is thought to stem from the Old French *braiel*, come down from medieval Latin. There is also a Gaelic phrase, recorded in Lewis, for that same action: *an t-abhsa*, from the Norse *halsa*, 'to clew up sail', as used in the Lewis phrase *abhsadh a chromain-luch* – 'shortening sail kite-fashion'.[5] It makes the analogy with a gannet folding its wings to drop. This is poetry of the most practical nature. The pressure came out of the mainsail and we were able to make a sweet turn back into shelter.

I now have Admiralty chart 1462 out from the press: *Harbours on the North and East Coasts of Scotland* reveals that none of the Moray Firth harbours have deep water all the way in. Most have a sudden shallowing in their approach. That makes steep waves inevitable when swell and waves pile in. The scaffie combined good tracking with good turning ability. As a working fishing boat she was limited, due to her lack of volume, and she was vulnerable. The cumulative experience of seafarers and builders was to combine to pass on many of her qualities to later and larger vessels, built to take their share of the great harvest of herring.

It was on the west coast I was to fully appreciate what a handy craft the scaffie was. Sandy Macdonald took me out on *Gratitude* from an anchorage in Loch Sunart. She was balanced. We went short-tacking between islands so Sandy could demonstrate her qualities.

The boatbuilder happened to be an expert sailor and that fed into his drawings for the rig. I found you could depend on her making the turn. As there were two of us, I could allow the flying jib to 'back', helping us tack as I let the inner staysail go over. Then the jib would be hardened on the new side and we would accelerate. Sandy had gone for the compromise of half-decking her. The sheathed plywood added very little weight but allowed any water shipped to run off at the side decks or stern. She had no inboard, only a small outboard on a bracket, and I don't think we touched it that morning. *Gratitude* would be limited as a workboat but was simply one of the finest day-sailing boats I have ever had the pleasure of helming. With these variations and on that scale (just over 20 feet on deck), she could very easily be the basis of a fleet of like pleasure craft.

NOTES

(1) '*The Evolution of the Scaffie*', on *McIntosh Boat & Shipbuilders website: http://glennmci.brinkster.net/scaffies/scaffies.html. Taken from Captain John Washington, 'Fishing Boats (Scotland): Copy of Captain Washington's Report on the Loss of Life and on the Damage Caused to Fishing Boats on the East Coast of Scotland, in the Gale of the 19th August 1848', London, House of Commons, 1849.*

(2) Eric McKee, Working Boats of Britain: Their Shape and Purpose *(London, Conway Maritime Press, 1983).*

(3) 'The Evolution of the Scaffie', as above: http://glennmci.brinkster.net/scaffies/scaffies.html.

(4) The Angus Macleod Archive website: www.angusmacleodarchive.org.uk.

(5) George Henderson, The Norse Influence on Celtic Scotland *(Glasgow, J. Maclehose and Sons, 1910).*

4
THE
PLUMB-ENDED
FIFIE

THROUGHOUT THE NINETEENTH CENTURY, THE range and volume of the herring industry continued to grow. Towards the turn into the twentieth, this was an explosion of commerce. The 'Scotch-cure', which was adapted from an earlier Dutch method, resulted in a proven product for export. Quality control was crucial and that meant that only the freshest of fish could be used. As the vessels ranged further from safe havens, speed became a major issue. The catch was worthless if the crew couldn't make the market before their fish deteriorated. Decking became vital, for safety and to provide some dry bunks for the crew and protection for the silver.

The swift development as well as the sense of opportunity are caught in Neil Gunn's *The Silver Darlings*. In the excerpt below, Finn has commissioned one of the larger of the open boats. From her given measurements, she is not as short in the keel as the scaffie, with her pronounced curve at the bow and rake at the stern:

> He was yet to own a boat of over 40 feet, all decked, but such a boat for the herring fleet was still far in the future. 'South-built', with 30 feet keel, 34 feet 6 inches over all, and open from stem to stern, she seemed a large and splendid vessel to her crew.[1]

Fifie (near-plumb ends, based on Reaper*)*

I doubt that Neil Gunn plucked these dimensions from the air. According to the records of McIntosh of Portessie, a scaffie with a keel of just over 30 feet would be over 40 feet overall. Gunn has caught the signs of changing times in his historical novel. This is a portrait of a skipper keen to go the distance. The scaffie became less favoured and the powerful Fifie, with her long keel and stately, plumb ends, satisfied the need for speed and resisted drift. A longer ship is only faster if she can carry enough cloth to power her to the full. But she could also carry more of the valuable catch. Against that, there is a far greater investment and more hands are needed to work her. The cost of gear will rise in proportion. Fishing is gambling. Both the statistical evidence from Fishery Office registrations and the documentation by the young art of photography reveal that the fishery was carried out by vessels of very different scales in most of the herring ports.

Historic vessels are more than picturesque because they affected the lives of so many. This is acknowledged in the efforts, often by volunteers, to maintain important examples by restoring them and then keeping them in commission. Thus we are able to take a close look at three surviving Fifies. They are of different scale and also have other variations.

On 15 September 1890, a trim Fifie of 45 feet overall was launched at Arbroath by James Weir Boatbuilders. She drew 6 feet and was close to 14 in the beam. Like many of the scaffies before her, she was powered by a dipping lug forward with a standing lug as an aft or mizzen sail. Over the years she had several Kelvin motors and carries a K3 still, rated at 66 horsepower. She has probably survived because she continued to work. It's fresh water, lying, that destroys even close-grained larch and oak. A coorse east wind will dry and crack even the resinous pitch-pine, the most favoured of timbers for the larger vessels, which were carvel-built with flush planking.

By 1976 the last in the line of her family owners had retired from the sea. Hobson Rankin took her on as a labour of love. Working with a co-owner, the vessel was returned to sail-power and kept afloat. She gave me my first experience of the bigger type of dipping lug when I was invited aboard during the inimitable Wick Festival of Poetry, Folk and Jazz, run by librarian, poet and painter David Morrison in the early 1980s. I found my way to the harbour and was drawn to a long black shape, with its yellow-gold cove line and signature arrow-tip flourish. This was the craft launched at James Weir's in 1890. The generous guys were taking anyone interested out for a sail round the bay. Their steady Kelvin, poetry in its own right, took us clear of the long breakwater. Then we hauled together on the tackle to hoist the mainsail. It was light breeze, but I trust my memory of our tracking and our turn.

All that planking below the waterline – the keel running near the full length of the boat – really did keep her steady in a groove and unshaken by a short-chop. They would need a bit of way on her and a bit of room to swing her length around. We were briefed in lining up to meet the yard as it came down smartly but under control. We would not attempt to dip the spar around the mast to transfer the sail to the other side. Instead, it was all lowered and unhooked. We could then pass it aft so the forward tip of that yard could return forward on the other side of the mast. The hoop of iron or 'traveller' which would hold the yard close to the mast was hooked back on. While this was happening, the sheet tackle was also transferred across. The halyard tackle, which would also act as the mainstay, was transferred to the new weather side at the same time. We did not lose too much ground before the sail was up and driving again. I thought of Murdo Smith (Murchadh 'An Fhionnlaigh), fisherman and my Lewis grandfather, as we regained the outer harbour. He would likely have worked on very similar craft to this, at times. Wick would perhaps have been the first port of call after leaving from Stornoway, unless they were bound for the Orkney or Shetland fishing.

You don't really see a boat sailing when you're on it. In 2007, I was aboard a vessel which had transited from Lewis to join in the Moray Firth Flotilla, mainly former working craft. The event was directed by Sinclair Young, co-owner of *Obair-Na-Ghaol*. We were on our first day out from Wick, south-bound for Lybster. Seas were very high. Our own 33-foot open *sgoth Niseach* was comfortable, her full beam and buoyant stern, helping us rise to the big ones. But we reefed her down and tacked and gybed to keep pace with a historic craft which had been towed over from Norway to join the flotilla. The inshore craft was struggling in the big water while the *sgoth*, developed for offshore fishing from Norse types, felt safe. Then we saw *Isabella Fortuna* come over the top of a dip and remain, lodged high. She seemed a long way above us. This is where that long keel comes into its own. A *sgoth* is short-keeled, a bit like a scaffie in that respect, though a very different shape. We could use that to our advantage to work like a collie at sea, and the simplicity of our single dipping lugsail helped. But the Fifie, since generously passed on to the Wick Historical Society, seemed to have to do very little at all. The Norwegian boat, *Knut*, was plenty fast though she looked jittery, surfing down the big waves. *Isabella Fortuna* just hung in there, keeping close. The crew of the *Isabella* hailed us to check we were happy to hold close to the Norwegians as we seemed to be in a very handy craft.

All my own team were more than happy to slow our own progress and hang out with our neighbours so I just lifted my arm to wave *Isabella* on. What a sight she made, two tan sails above the clean black and cream foam at bow and stern. A couple of days on, out of Helmsdale, we were treated to the sight of the larger classes of Fifies driving on. These are also historic craft which have had major restorations and both are run by charities.

One of these was *Reaper*, built at Sandhaven in 1902, first registered as FR958 and also carrying a dipping lug main and a substantial standing lug as mizzen. She could send a jib out on a long bowsprit which could be pulled back on deck, in harbour. Her later working years, now engined, were spent in Shetland, first at the herring and latterly taking small cargoes between the islands. Her working life was over in 1974. She was later bought by the Scottish Fisheries Museum at Anstruther. This remains her base. A series of renovations and repairs, with a range of funders, have kept her in commission. A boat club, linked to the museum, runs her and she takes part in a circuit of visits to maritime festivals. Visitors are welcomed aboard and their generous donations keep history alive.

Thinking back to that day of the flotilla, it was fresh all right, bright with it, but there was no sea running as the fleet worked their way into the bight of the Firth. Small craft like ours were bound into Cromarty. *Reaper* and her fellow Fifie *Swan* would moor elsewhere. We were in just the position to watch the big ones fly by. I thought *Reaper* might have a reef or two in but she had both full lugs up as if racing for market. I'd already seen how her skippers, mostly retired fishermen with a lifetime's experience of warping in and out of tight harbours, could manage her under auxiliary power. This took judicious use of warps and a crew who had also swerved long boats in and out of short entrances. Now I saw how the team on *Reaper* could drive their ship with pride. A small steam capstan allowed for the hoisting of the substantial weight of such a spread of canvas and the tackle which supported it. Such developments allowed for the herring fishing vessels to be built on this scale. Her current one was built by McDonald Brothers of Portsoy in the 1920s but is now driven by compressed air. The power and pace of *Reaper* were as impressive as any warship. But this was a craft built to provide.

I'd also been aboard the *Swan* before. She was built in Lerwick and launched in May 1900. At 60.5 feet in the keel and 67 on deck, she was the largest of the Fifies built at that port. At first she carried a similar rig to *Reaper*. In 1908 this was altered to a handier gaff ketch arrangement, with two foresails. She was rescued from a muddy grave in Hartlepool and transported home for restoration. This has also taken an inspiring combination of vision and administration, with huge volunteer support. Since her relaunch, with the gaff rig kept as a typical Shetlandic variation, she has seen constant service in sail-training. I joined her on one of her visits to the Western Isles, mainly working with school groups. She has a comfortable motion. As the strain is distributed between several sails, the rig is easier to handle than two huge lugsails. My elder son, Sean, helped rally a group of schoolfriends to be able to join her for a leg of the Tall Ships race that took them from Bergen to Shetland. That wasn't yesterday, but all remain best of pals. The ethos aboard worked its spell. A charitable trust continues to maintain her by keeping her in use, often in education projects. Membership of the boat clubs linked to *Swan* and *Reaper* helps that work.

The sight of the gleaming green *Swan*, with her very different shape of wings, was counterpoint to the longer and higher *Reaper* on that Moray Firth transit.[2] I remembered the greeting when I boarded *Reaper* at Anstruther. 'Git that bonnet in your pocket. You're on the east coast noo.' It was green. This fisherman's superstition was new to me. A *sgoth* built at Port Nis (Port of Ness) could be green and so it seemed could a craft from Lerwick. Even these limited experiences, on chosen days, give some insight into what these fishermen faced at a time before reliable weather forecasts, communications and safety equipment. You can well understand how taboos and legends survived. Sometimes the changes in conditions are so sudden that they seem to need some explanation. A tradition widespread around the Moray Firth tells of the woman who can curse the vessels of rivals. For a price she will create the fishing grounds in her own enamelled vessel. Shells are set afloat and small waves set in motion until the rival vessels are swamped. Another story with endless variations, told east coast and west, is of the woman who can sell you a favourable wind. A version, probably come from the Moray Firth but settled in Stromness, tells of the three straws. Their ends are whipped neat and tight, but in threads of different colour. For safety reasons I cannot divulge these colours here. One will bring you a fair wind when you cast the straw overboard. So why should you need another? You don't, but no sailor can resist driving his boat to the limit. The second colour can be cast if you feel she can take it. But on no account can you mix that up with the third one. That must never be released, but it has to be carried for the spell to work. In the tale, someone on board does say she could take a bit more, and sure enough the second straw has them heeling over with the waves lapping the top plank. They are so near home so fast that another crewman says, what harm could the last one do now?

As soon as that straw hits the wave the sky darkens. The tempest takes their keel clear of the water. They are hurtling through the air, clinging to the gunnels with their fingernails, wailing and wishing they'd had a bit more sense. Then there is a crunch as they are cast at the very feet of the woman who sold them the winds. 'Ye daft chiels,' she says, 'Mind I tellt ye clair as the licht o the morn nae tae cast yon third straw. Your boatie's back far it startit.'

NOTES

*(1) Neil M. Gunn, The Silver Darlings (London, Faber and Faber, 1941; 1986)
p. 571.*

*(2) 'The History of the Swan', The Swan Trust website: https://www.swantrust.com/
about/history.*

5

THE ULTIMATE
SAILING DRIFTER?

FOR ALL THIS TALK OF horses for courses, folk will always ask what is the bonniest boat of them all. East coast or west, northern isles or southern, you will still hear this discussed endlessly by those who rest a foot against a rail at a harbourside. The vessel I would most love to helm, *Muirneag* SY486, no longer exists. And yet she does. There is strong documentation of her from her builder's records. That is augmented by measurements taken as she was beached in 1947 for breaking for fenceposts at Balallan, Loch Erisort. These were taken by George Macleod at the time, and drawn up by Harold A. Underhill, of Glasgow. These lines are still available and were used as the basis for Mr Macleod's 1955 model, now housed at the National Maritime Museum, Greenwich. The data, photographs and other archive materials as well as the same drawings were later compiled by model-maker Gordon Williams. His version took 2,294 hours to build[1] and is now in Museum nan Eilean, Stornoway. The Scottish Fisheries Museum at Anstruther displays a model by David P.H. Watson, of Connecticut. Before the Covid lockdown in March 2020, I was able to visit the workshop of retired Stornoway shipwright Dick Stenhouse. I could study his copy of the detailed plans which resulted in his own accurate scale model of this same vessel.

This case study surely raises the key question of why an inanimate

Zulu (steep rake at stern, based on Muirneag*)*

object can inspire such devotion in celebrating her shape. The models help answer this, even more than the emotive photographs held in many public collections. There are also a few feet of moving film[2] which show the last of the herring drifters that worked under sail alone. She was registered in Stornoway and owned and worked from that port all her life. The fragments of her also remain on Lewis but *Muirneag* was, to many, the epitome of the Zulu class of drifter. The nickname of 'Zulu' stuck, perhaps because something made the fishers admire the tenacity of the warriors who were standing up to British imperialism at the time. The form was born in the shipyards bordering the Moray Firth and SY486, launched from the yard of William McIntosh, Portessie in 1903, was among the last to be constructed. Markets were buoyant and companies and skippers were becoming confident enough to commission the more expensive steam drifters.

The class was born not many miles away, at the yard of William Campbell at Lossiemouth. In 1873, a vessel like no other was floated. It took a confident skipper to break with proven tradition, but this one underlined that, giving her the name *Nonesuch*. She was clinker-built, but by the mid 1880s the Zulus were being built on a 50-foot keel. This was beyond viability for that construction and so the new big boats, averaging 65 feet overall, were of carvel construction. All had a nearly vertical bow but a stern raked like that of the scaffie. This was the ideal compromise between seakeeping and the ability to turn in a tight corner. With a steam capstan and masts with a huge girth, she could carry the sails that would power her up. When she leaned, her waterline was longer. Every port will have its legends of these powerful craft, decks awash, racing to get the best price for their fresh herring.

A contemporary newspaper report in the *Banffshire Advertiser* gives a clue as to why Alexander MacLeod of Point, Lewis, went to the McIntosh yard for his new drifter:

> This long-established firm has gained a most favourable reputation for the strength and fine models of their boats, the strength not lying so much in extra heaviness of framework or planking as in the careful workmanship and general build. Messrs Mackintosh adopt a system entirely their own, in which the greatest possible strength is obtained without making the boat unduly heavy, and the high appreciation in which they are held is shown by the fact that during a period of unusual dullness in boat-building they have been fully employed. The boats just launched are much about the same dimensions – viz. – length of keel, 50ft, length overall 65ft, breadth of beam 19ft and depth 12ft.[3]

The carvel method leads to a heavier construction. Strength without penalty of weight is not only the aspiration of designers and builders of racing yachts. Gordon Williams decided to leave part of his model open to reveal the intricate details of construction. He describes just how careful detailing could save weight without losing strength: '*Muirneag* herself was enormously strongly built (as were all the McIntosh boats), with many of the crucial deck-beams (carlings, half-beams) dovetail jointed into the cross-beams. This ensured that these joints would stay tight, and never pull out under stress.'[4]

Once more, it is the model-builder who communicates the finesse in this culmination of the Moray Firth sailing drifter. He had to get his head round the shipwright's methods in achieving the shapes and dimensions stored in the plans. Williams adds:

> There are 58 frames in *Muirneag*'s hull, and in common with most other boats, each one is uniquely shaped . . . The inside and outside edge bevels for the planking were also drawn, together with the scarf joint positions and drainage holes in the floors. In the larger midships section of the hull, the frames have alternately 6 and 7 parts each – floor, first futtock, second futtock (or top timber) and short timberhead – this on the real boat was for easy replacement if damaged.
>
> At the bow and stern the frames are smaller, and have mercifully fewer parts . . . the natural shapes of the original oak board would have been utilised in the frames of the full-sized boat. This was a very time-consuming task . . . all first and second futtocks, floors and top timbers marked out individually with regard to grain direction, all 319 of them.

Mr Williams intersperses his construction details with similar detail on the method of reproducing the original in the smaller scale, working in miniature and selecting materials. The detailed photographs on his website also reveal a work of art in its own right. James R. MacGregor has written a paper which outlines restoration works on a very different scale to the issues facing the model-maker. He also provides detail on other surviving Zulus and generously shares his research in the form of a PDF you can download without charge.[5]

But we still have not come close to answering why a vessel,

whatever the scale, should inspire people to devote so much of their lives to it. We can start with Neil Gunn's *The Silver Darlings*, which celebrates the herring fishery as a means for people demoralised by Clearances and unscrupulous landlords to find their own way. A widow's son like Finn, in the novel, could work his way to commission the pride of the fleet. Such aspirations certainly came to pass in real life. A man from a crofting family who probably began his career at sea coiling warps in the heaving forepeak of a Fifie could commission his own Zulu, of 62 feet in the keel, 82 feet on deck and drawing two fathoms. This was *Muirneag*.

Sandy MacLeod of 5 Knock, Lewis, often outfished the powered craft and always worked his vessel under sail. At the age of 80, he took her out for one last night before she was auctioned. The oak that had been bevelled and scarphed by the McIntosh shipwrights would become long-lasting fenceposts. This irony resonates on.

Many have dreamed of rebuilding the *Muirneag*. When I kept an archive of recorded conversations linked to the old sail loft, a historic part of Stornoway harbourside now restored, I was handed one rusty boat nail or 'spike' by John MacLennan, then CEO of the Port Authority. He guaranteed this was from the Zulu. That has now been passed to the current CEO, who happens to be related to the family who commissioned *Muirneag*. Mr Glen McIntosh, a descendant of her builders and creator of the McIntosh shipbuilders website, visited Lewis on a pilgrimage. He photographed fenceposts which suggest shaped frames and he assembled some ironwork. These could be mementos or museum exhibits. Is it just about possible that a few fragments of the old boat could be worked into a recreation of her form? Dan Johnson, of Johnson and Loftus boatbuilders, Ullapool, travelled to the Balallan area to do his own research on behalf of a customer looking at the feasibility of such a project. This would be a replica, but if original material is contained within the new structure she will arguably be a rebuild – even

Cutty Sark now has only a tiny proportion of original material.

Let's leave the structure aside for now and consider how a legend develops. Her name has resonance on her home island. *Muirneag* is one of the few significant hills in North Lewis. Moorland navigation can be trickier than at sea and shepherds would take their bearings from the high ground. Out in the North Minch the peak of *Muirneag* would be sighted and lined on Tiumpan Head lighthouse to form a transit. A second transit for the longline fishers, seeking a bank where food and so fish amassed would intone '*Muirneag agus Dibidail*', lining the hill on a visible 'geo' or crevice on the shoreline. The name of MacLeod's vessel also suggests a girl held very dear.

But Sandy didn't spare his darling. His vessel would cover the miles to follow the fishing round the coasts, often working very close to her place of build. He is quoted as saying he never worried about the hull, only the spars, as he drove her on full sail when the others in the fleet had two reefs in. Her main mast would have been massive. Edgar March quotes the son of the builder of *Muirneag* in his book *Sailing Drifters*: 'Masts were of Norwegian white wood, yards were larch. The biggest foremast Mr McIntosh remembers was 6ft 9in. circ., or about 26in. diameter, and these immense masts stood unsupported by any standing rigging, the halyards and burton on the weather side being the only stays. Ballast was some 30 tons of stone from the seashore . . . capacity was approximately 80 tons.'[6] A *Stornoway Gazette* article summarises her qualities: 'She was a safe and powerful seaboat, whether close hauled or running free, hardly ever needing her sails eased in a sea.'[7]

Such legends inspire literature. Norman Malcolm Macdonald, a native Gaelic speaker from a fishing family who was raised on the shoreline of Broad Bay, Lewis, was an innovative writer. His moving play *Anna Caimbeul* has been a Radio 3 production as well as powerful live theatre. Norman once told me he'd set out to write the first Japanese Noh play in Gaelic. The critic Douglas Gifford judged his writing on the sea in his novel *Calum Tod* as even beyond that of the great Orcadian writer, George Mackay Brown. Here is Norman's description of a sailing drifter running for the market in his 2000 novel *Portrona*:

> After the psalm and the supper and the waiting, the hauling of the nets, the capstan turning, we shake out the gasping fish, the hold fills, the boy coils, coils in his wet cubbyhole, in his weaving world of black wet rope.
>
> We turn for home. Portrona beckons in the pearl and gold dawn. The wind with us, she takes it, hear her hiss through the water. The Zulu boat heeling, straining boards and sheets and canvas. Hear her chuckle past Tiumpan, Bayble Island, the Chicken. She heels so far, at the Beasts, herring slips from her decks back into the sea.
>
> Arnish, Goat Island, Number One, Portrona Quay before us. We're not the first but we're not the last either.[8]

Many craft of the Zulu type were engined and many were re-rigged as cruising yachts with a handier sail plan. A few do remain afloat. *St Vincent*, which was registered in Castlebay, was originally built by Stephen of Banff in 1910. At about 49 feet overall, she is of intermediate size for the class.

I was able to sail up Loch Broom and berth on the pontoon finger that juts out from the Johnson and Loftus boatyard. There you meet an ingenious wooden slip, constructed to enable slipping of the *St Vincent*. The last time I'd seen her she was afloat at Burntisland and seemed pretty well intact, though her rudder arrangement showed that she had gone through some reincarnations as a working fishing boat. Now her garboards (first planks on the keel) were removed and it looked as if a large proportion of her planking would be renewed. Dan showed me the huge oak frames cut to replace both original ones and generations of repairs. As a boatbuilder trained in yacht joinery, he had found the fit of the original timbers revealing. He explained how this had been done at speed. Joints were butted together, leaving a V-shaped gap at the curve. This was simply filled with a wedge-like piece of oak. These powerful vessels were built fast to take their share of a Klondike of silver. Because the framing was so massive, there was tolerance. As long as the joints were staggered, they did not have to be more sophisticated scarphs. Built to a price, the boat would be expected to make a return on the investment in a few seasons. Neither builder nor owner would have imagined this Zulu surviving for 111 years, to date.

The best way to gain a sense of the scale and shape of the great Zulu is to visit the Scottish Fisheries Museum at Anstruther. The organisation have done great work in keeping the Fifie *Reaper* in commission, but it's just not possible to renovate and keep afloat every historical craft. Among the museum's shore-based collection is the essential form of the 80-foot (24.4-metre) Zulu *Research*. She was built in Banff in 1903. Registered LK62, she last worked in Shetland in 1968. The deck is missing and the stern apart, so heavy timber braces have to be rigged to help maintain her shape.

There is also such a thing as a 'Zulu yole', which like scaffie and Fifie yoles, exemplifies the essential shape, though the smaller craft will tend to be beamier in proportion. One found its way to the Ness district of Lewis, and her very distinct shape stands out in period photographs with lines of *sgoth Niseach*, with their very rounded sterns. Up till about 2015 or so you could see her shape by a North Lewis roadside but up high on a trailer, exposed to the gales. The inevitable happened, and you wonder if some passer-by with an eye for a bonnie shape ever measured and noted the lines which would let her be made again. You could imagine an enterprising builder moulding this shape in GRP (glass reinforced polyester) and marketing a craft of 24 feet or so as a pocket cruiser with a turn of speed but responsive to her tiller.

The story of the *Muirneag* seems to me to encapsulate how the ambition of a skipper in one locality will drive him to seek out a proven builder who would take account of suggestions from that skipper's own experience. It does not matter if that builder is 'local'. Successful skippers of prawn-trawlers in Stornoway would continue to look across to the Moray Firth yards to create their ideal. In the same way as Sandy MacLeod had looked to McIntosh for his Zulu, Alex J. MacLeod commissioned his stern trawler *Wave Crest* (SY3) from J. and G. Forbes of Sandhaven, in 1968. She came with a hull of gleaming larch but her shape seemed anything but 'traditional'. She had her wheelhouse very far forward up the incline of a high, flared bow. This left a wide and long working deck area all the way to her transom stern. She would make a good living, mainly working the local Shiant Banks, for her innovative owner. He clearly put practicality close to the top of his list of requirements.

NOTES

(1) Gordon Williams, 'Muirneag SY486: 1903–1947: A Short History', Muirneag SY486 website: http://www.muirneag.net.

(2) 'Muirneag – A Stornoway Fishing Boat', part of the Dualchas na Mara Project at Museum nan Eilean, funded by Bòrd na Gàidhlig and Museums Galleries Scotland: https://www.youtube.com/watch?v=eP4hLxSx-3E.

(3) Banffshire Advertiser, *19 April 1888.*

(4) Williams, 'Muirneag SY486'.

(5) James R. MacGregor, 'Restoration of the 1910 Zulu St Vincent', https://www. researchgate.net/publication/330016077_Restoration_of_the_1910_Zulu_St_Vincent.

(6) Edgar J. March, Sailing Drifters: The Story of the Herring Luggers of England, Scotland and the Isle of Man *(first published London, Percival, Marshall and Co., 1952).*

(7) Quoted on McIntosh Boat & Shipbuilders website: www.glennmci.brinkster. net. See also reproduction Stornoway Gazette *notice on passing of Sandy MacLeod, master of* Muirneag.

(8) Norman Malcolm Macdonald, Portrona *(Edinburgh, Birlinn, 2000).*

6

VERSATILE MOTOR
FISHING VESSELS

WORKING OUR WAY ALONG THE southern coast of the Moray Firth to the challenging Rattray Head, we are also following a history of boatbuilding for the fishing industry. This is a huge subject in itself. Histories of particular craft have been written and there are several excellent studies of diverse Scottish fishing vessels by those who were inside that history, from a boatbuilder's or a fisher's point of view. One way of looking at the huge variety of the shipwrights' products is to take a journey through time as well as place. Changes in fishing methods and legislation brought changes in the hulls and the fittings of the vessels. In the context of this alternative tour of Scotland, let's look at just a few examples. Each was custom-built to serve the needs of the customer's fishing methods at the time.

Marigold changed things. In 1927 William Wood and Sons of Lossiemouth launched a new vessel of 50 foot overall and a gross registered tonnage (GRT) of 23. At this time, steam drifters and steam trawlers were still packing harbours all round Scotland, but this new vessel was installed with one of the products of L. Gardner and Sons of Manchester. This firm had moved from inventing and producing bespoke products, including dentists' chairs, to building higher volumes of engines. This was a 'semi-diesel' with three cylinders producing 50 horsepower. It burned heavy oil but there was a 'hot

The multipurpose MFV 9 (drift net and seine net)

pot' system for igniting it at less pressure than was needed by a 'true diesel' motor. It was not an invention of the Gardner family, and other examples were produced in Scandinavia and the USA, for example. But this company became known for reliability. In the marine world, lives as well as livelihoods depend on that. The new unit produced enough power to serve the first of the Scottish fleet specifically built to work the seine-net method. The hull itself was close to the Fifie type: near-vertical at each end.

The word is that herring fishers, following the route of trade, had seen how Danish vessels landed the prime whitefish that were achieving high prices. Sole, turbot and plaice were among the most sought-after species at the markets. These were worth taking care of and speeding to Glasgow or even Billingsgate by rail. A seine net is weighted at the bottom to reach these species. A line of floats holds its mouth up and open. The power of the boat will allow for long lengths to be run out before they are pulled taut to form a bag. The fleeing bottom-feeding fish cannot wriggle out of the sides so are gathered to fall into the lower section of that bag as it is stretched, then raised.

Within a year, a second, similar, craft was commissioned for seine-net fishing. Running costs were much lower than those of the steam-powered craft. The story is best told by a local. This is from the folk history of Lossiemouth on the 'Lossiefowk' website. It is the narrative of John Imlach, reproduced with permission from Brian Ogilvie, his grandson:

> The steam drifter as far as Lossiemouth was concerned was on the way out, and many of the older ones were sold for scrap, others broken up. The new and better drifters were 'sold for a song', as everybody wanted to go in for, or get a berth on some of the new diesel motor seiners.
>
> At this stage in the history of Lossiemouth, much praise is due to the traders in the town, the farmers in the surround district, towns-folk in Elgin and the area round about, for without the financial backing they gave, the fishermen of Lossiemouth would never have the total of 90 seine-netters operating by the year 1937.[1]

You get a picture of an extending network of commerce and dependence, onshore as well as at sea. Another account suggests that the innovation was due to the enterprise of a skipper related to 'Daad' Campbell, who commissioned the first of the Zulus. This goes on to describe the build-up of seine-netters built by Wood, Slater and Dunn before the end of the 1930s: 'By 1939 there were over 80 such boats operating from the port.'[2] That is one harbour alone. These vessels had the seaworthiness and power to follow the fishing and land at different markets. Documentation of the fleet of this one small port speaks for many similar townships. Lossie craft were, in time, working from Ayr to Scrabster.

If earlier craft fished the drift net for herring in season and long-lined for whitefish in winter, could later craft not also be multipurpose? At least one type of dual-purpose vessel does not look like a compromise of any kind. I'd say these long, slim boats, built in the 1960s at about 60 to 80 feet overall, epitomised what would come to mind as a classic fishing-boat shape. They had clear deck-lines which revealed a pronounced sheer-line from the high bow to a late uptilt at her cruiser-type stern. The stepped wheelhouse gave a fairly good view forward without taking up too much deck-space. In season, that would be festooned with the cages which kept the high poles of the headline buoys needed for the seine net. An article in *The Fishing News*[3] (3 April 2017) reprinted contemporary photos of the Sandhaven-built FR25, *Ritchies*. She can be seen entering her home harbour in her differing seasonal plumage. These craft also carried a mizzen sail, to steady them at sea. Usually they had Gardners too, but now full diesels rated more like 150 horsepower. They had the power and the hull length to give them the speed that let them retrace the routes of their sailing predecessors. Some would continue to berth from Lerwick to Lowestoft, as the markets continued to follow the migration. Others would work nearer home. Anyone who has worked on the North Sea or been on one of the ferry crossings in a bit of weather will know that this was no easy option. The first RNLI lifeboat station in Scotland (1800) faced the North Sea from Montrose. Fraserburgh lifeboat station was established in 1858. There have been three Fraserburgh lifeboat disasters in recent history and a chain of wrecked boats and loss of lives before that. At the inquiry that followed the loss of the *Duchess of Kent*, on service to the Danish vessel *Opal* in 1970, a Board of Trade surveyor spoke of the inevitable accidents which must result from the seas generated by gales in this area.

Still the vessels put out to those seas and still volunteers launched lifeboats in the full knowledge of the risks they were taking. The seaworthy nature of the design and build of working craft reduced the risk factor but nothing could remove it. Some did make fortunes, but the majority only made their livings. Even that needed a will to adapt. As very little needed to be altered on the vessels designed to shift easily from drifting to seine-netting, they could make an opportunist shift of gear between landings. Before the establishment of species quotas, they could take a 'flyshot' of whitefish while a species was running.

We are looking at vessels built or based along a coast but adapting to different fisheries and methods. Breakwaters and harbours were also a crucial part of fisheries development, and a huge influence on the design and build of the vessels. There was little point in building a more powerful boat if her length, beam or draught meant it couldn't work out of an existing haven. Engineering works helped drive the fishing industry, and so its boatbuilding, on all of Scotland's coasts. There is an excellent study of such works on Scotland's northern area and on the west coast.[4] Research, including site visits by Joanna Gordon extended the work done in collaboration with Angus Graham, who died before the study was published. In the introduction, describing the scope of the study, Joanna Gordon makes it clear that there is a huge difference between developments on the north-east coast of Scotland and the majority of the west. The indented coastline of the west provided natural shelter and anchorages. Vessels could only be built and worked from most east-coast settlements if sea-walls were built first. Mooring and landing places were also needed on the west coast but often there was natural shelter in the geography to build on.

The thought of long, multipurpose boats warping their way between high harbour walls makes me think of the longlining boats I first noticed in Kirkcaldy harbour when our family lived in the Central Belt. These would be mainly black-painted wooden boats with white-painted steel whalebacks. I saw them again in Stornoway. The KY boats (and some from other east-coast ports) would tie up in Stornoway to take on herring or mackerel for bait. Large baskets were filled with coiled lines and fist-sized hooks placed in sequence around a cork rim. Their catch would be most prized for quality. My father told me how my Fraserburgh grandfather would have his pick of the catch as he worked at the harbour. He would select line-caught fish. When any of the family said, 'Not fish again' his reply would be, 'There'll come a day ye'll mind ye said that.' Every time I buy fish, retail price, I think of these words.

As a Lewisman with the east-coast surname of Stephen, I'm fairly conscious of Scotland's coast-to-coast interchange through the fishing industry. But it was former lifeboatman John MacLennan who reminded me that one of the east-coast line-boats was the subject of an epic lifeboat service after suffering machinery failure out on the Atlantic side. Vessels such as these fine, long, multipurpose boats 'migrated' more and more, coast to coast. Because fishing vessels have to be registered, port to port, histories are easily traced. More and more, we see vessels built in one area for one fishery being bought and sold round Scotland. By the early twentieth century, the larger vessels would be moved from east to west coasts. Often, the three major canal systems were used. This came at a cost, but skipper and crew could avoid waiting for favourable wind and tide to transit Pentland Firth. The shift from local build for local waters had already happened with the commissioning of larger Fifies, Zulus and steam drifters. The building of distinct craft developed over generations to suit local conditions did continue, but mainly for smaller boats of about 30 feet and under.

I was able to gain a glimpse of a later phase of boatbuilding for the fishing industry in the last years of the twentieth century. An innovative education project in Aberdeen city and Aberdeenshire brought together a team of artists across forms from dance to poetry. We began with visits to McDuff shipbuilders in Banff and the netmenders which were then building trawls for twin-rigging. We had a week to study and respond to the culture of the communities living at the edge of the North Sea. Then we would reply to what we'd experienced by devising collaborative lessons for Primary and Secondary schools, exploring themes in partnership with teachers.

The first thing that hit you in the McDuff yard was the resinous smell of Scottish larch, or 'larick' as the shipwright termed it. This is not a hardwood but a tough softwood with good durability in saltwater. European larch is not a species indigenous to Scotland. Estates with an eye to the future planted new forests when native oak was close to exhaustion after forests were felled for shipbuilding. Even in the late 1990s, some skippers still favoured timber. The vessel on the stocks towered high and stretched out for at least 80 feet. The backbone structure looked massively strong – 'boatskin' larch planking is heavily selected for quality.

Frames were bolted together and braced first before the thick planks were steam-bent and clamped in place. Timbers were first faired with the age-old but efficient adze. We were told that apprentices of old worked barefoot to teach them respect for accuracy in swinging that honed edge. The process is captured in 'Herd & Mackenzie Boatbuilders, Buckie', a most emotive short film, in strongly lit colour. These might well have been the last days of commercial shipbuilding in timber in Scotland.[5] The methods employed in the film are the same as those we saw in Banff and, until recently, could have seen in Sandhaven, Peterhead or further down the coast. The adze is featured, but another man follows the man driving huge spikes, or boat nails, by dressing the plank with an electric finishing-sander.

Shipbuilding has survived in the Banff area by adapting once more. The vast majority of designs are now drawn for production in steel. They will often be deep and high, to make use of every millimetre of the length permitted before a different set of regulations apply. The last of the great wooden fishing boats such as the one I gazed at in McDuff were sophisticated in their fit-out.[6] As before, the cumulative experience of skippers went into the custom-finished boat. Like most of the later timber motor fishing vessels (MFVs), a shelter-deck of steel would be fabricated to cover most of the deck area. Crews were better protected than they used to be. The wheelhouse projected above that shelter. Most were rigged for towing twin trawls, making even more demands on the machinery. Units were mainly supplied by Caterpillar (a world-wide corporation founded in Illinois in 1925), sometimes Deutz (a German company with a branch in the Midlands of England).

That reminds me of a phrase I first heard in the Grampian district: 'It was bananas sent men to the moon.' Trade brings an exchange of ideas. These sometimes result in technological breakthroughs.

NOTES

(1) 'John Imlach's Memories', Lossiefowk Archive website: https://www.lossiefowk. co.uk/articles/imlach.

(2) David B. Thomson, 'Our Fishing Heritage', Electric Scotland website: https:// electricscotland.com/thomson/fishing01.htm.

(3) 'The Last of the Dual-Purpose Herring-Drifters and Seine-Netters in the 1960s', Fishing News website: https://fishingnews.co.uk/features/the-last-of-the-dual-purpose-herring-drifters-seine-netters-in-the-1960s/.

(4) Angus Graham and Joanna Gordon, 'Old harbours in northern and western Scotland' (Edinburgh, Society of Antiquaries of Scotland, 1987).

(5) 'Herd & Mackenzie Boatbuilders, Buckie', https://www.youtube.com/ watch?v=Id4rfH9gxy0.

(6) See also James A. Pottinger, Wooden Fishing Boats of Scotland (Stroud, The History Press, 2013).

7
THE HERRING FISHING
– A NEW METHOD

THERE'S NO DOUBT THAT INFLEXIBLE quota systems led to large numbers of dead fish being dumped. The question now is, even with more sensible regulation, could that scale of catching ever have been sustainable? As someone with no first-hand experience of trawling, I had to look to diagrams to fully understand modern trawling rigs and their impact on fish populations. The most clear illustration I've found, to date, is in a Scottish Government report titled 'Selectivity in Trawl Fishing Gears'. Several other studies are summarised in the same Scottish Government publication on lessening discards.[1] There is a systematic but readable outline of trials with different commercial vessels. Each section summarises findings on how a specific measure fared in its attempt to reduce the proportion of 'discards', or unwanted but dead fish in the net. This has long been a controversial subject. Any change in mesh size and type for conservation reasons can make new investment necessary. Against that, there is huge waste and destruction when heavy trawls are dragged along the seabed, day and night. Species not included in the vessel's quota are dumped back, dead, along with immature fish. Then the boat trawls on to pursue the species it can put to market. The questions of fisheries legislation and internationally agreed restrictions are complex, but it's clear to most people that 'discards' of dead fish only benefit seals and crabs. Yet it

First of the purse-seiners

just does not seem possible to get a grip on the range of contemporary Scottish fishing vessels without some understanding of the tension between 'progress' in catching power and 'conservation' in holding that power back. If immature fish are decimated, of course future stocks will suffer, but in a spiral. If different species are killed and dumped in the pursuit of others, the damage also accumulates.

So before we move on round the coast, let's take a look at a couple of other boats. Their personal histories might help tell a story with many twists and turns and signs of change.

The Peterhead-built and -registered *Glenugie III* (PD347) was built by Richard Irvin and launched in 1964. At 78 feet and 65 GRT, she was towards the larger end of her type. Like *Ritchies*, she was one of those listed as being built for working with either drift net or seine net. But she was to pioneer another method still. By the late 1960s she was involved in trials of working the higher capacity purse-seine net, for herring. In that same period other vessels were trialling pair-trawling. The purse-seine could be used mid-water or on the bottom.

As before, the catching power of a new method led to a demand for purpose-built new vessels, sometimes aided by government grant and loan schemes.

The livelihoods of those ashore in boatbuilding, engineering and processing were secured but the pressure on fish stocks was rising. As new vessels were being designed and the yards adapted to greater use of steel, *Glenugie III* had a few changes of owner and was re-engined at least once. Eventually the North Sea claimed her. After springing a leak, she sank, some 90 miles out from the east coast of Orkney, on 3 November 1993. All her crew survived.

The method she tried proved to have a catching power beyond all expectations. This led to a new generation of ships, bristling with improved electronics. Herring and mackerel quotas could be caught in a few nights. Bans followed, in the North Minch for example, and the surviving drifters and ring netters were tied up too. Just to give some sense of the scale, a third-generation pelagic vessel arrived in Symbister harbour, Whalsay, in January 2020. The new *Charisma* is 75 metres, rather than feet, overall. The hull of LK362 was built, in steel, in Poland and her machinery was fitted in Skagen, Denmark. Her first shot took 800 tonnes of mackerel to be processed by the electrically operated machinery aboard. The argument for such investment is that there is less waste when the catch is treated better and faster and new machinery can have a lower environmental impact. The argument against is that the method itself, used on that scale, is simply too effective.

What of developments in vessels built for the demersal (fish usually feeding near the seabed) sector? Let's take a look at another late example of a wooden boat with steel superstructure, built to work a twin trawl. In 1986, Jones of Buckie launched such a vessel, then named *Still Waters* and about 78 feet overall and 79 GRT. The vessel I'd seen under construction at McDuff would have been very similar. *Still Waters* worked first in Shetland under various owners before returning to the Moray Firth as *Zenith*, BF106. She was to take part in trials which compared how changing 'bobbins' and 'discs' in her ground gear affected 'discards' of flatfish species which could not be marketed. In summary, catches were reduced but a higher proportion of mature fish were in that catch.

Legislation only allowing specific proportions of untargeted species led to an alternative illegal economy of 'black fish' as well as the dumping of large volumes of dead fish at sea. Many skippers can accept that there have to be effective ways of lessening destruction if boats are to work on and new ones built to replace them. Former 'decommissioning' schemes were designed to reduce catching power by taking chainsaw and bulldozer to many examples of the work of the shipwrights I had been lucky enough to observe. Science and fishermen's experience or 'instinct' will have to work together if any commercial fishing – and so boatbuilding – is to survive.

From Peterhead to Shetland, it's not only big boats you'll see at our harbours. There will still be a few of the wooden creel boats, some of them built at the same yards that produced the drifters, seiners, trawlers and pursers. Newer vessels will usually be production boats moulded in GRP. This is the other approach to profitable fishing – keep the scale and so the overheads down. The vessel will target quality langoustine, crab or lobster and gain a premium from selling to the restaurant trade. Often, this approach will use a method that takes only a few gallons of diesel and where the 'discards', such as lobsters 'berried' with spawn, can be returned in good condition. A convincing argument is made on the website of the Scottish Creel Fishers Association.[2] The numbers engaged in fishing with small craft run by one or two persons all add up. The argument is that more people would benefit and stocks would be protected if trawling for prawns with its inevitable 'bycatch' was replaced with more creel-fishing. The group also argues for reinstatement of a general three-mile limit exclusion zone for trawlers. The 'openseas' site claims that creel and dive boats add up to 75 per cent of the Scottish registered fleet.

Most of these will have a small wheelhouse forward and a wide, clear space aft to lay out the gear. Before we get too romantic about the picturesque and colourful small craft, we should also remember the particular risks. If a 20–30-foot boat is caught out in sudden bad weather, it is vulnerable. If a fleet of creels snags the bottom when hauling, the boat quickly becomes unstable. If she is seeking lobsters, she will be nudging as close to rocks as possible. Any significant change in wind direction and gear will have to be recovered from a lee-shore before it is tumbled and destroyed. It's quite likely that gales will tangle and even demolish an investment in new gear. And when a long fleet of creels is being shot, all it takes is a boot in a bight of line and a crewman might well be pulled over the side.

Against all that, you have a sustainable method where overheads are not so crippling and the owner-skipper is likely to have a great deal of independence. He will have to negotiate territories with his neighbours, of course, but that is often amicable. We need not be looking back, either, to the boats and gear of the past. In June 2019 *The Fishing News* reported on a new addition to the creel-fishing sector, now working from a pontoon in Peterhead. *Onward*, PD349, is a new catamaran coming in under the 10-metre mark. This is a stable platform to work from. At a design speed of about 10 knots, she will be fairly light on the fuel bill. She has already been through an 800-mile delivery trip from Southampton via the Caledonian Canal. Her skipper and crew judge her ideal to seek brown crab in the very open waters of Peterhead Bay.

As we are taking a sweeping tour of a vast array of vessels, let's pause for breath. The subject of fishing at different depths for different species brings a story to mind. East coast or west, fisher folk, or those who will queue for their catch, often talk about the 'king of the sea'. There's more than one version of a song, especially strong along the coasts we've been considering, which says that is the herring. I was fortunate to hear Peter Hall, researcher, concertina player in The Gaugers and singer in a strong Doric voice, sing that song in Aberdeen Folk Club. But there's a yarn that says the fishes themselves weren't that happy about the matter being decided by human beings. Once, they decided to hold a conference to settle the matter.

Large and small, fast and slow, they all made their way to the gathering. You'll excuse me not giving away the exact location. The flounder was making slow progress, shuffling through the sand, keeping an eye out for any opportunist dogfish or skate. He persevered because he thought he had a fair chance, himself. He was one of the few fish clever enough to change his colour to merge with the bottom. Above him, the more streamlined species swam on at different depths. Among them was the powerful porbeagle shark. He definitely fancied his chances. Nearer the surface, there was just a shimmer as great shoals of mackerel and herring sped along.

The flounder was getting tired. This seemed to be taking forever. He met a gurnard going back the other way, fins just about walking along the bottom. 'Is it all over then?' asked the flatfish.

'Aye,' says the other.

'Who was it they chose then?' asked the flounder, fully expecting to hear his own name.

'There wis a bit o' a stooshie but they settled on the herrin. He covers a yon miles an only sooks in plankton. Never hairms any ither body.'

'I doubt that's it a' settled then,' said the flounder. He curled up his lip as he spoke. It stuck that way, with a funny twist. You might have noticed, the flounder still has that twist to the mouth to this very day.

NOTES

(1) Summary of research into methods to reduce discards on the DiscardLess website: http://halieut.agrocampus-ouest.fr/gears/index.php?action=fiche&code=103&type_code=GS&atl_version=0&idlang=uk.

(2) Representation of creel fishers' interests on SCFF, the Scottish Creel Fishermens' Federation website: http://www.scottishcreelfishermensfederation.co.uk.

8
THE
DEEP-SEA TRAWLER
– COAL AND OIL

SOME PORTS ARE DEEPER THAN others. Bigger boats tend to need a bit more water under them. That has to be a factor in deciding the locations where both boatbuilding and commercial fishing with long-range vessels flourished. Banff and Buckie, Fraserburgh and Peterhead too, all have a history of building in wood and steel and now also in GRP and aluminium. The method of fishing has a bearing on the scale of craft, as well as the distance they need to cover. Many also have to work a compromise on this, chasing herring and whitefish in season. Fishermen remain in business by adapting, and shipbuilders do too. There are excellent books and articles that build on the first-hand knowledge of their authors to give the details of particular ports, fisheries and boatbuilders (see Further Reading). The focus here will be on telling the stories of a small number of contrasting examples of the vessels which now have their lines etched in memories.

Aberdeen is a railhead as well as a deep-water port. Like Hull, it is well-placed for reaching both the nearer North Sea grounds and the distant waters. In its day it was also a herring port, but the image in mind now is of the trawler that could tow heavy gear along the seabed to keep a wide net-mouth open. That would swallow the cod, haddock and whiting, the plaice, sole, witch, megrim and precious turbot. These would be herded by heavy trundling balls of iron as water-pressure worked against great boards of timber or steel, to spread that mesh. Even pulling at 3 or 4 knots, most of the fish would fall back to the 'cod-end'. Some of the smaller ones would escape the mesh and the size of that would be regulated, through the times, to allow more of these to grow. But it was a messy business, and immature specimens were crushed among the plump and prime ones.

It took a powerful craft to reach the grounds, work in all weathers and carry the fuel, ice and catch needed to sustain the industry. This was provided by sail and steam before diesel engines took over. Very good records have been kept, and both Aberdeen Library and Aberdeen Maritime Museum have done a thorough job of making these available. Let's take a closer look at the development and then follow a single case-history of an Aberdeen-built trawler.

The port of Aberdeen played a critical role in the trawling industry from its very beginnings. A converted steam tug showed the way but a PhD thesis submitted to the University of Hull by Michael Stuart Haines lists the Aberdeen-built *North Sea*, built in 1888 for one William Pyper, as one of the first purpose-built steam trawlers.[1] Build and running costs were higher than those of a sailing craft, but monthly earnings could average £270 as opposed to £120. The rise in trawling is reflected in statistics for the tonnage of fish moved by rail from the ports of Grimsby, Hull and Aberdeen. From only a very small proportion in comparison to the English ports, Aberdeen's share rose steadily with the building of the steam trawlers. By the early 1900s, that was nudging towards half the tonnage landed at Grimsby and about two-thirds that of Hull. The steam-powered vessels worked well into the 1950s. There is contemporary film footage as well as first-hand accounts to document the machinery and the grinding labour needed on deck to drag the seabed.

I am of a generation in Scotland which grew up with the incantation that Aberdeen had trawling the way Glasgow had shipbuilding and Kirkcaldy made linoleum. I do remember how high

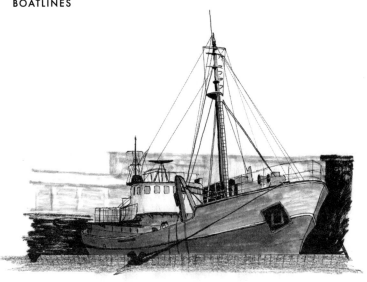

A deep-sea trawler (Aberdeen)

the bows seemed and how rounded the steel sterns, when visiting the city on holiday as a child. There seemed to be a lot of coal and smoke and soot about. I was to return in the mid 1970s as a student. It was a time of huge change, but a gang of us would rise early to catch the fish auctions. Across from the landings from a new generation of mid and far-ranging trawlers, there were the remnants of the old fleet, not yet scrapped. Artists like Ian Fleming and Will Maclean sketched and studied the generations of vessels. Both made prints too, at Peacock Printmakers. There was an exhibition called 'A Pound a Time'. You could buy an original screenprint, numbered and signed from editions of 100. I did just that and still appreciate Fleming's vision of echoing whiteish gull-wings over a harbour. Aberdeen Art Gallery continues to keep a strong print section and the trawlers are part of that. As long as you didn't have to suffer the jolts, stinks, coal-dust, slime and grime, the textures of toil made a strong subject.

I never did go down the ladder to land on one of those decks of scuffed steel. But I did hear how a skipper might have to round up his crew from the pub and steer them into the taxi to get them to the docks. The talk gave a sense of the deckhand's life as being similar to being on a war footing. The enemy might be ice building in the rigging to destabilise a trawler trying to plough the North Atlantic. Two first-hand oral accounts confirmed the impression. My fishing buddy Gregor, met in the Ochil hillfoots, a step back from the Firth of Forth, shared the first. His father, from the Loch Broom area and with the culture of boats in his DNA, was a Merchant Navy skipper. Gregor sought to combine a passion for angling with the urge to go to sea. In the 1970s you could attend college onshore to learn seamanship and netmending. Then you would get taken on as an apprentice deckhand with hope of working your way up.

Gregor was sparse in his detail, the same way I'd noticed my father and uncles would skip all but the outline of an answer to the question of what they did in the war. In a word, it seemed to be about endurance. You had to work through sickness, then sleep deprivation, then cold. You needed an incentive. For Gregor, it ceased to be the desire to gain a ticket which would get him into the wheelhouse, but what he could buy with his part-share if he could keep out of a warm pub when they at last docked. For him it was an electric bass, and that took him to the streets of London.

I was to meet another man who first went to sea as an apprentice on deep-sea trawlers. Mike would push a dinghy out when his mates would set off on their pushbikes. He'd make himself boxes of sandwiches and rig a cover on the boom so he could keep exploring over a full weekend. The creeks and channels of Suffolk would teach him tides and transits. At 15 years of age, he got his start on a Hull trawler, likely working similar deep-sea grounds to the Aberdeen fleet. He described the exhaustion that took over from sickness on his first trip. He'd be shaken up from the heap of coal where he'd tumbled and pushed out to work. But he never escaped the grip of the sea. He did work through his tickets. The deep-sea trawling was his way to gain hours and skills that were to lead to his Merchant Navy certificates. Maybe they reckoned if you could navigate in the conditions aboard a 'rustbucket' trawler, you could drive a ship anywhere. He now had a pension from the Canadian merchant marine.

He came 'home' to do his Yachtmaster. Delivery trips were to take him to the Med and far beyond. A lot of trawlers did go down, back in the day, but he was pleasure-sailing, in his retirement yacht, out of Woodbridge when his number was very nearly up. After skating on iced decks as a teenager, it was a colourful cruising-chute on a fine day which nearly cost him his life. If the stern-ladder had not been down in the water, he could not have grabbed it after he'd been swept over the rail. He was not a well man by that time and still does not know how he hauled himself back aboard. Mike's story was, to me, one more reminder of the risks in any seafaring, but the even greater ones in commercial fishing.

It's one thing to appreciate the boatlines of various skilfully built craft, but these forms should not be thought of as merely picturesque. Trawling did not become an easy life with the advent of vessels fuelled by diesel oil. Documentation, so well-presented and made available with such generosity, catches the time. There is pride in the new ships and their efficiency, ranging as far as Greenland waters. A chronicle of Northstar Shipping focuses on the role played by the Craig family of shipowners:

> A number of steam trawlers and line vessels were built at Aberdeen and I can remember as a young boy my father taking me to visit J. Duthie's shipbuilding yard near Greyhope Road in Torry and witnessing such a fishing vessel being launched. Other shipyards were also actively building, especially Hall Russell at Footdee, which built naval and merchant vessels, plus some trawlers, while John Lewis & Sons of Torry became largely involved in building fishing vessels of various sizes.
>
> The Aberdeen trawler fleet of the 1960s was potent, with a large number of smart diesel trawlers displacing ancient, worn

out steamers that were then consigned to the quay at Point Law to await a final tow to the breakers. The Craigs were at the forefront of the modernisation drive, with the *Mary Craig* setting the trend, her clipped lines set off with rakish funnel and the first 'lantern-style' wheelhouse ever to be seen on a Scottish-owned fishing vessel.

By the late 1950s it had become obvious that much of the Aberdeen fleet had to be replaced. Steam was outmoded, expensive and dirty; the future lay with diesel – modern, clean, economical.

And transformation it was! Over a period of little more than 10 years, the Granite City's fleet of trawlers was totally modernised. Steamers were swiftly dispatched for scrapping . . . largely displaced by sleek motor vessels.[2]

The sophistication and the scale of the new-generation trawler brought both admiration and apprehension from William W. Warner. This American author had already written a Pulitzer Prize-winning book on the maritime world (*Beautiful Swimmers*) when he made several trips on the 'fishing liners' that were to range over most of the world's seas. One chapter reflects on trawling in the Barents sea. He was on board a Hull-based vessel, but she was among a British fleet which included trawlers working out of Aberdeen. His crisp writing in *Distant Water* catches the mood of the hunt which was still there in 1977, despite increasingly effective electronic aids and a level of comfort Gregor and Mike could not have dreamed of.

The dominant undersong of the trip was not the sea conditions, nor the quality of the catch. It was the threatening messages coming over the radio. Cold War tensions were high, and the British fleet were working disputed waters. The chapter could well have been describing the 2021 communications between Russian vessels and a British warship seemingly tasked to test exactly what the current limit is. There is also an important reminder of the contemporary debate on the pros and cons of joining the European Community which had to include signing up to its Common Fisheries Policy. The contrast between the approaches of the governments of Norway and the UK is revealing. Yet Warner's perception seems to me that the immensity of the advances in the vessels and their equipment could never be sustainable without regulation of some kind.

Once more it is the first-hand comment which rings true. Captain George Renardson, master of *Kelt*, was recorded by Warner in October 1977 saying: 'When we first came to these grounds up here in the Norwegian Arctic, we used to call the fishing "dip and fill" . . . That's the way it was – short tows and always a full bag. But you see how thin it is now. Sometimes I think we're getting too good for the fish.'[3]

When it comes to the fishing industry, nothing is forever. *Lindenlea* was one of these new-generation trawlers. A409 was built of steel at the John Lewis yard in Torrey, completed in March 1960. At 121 feet overall, her GRT was 281. She was powered by a six-cylinder, oil-driven engine from the innovative Mirrlees, Bickerton and Day. This company began in Glasgow but developed several branches, this one in Stockport. Trawling depends on abrasion. One trip would take the shine off the flanks of the pride of owner, shipbuilder and skipper. Even in a two-day turnaround in port, there would be a jostling for a position in the landing bay and a place in a close-packed raft of chafing steel. Looking down from the fishmarket quay, you could still see just how well-drawn these lines were. A whaleback would shed most of the big waves. She might meet these in minutes, crossing Aberdeen bar, if there was any east in the wind. She would certainly encounter crashing tonnes of green water on the banks off the Faroes or Iceland.[4]

There is a likely explanation in the physics of naval architecture for that stern, just a bit ovalised from the round. To my eye, it just seemed the perfect ending, to balance a cutting edge at her bow. That, or maybe her catching record, was appreciated by four different trawler companies, with George Craig and Sons being the last one. Her records then hint at another huge shift in Scottish maritime history. In 1985, now the *Grampian Princess*, she was converted to a safety standby vessel to tend the North Sea platforms. The history of one ship speaks of a huge change in the industry and of course the shape of the ships you will see, looking down Market Street, Aberdeen or at Peterhead or at Hull or Great Yarmouth. These will now be high-bowed supply and safety vessels, purpose-built. The Craig company saw the writing on the wall and moved their main focus in good time. The family history does outline international politics as the reason for such a sudden shift. The demise of the trawling fleet is ascribed to the combination of the 200-mile limit in Iceland and the rules accepted with joining what was then the Common Market. The pursuit of species vital to the food chain by Danish vessels is also mentioned. Apportioning blame could never be an easy thing. If we are to learn from the past we have to admit that vessels all round Scotland's coasts also took part in this 'industrial fishing'.

It's not for this book to analyse these reasons or to propose other factors which contributed to the drastic reduction of the Scottish fishing fleet. However, it's just not possible to study the diverse examples of boats which affected so many lives without asking why they took the forms they did. Drifting or trawling, the scale of the vessel and the scale of investment was of course dependent on the return. The time has come to face the fact that fish, pelagic and demersal, are finite. When our vessels became even more efficient, helped by vastly improved electronic aids, their catching power increased. When size and machinery allowed them to work at sea for longer periods, their days at sea had to be artificially limited. The fleets of the independent Icelanders and Norwegians are restricted too, by their own governments. In the same way, the future of the towering standby-boats might also be dependent on adapting to change. Already some are serving offshore windfarms rather than oil and gas platforms. Short-term measures to address energy shortages due to the Russian invasion of Ukraine may give some of the North Sea supply boats a reprieve.

We can follow the story of *Lindenlea* that bit further. As *Grampian Princess* she was decommissioned from safety vessel service. In 1991 she made her last journey under her own power, to Thames Shipyard, Kent in the company of a second former trawler. In 2002, both were towed to Ipswich, Suffolk. There were plans for conversion but these proved too costly. A ship-spotting website carries a photograph submitted by Terry Egalton in 2006.[5] It shows the *Grampian Dawn* (ex-*Ben Strome*) in the foreground and *Grampian Princess* (ex-*Lindenlea*) moored behind her. They reveal the neglect which was to sink them and lead to their breaking-up in 2012. They also cannot hide their pedigree. That raised bow, sharp enough, sweetly steps down to a gradual descending sheer to glide down to that characteristic stern shape.

NOTES

(1) Michael Stuart Haines, 'Britain's Distant Water Fishing Industry, 1830–1914: A Study in Technological Change' (PhD thesis, University of Hull, 1988: https://core. ac.uk/download/pdf/2731582.pdf).

(2) Unfortunately, the chronicle is no longer available on the Northstar company website since its sale in early 2022. Records may be available at Aberdeen City and Aberdeenshire Archives.

(3) William W. Warner, Distant Water – The Fate of the North Atlantic Fisherman *(New York, Little Brown and Co./Atlantic Monthly, 1983).*

(4) Gabriel Hechtman, 'Aboard a Scottish Fishing Trawler: Not for the Indolent', New York Times, *8 December 1974 (https://www.nytimes.com/1974/12/08/archives/ aboard-a-scottish-fishing-trawler-not-for-the-indolent.html).*

(5) 'Grampian Dawn and Grampian Princess', on Shipspotting.com: http://www. shipspotting.com/gallery/photo.php?lid=277596.

9
A BOAT TO TAKE
A SALMON

ANOTHER SPECIES OF FISH BROUGHT other methods of fishing and a type of craft very different from all the others studied so far. Neither the methods nor the vessel changed much for centuries. Like the herring, it once seemed an inexhaustible bounty. Yet numbers of the species have fallen so far that, at present, only one small netting station has a dispensation to continue. This is a fish which cannot be slotted easily into either the pelagic or demersal category. It ranges through depths as it ranges through Atlantic waters. Weirdly, though we can investigate the surface of Mars, we still can't track the exact routes of its migration. From tagged catches, it looks like these strong swimmers leave Scottish waters to hug the long coast of Norway before swinging a left to forge on till they meet the Greenland coast. That is also followed, down and around, though it now seems as if at least some of the species then cross to come back down the maritimes of Canada before making the turn back home.

The Atlantic salmon follows its nose to its own place of birth and returns to the freshwater environment where it hatched to lay its own spawn, or milt. Some will winter only one season in the sea and return as a 'grilse' of something between 3 and 7 pounds or so. I'd guess the average weight of a grilse has probably fallen from about 6 pounds to about 4, in my lifetime. Fish which spend a second winter at sea can

A salmon coble (most Scottish coasts)

be much larger. Salmon, in Scotland, are now worth more alive than dead. Angling permits and guided fishing bring in revenue rather than wild fish, trapped for the table. It is illegal to sell a rod-caught fish, though a few can still be killed and eaten if the catch-figures for the river are over a given number. Wild salmon became more and more of a luxury when the products of fish-farming started to be sold in greater and greater bulk. Many argue that intensive fish-farming has had a devastating effect on wild salmon and sea-trout, partly by increasing sea-lice populations. There are other concerns on pollution, use of chemicals and the dangers of escapees affecting the genetics of wild fish.

Up until the 1980s, and maybe longer, you would still see a section for wild salmon landings at Aberdeen fish market. These were caught by two legal methods. The stakes which stretched out the coastal bag nets could be seen in season, jutting in lines from the surf around coastal villages like Portsoy. The artist Donald Smith, my late uncle and son of a fisherman, would spend time with the netsmen of Balmedie beach when he lived with his family, just up the hill. His painting *Netsmen, Balmedie Beach,* included in a posthumous retrospective (a collaboration of An Lanntair, Stornoway, Taigh Chearsabhagh, Lochmaddy and the City Art Centre, Edinburgh, 2019–2021)[1] reveals the Forbes family in their white waders behind a tractor. The stakes which held their nets rise up behind them. Last time I walked that coast I found one of the craft that laid these staked nets on a hard-standing in the dunes. It seemed more of a memorial than an exhibit.

South of Aberdeen, at Stonehaven, Johnshaven, Catterline or Montrose, the netting stakes could also be seen into the late 1990s. Migratory salmon, joined by schools of sea-trout when close to Scotland's shorelines, swim close to the coast to get a sniff of freshwater currents. The bag was at the end of that line of stakes. These supported a long stretch of 'leader' which would divert the fish. At either side, the salmon would have to enter an outer 'cleek' before being funnelled further into the 3-foot opening of the 'doubling' section. Very few fish would find a way back out from that point. They would be gathered through a 6-inch opening, to be contained in the 'fish court'. If you visit Tate Great Britain you can see a lively image capturing the drying nets which could be seen from Portskerra to the coast between Forth and Tweed. Bold expressionist sweeps of colour capture the scene in a large-scale painting, oils on board, by Joan Eardley (1921–63). The artist came from Glasgow to live for periods in the village of Catterline, which is nestled into the fall from clifftop cultivation to a boulder-beach and breakwater.[2] The painting shows the line, block and strut, rigged to dry the salmon nets.

Small craft were used to service the bag nets but it was the second legal fishing method which led to the centuries-old design used for coastal salmon fishing. When I was a student, these simple craft could still be seen working between Balmedie and Aberdeen City. At the mouths of Spey, Deveron, Don, Dee and Avon, the salmon cobles would also be launched to cast their nets. Gear was paid out from the wide transom stern, while the other end was carried along the shore. A circle would be drawn and the outer end returned to make a loop. This would then be pulled taut and any encircled fish pulled ashore with it or back into the coble.

These cobles would be flat-bottomed to let them work the shallows. Stability was provided by beam, carried all the way aft. They would range from about 18-footers, used in sheltered areas, to over 30 feet, useful in areas where you might expect a bit of sea running in. A pronounced high bow would shed that water. It would be sharp enough to cut sea but buoyant enough to ride it. The requirement resulted in one of the most recognisable of boat-shapes. Its simplicity might disguise its clever nature. Most were clinker-built and clenched, like many of the other craft we've been observing. But there was no keel to suggest the lie of the first or 'garboard' plank or strake.

In this respect, the type of craft has something in common with the *curach* (usual Scottish Gaelic spelling) or coracle-type, usually thought of as Celtic. The concept was a buoyant dish rather than a craft where at least the first few strakes rise, near-vertical, from the keel, to provide a grip on the water. A main difference is that a *curach* has its skin stretched over a pre-made frame. A salmon coble's shape, like the vessels of Norse origin, is derived from the cut of its clinker-laid planks. That also provides strength so that a small number of interior frames are added at a later stage. These were formed from oak or larch, sawn to the curve, joined and joggled over planking. Though the word is also used for the beach-launched craft of Northumberland and Yorkshire, these cobles are completely different in character.

The finished salmon coble was propelled by oar at first, with maybe a long-shafted Seagull motor chuntering along in the later period. Larger examples were motorised, with a fitted inboard, often a slow-turning, single-cylinder diesel. But there were advantages in keeping it light and simple – a fixed propellor was an invitation to foul netting and long warps.

As the salmon-fishing stations were closed, many cobles became coastal features, probably because that shape is so recognisable. The craft set back from the dunes at Balmedie is just one example. A new salmon coble was built as a teaching project at the Portsoy Boatshed. It can be seen at their Salmon Bothy museum. Inside, you will also see models of some of the iconic vessels we've glimpsed on this swift tour. There is a very fine one of scaffie *Gratitude*. The contrast between coble and scaffie reveals how boat shape is affected by function.

Continuing southwards down the coast, Aberdeenshire to Angus, the coble was used in coastal communities. In bordering Perthshire, a variation of the salmon coble remains at work but we have to flit inland a bit to see it. John Ferguson of Stanley built the larger cobles for the downstream netting stations when that was part of the way of life. There was also a local tradition of building similar but smaller vessels for use by ghillies and anglers upriver. Now, a few discriminating folk still appreciate that a 16-foot vessel built from larch on oak will have a grip on the water. It will also provide a satisfying experience. The main materials will have been sourced from within a few miles of the place of build (Stanley, Perthshire). Her shape will echo that of the estuary boats with a few variations. Most of the frames or ribs will be steam-bent straps of oak, to save weight. A few, clever, frames will be extended above gunnel height to act as a rod-rest when rowing from pool to pool, or when 'harling' when that near-flat bottom helps the boat traverse the glides.

Mention of angling has brought another story to mind. This was first told to me when our family lived for a few years in Clackmannanshire, not so far from the Tay and Forth. I used to catch a few flounder at Kincardine and a trout or two in the Devon. Our very good-natured gym teacher, 'Tam', encouraged us to persevere with fly-fishing. 'A Blae an Black should do the trick. Aye, but there are other methods,' he said.

When they were building the Caley Canal there was a lot of navvies over from Ireland. They weren't going to leave all the salmon in there for the toffs. They were eating very well but the word got out and they were on their last warning. One night the gamie came across one of the navvies sitting there watching a float. 'And what have you got on the end of that?' he asks. 'A Kerrs Pink,' says the navvie. The gamie had heard they used such things as par-boiled potatoes to catch carp but no one ever heard of a fish taking anything like that in Scotland. 'On you go,' he says.

He pops in for a dram on his way home and tells the story in the pub. Right then the navvie comes in for his pint. 'We'll get a laugh here,' says the gamie. He asks the other fellow to open his creel and show them all how he got on. Well, there's a fine fat grilse in there, fresh-run and silver.

'You didn't catch that on a Kerr's Pink,' he says.

'No, the only thing I caught today on a Kerr's Pink was you.'

I'd forgotten the tale until I heard it again one evening. I think it might have been from a local guy in the pub at Applecross. Like salmon and sea-trout and types of vessel, stories migrate too.

The salmon coble was found on a few places on the west coast where a commercial salmon fishery took place. Sheena Walker grew up in the coastal village of Calgary on the west side of the Isle of Mull. Her father was one of the last of the licensed salmon fishers. She described helping him with the boat, setting out salmon nets. The photographer Gus Wylie captured the last days of casting nets from cobles on the Isle of Skye.[3] But it was only a mile or two from home, out of Stornoway, Isle of Lewis, where I saw one of the larger examples, adapted for lobster fishing.

I remember her as the *Passage East* when she appeared on our shores first. I would gaze from the wide stern to follow that exaggerated sweeping sheer to her nose. This shape seems to me like a boat from an illustrated children's book and yet it has stood the test of centuries. If it hadn't worked it would have changed. This example had bolted-on bilge keels so she could sit easily ashore, and these would also offer some resistance to leeway. I could see why a creel-fisherman would adapt a large salmon coble, and this was as large as any I've seen. All that clear working space aft and a low transom would make shooting a fleet as easy as it ever could be, though maybe not as safe. She might well have proved herself fit for the adapted purpose in the sea-lochs and Approaches to Stornoway. But the North Minch changes nearly as fast as the North Sea. Once, on coastguard watch, we received a new gale warning pretty much out of the blue. Then it became a storm warning. In fact it was a Beaufort hurricane – wind speeds of Force 12. That is above those of a 'violent storm'. Several craft were caught out, including creel-fishers who were trying to recover their gear before the blow. The adapted coble was now called *Westward.*

Stornoway lifeboat was launched in answer to a distress call from the *Westward*, one of several concurrent rescue tasks. With so much going on, all communications had to be as clipped as they could be. Lifeboat crews and fishermen tend to be very low-key in any case in their descriptions of events. I knew that conditions, even a few miles from harbour, would be engulfing. The vessel had attempted to anchor to avoid being swept out to sea, but that was not holding. At wind speeds upwards of 65 knots or so, the air would be filled with spray so that visibility would be like being in a blizzard. Even breathing, out on deck, would be a matter of gulping a breath when you could.

Years later, one of the crew, John MacLennan (now retired), was asked to give a talk to a local body. I was there, partly because he tells a very good story and partly because you are always separated from experience by communications technology when working, as I did, in an Operations Room. Typically, John spoke of cox Calum Macdonald's great seamanship in driving the lifeboat through the spray and holding station alongside the foundering vessel. He directed

John and a second crewman, 'Scotch', to board the *Westward* to transfer the persons on board.

John made it sound as if he'd been stepping on a bus. I thought back to all the other incidents that night and the descriptions of conditions. 'Tell us a bit more about that stepping on board, John,' I asked. John showed an image of the lifeboat taken from another vessel that night. You might think it was in the Southern Ocean. The rise and fall from one vessel to another must have been immense. Calum was awarded the RNLI bronze medal for the rescue of that crew in a swell of some 15 feet. The vessel was lost. I am now glad to report that John has written up the story of that night, and that of several other lifeboat services too. You can find his accounts, though still played-down, on the Facebook page of Stornoway RNLI Lifeboat and shared on other local social media sites.

NOTES

(1) Donald Smith, Donald Smith: The Paintings of an Islander, *Jonathan Smith and Professor Murdo Macdonald (eds) (Stornoway, Acair, 2019), p. 118.*

(2) Patrick Elliott, Joan Eardley: Land & Sea – A Life in Catterline *(Edinburgh, National Galleries of Scotland, 2021).*

(3) Gus Wylie, Hebridean Light *(Edinburgh, Birlinn, 2003). Gus Wylie followed several salmon fishers and exhibited studies of the Hebrides in black and white photography with an exhibition, and a book (with colour photographs), including studies of the Skye salmon-netting.*

10
FROM WORKING CRAFT TO YACHT DESIGN

FROM ANSTRUTHER TO EYEMOUTH, YOU'LL see them. Among the low-maintenance creel boats of GRP, your eye will go to a vessel which is someone's pride and joy. Very few commercial workboats are built in timber now, due to cost and maintenance, but the life expectancy of a timber craft is long. That life can be extended, like Grandfather's shovel, by replacing parts. Usually there are local styles in the way these craft are painted. Perhaps the nameplate will be carved with a scroll. A 'cove line' near the gunnel might be in a particular yellow, out from a black skin, and it might end with an arrow-shape. The fishing numbers might be painted on with contrasting shadow-lines to give an appearance of being solid.

As to the shapes, there will be variations as there are with all other working boats. In Crail, Anstruther, Kirkcaldy or Newhaven, or any haven in Scotland, you will usually see at least one survivor. These creel boats will tend to be more like a Fifie yole than a Zulu. At 20 feet or so, she will want all the grip she can get, and all the load-carrying capacity. She will be plump. Smaller craft tend to be more beamy in proportion. When a boat was costed by the foot, that gave more volume, so more value. A very few might have an auxiliary sail still, perhaps hoisted when a stubby mast is raised from its 'crutch'. Typically, she will come to a point in the bow, on deck but not that

Victoria 30 (Chuck Paine design)

sharp. There will be fullness to give buoyancy to a vessel that will be bobbing close to dangerous reefs most of its working life. The beam will often seem to be carried aft, way beyond the middle, and then suddenly turn into a stern. That will often be rounded too, so the whole shape is more like an oval. In fact, it is often very like that of a lemon. The poet and visual artist Ian Hamilton Finlay came up with the concept for a series of cards and screenprints, based on that sharp-witted observation. I'd argue it is more accurate for the smaller classes of inshore craft rather than the incarnations of large Scottish fishing vessels.

Another twentieth-century Scottish artist, John Bellany, returned with compulsion to the Port Seton fishing fleet for the images, myths and omens that illuminate his intense paintings. An early example, showing the building of a working boat, has recently been bought by the Scottish Maritime Museum. These boats have survived because their very quiet domestic beauty is derived from them being just about perfect for the job. If a plank is staved in or rotted, it can be renewed. A BMC motor, out of a taxi, or a marinised industrial unit from Ford or Kubota, will run all day on a few litres of diesel. A hydraulic capstan, set not far from the tiller, can be easily reached and steadily do all the hauling. Usually she will be 'three-quarter-decked', with a hatch over one hole for the catch and gear and a removable canvas over the cockpit area. An arm can stretch to steering, gear lever or hauler, without the need to perch on a jumping and slimy deck.

You might ask if there was no large-scale boatbuilding this far down the coast to match that done in boom days further north. There was plenty. People tend to associate Scottish shipbuilding with the west coast and the Clyde in particular. In fact, many of the great sailing ships were built by Hall, Russell and Co., Aberdeen. The stairway at Aberdeen Maritime Museum opens up vistas of the half-models made as a first step to achieving the shape of elegant but strong ships. The clipper *Thermopylae* was built for the Aberdeen Line by Walter Hood and Co., but at 212 feet, such ships are out of the scope of this book. Hall, Russell also ran a yard in Burntisland. There was the Robb Caledon yard in Dundee and several major yards in Leith.[1] At Arbroath, the yard of Mackay Boat Builders was established in 1967. They have kept going by diversifying. They have an area where the environment for build and repair in GRP can be achieved but they also do repairs to historic craft such as *Reaper*. This company also has a contract for the long-term repair and maintenance work which keeps the polar exploration ship *Discovery* on public display in Dundee.

Another example is James N. Millar and Sons of St Monans, Fife, established in 1747. Up until 1976 the yard would alternate between making large-scale commercial craft and turning out a yacht or two by established designers when the fishing was quiet. They built more than one vessel drawn by Robert Clark, who was the designer of Francis Chichester's solo Transatlantic winner, *Gipsy Moth III*. They also made many smaller yoles, mainly for creel-fishing. These are highly developed examples of the 'double-enders' already described – full-bodied Fifies but with a most pleasing and practical canoe stern. That has good lift but it will cut a following sea to take most of the power out of it, without harm. James A. Pottinger reprints a photo of a handsome pair of these in harbour.[2] He proposes that the distinctive stern was carried into the design of the 'Miller Fifer'. These would not be the first or last yachts built to make use of the proven seakeeping features of working craft.

The shape has been developed by generations of experience rather than by systematic testing in controlled conditions. Even if you have no technical knowledge of the subject, observation of the shape of one very fine example may suggest that sometimes what we call beauty is a sense that a shape, well-nigh perfect for its purpose, has evolved. *Girl Elsie* was ashore at Cockenzie harbour, south side of the Firth of Forth, when I photographed her in the summer of 2021. There is definite sheer bow to stern, but in a run that is subtle rather than extreme. She would shed water, going into waves. Breakers would be parted by her fairly sharp stern. But her underwater shape, at both forward and aft sections, is more round than the lie of the planking above. You just know this vessel will have astonishing buoyancy for her size (about 8 metres or so) and a hefty load-carrying capacity.

I was not surprised to hear from her owner, reluctantly preparing her for sale, that she had been built across the Firth at St Monans. But the next part of his story is a reminder that vessels are moved around the country, bought and sold. And, like the great sailing drifters before them, more recent creel boats will be built to take account of the given needs or wants of the one who commissions the boat. I was told that *Girl Elsie* was built for working creels in Pentland Firth, out from Stroma. That island, inhabited until the 1960s, was once famed for its own particular craft. *Elsie* was commissioned at a time when the

Stroma yoles were no longer being built. She is nothing like a replica of those, but a different solution to meeting the same demanding set of requirements. She had to be capable of transporting fleets of heavy creels and the catch. She had to work in waters with great tidal velocity, which often would be colliding with waves driven from the other direction.

This man had fallen in love with that shape when he went to view the boat on the north coast, near John o'Groats. Her name helped. It's often thought that changing the name tempts fate, but his grannie's name happened to be Elsie so that would do fine. Lorries were returning south without loads so she had come that way. He had kept her Kelvin going, when parts were no longer made, by making them himself. At last a steady Perkins three-cylinder was installed but he had kept the Kelvin because that was just the right thing to go with that boat.

Our conversation was a reminder that boats built for work or pleasure are often containers of emotion. The history of Millers of St Monans also prove that distinctions between workboats and yachts are blurred. The canoe-sterned Scottish working boat was to influence the American yacht designer Chuck Paine. His publications describe how observation of these craft fed into the first of his designs that went into build – the American-built Frances series and the UK equivalents. This developed further into the Victoria 30. Her lines clearly show a homage to the lemon-like seaboats of the Fife coast. The blog of Thomas Armstrong places photographs of typical working boats beside reproductions of the designer's working sketches to reveal the influence.[3] The yachts that resulted, at 26 to 30 feet, built in timber first and later moulded in GRP, have an excellent reputation as seaboats. Voyages which have been documented include many crossings of the Bay of Biscay. *Gallivant,* a Victoria 30 presently in Inverness, brought the couple who owned her to cruise the Norwegian coast more than once and also out west to St Kilda.

Another contemporary boat designer who acknowledges the working craft of Scotland is Iain Oughtred. The Australian sailor, now a resident of Skye, has adapted the traditional small craft of Norway and Shetland for building in glued plywood construction. It is his pocket yacht designs, 'Wee Seal' and the larger 'Grey Seal', which show, like Paine's double-enders, how the proven sea-kindly shapes have been adopted and adapted. I was present at the first launch of a Grey Seal built in a wind-powered workshop by Topher Dawson on the Scoraig peninsula. Topher had worked from Iain's drawings but adapted the build back to traditional copper-fastened, larch construction. Iain had drawn a variation of a gunter rig, similar to that used for a time on Shetland racing yoles. This one had a sweet-curving yard, reminiscent of that used by our neighbours across in the Netherlands. She was shoal-draught but used a lowered centreboard to counteract leeway. I saw then how she sailed well on all points. This was the sheltered water of Little Loch Broom. Some years later I saw, from the *sgoth an Sulaire*, how well she coped with a North Sea swell as part of the Moray Firth Flotilla. She was both handy and fast. In shape, it was a pronounced sheer and a timeless canoe stern that defined her. I saw her as a pleasure craft with working-craft influences.

Motor-sailors, marketed as the Miller Fifer, mainly built to 26, 28 or 33 feet, became a sought-after pleasure craft. These integrated features of the Scottish working fishing boat, such as a sheer described as 'proud' in the trade, protective bulwarks and that distinctive stern. The wheelhouse, which gave protection, also helped this impression, as did a very solid build, though with greater use of mahogany in interior and trim. The yard was taken over and the focus changed to manufacturing workboats in steel. Last time I visited, there were still abandoned plates with the remains of mysterious graphics that meant something to the welder. These sprayed scripts are like a futuristic typeface. I found a quote from type designer Eliott Grunewald that I think describes what I saw: 'Something illegible still has something to say.' I'd suggest that could be applied to the signs and survivors of vessels created by closed industries.

As with so many of the world's coastlines, there are now far more pleasure craft than workboats to be seen around Scotland. Marinas continue to expand, which indicates that putting out to sea is still a driving force to many. But there is one more elegiac note to sound before we move on down the east coast. Dysart was the small harbour that hosted one of the most competitive of racing scenes for small craft. This was recreation for many of the Fife miners. Their vessels may have begun as working Fifie or Zulu yoles, at about 18 to 20 feet, but these became drastically modified. Frames and planking became lighter and masts higher. At the peak of their development, they became sophisticated racing machines in the same way as the 'Shetland model boats' came a long way from their Norse forebears.

Tackles were rigged to hasten the dipping of the huge single lugsail, but that still required good coordination from the crew. She would be tender, being so light and narrow in the beam, though with buoyancy in her stern-quarters, especially useful on the run. They did carry ballast, but probably not enough of it. Crew would have to shift pronto or all would get a ducking. Like the larger sailing drifters, the Zulu type was easier to tack and more manoeuvrable with its shorter keel. That would be an advantage rounding a buoy. But the plumb Fifie would have the edge on keeping a long track and often be that bit faster, with a longer waterline. Sadly, the Forth Maritime Preservation Society, which kept surviving examples alive, has folded due to lack of members but two examples are still maintained by the Dysart Traditional Boats Group.

I have often had the pleasure of sailing *Cuach*, a very racy Zulu skiff built as a recent homage to the Dysart yoles. Sandy Macdonald had been fascinated by the Dysart racing as a young man. When he had access to some clear boatskin larch, he set out to make his own version. He towed the completed craft, shimmering with its varnish coatings, to the Scottish Traditional Boat Festival at Portsoy. Ashore, all could see saw how fine the frames were and how tall the mast. Even with lead ingots, packed to her keel, she is tender. Precise distribution of crew weight is just as important as sail trim. But it is exhilarating. She tilts and heels easily but she has the power to accelerate. Even with the 45-degree rake at the stern, she needs a fair bit of momentum to come tight through the wind. That bow is pretty well vertical. Off the wind, she can roll, but there is more lift in the stern than you might think. A close look at her underwater shape, when she is out on her trailer, reveals all.

Once I took on the task of delivering her up a sea-loch while the west wind was funnelling down it. We were short-handed, with just two on board. Each person had to multi-task. It was breathless, but tackles at each side eased the work of letting one stay go and hardening the other as we tacked. We had organised additional reefs in the sail so that her high rig had a full six rows. We found it was critical that the cloth carried was proportional to the changing wind strength. Even in 10 knots or so, she sailed much better with one in. Above that, you really had no choice. The spray would come over that sharp bow section as an indicator and reminder. But she cut through short-chop and kept her speed up.

She is not really successful as a training boat for young skippers to go on to take charge of larger lugsail craft. *Cuach* is just a bit specialised, and requires good sailing skills to start off with. She is, however, a fine craft for dinghy sailors to get a taste of sailing a very powerful vessel of traditional construction and rig. She can now be seen afloat in Tobermory Bay, just across the Sound of Mull from the farm still run by her builder. It must give him pleasure to see the miners' joy experienced by another generation on another coast.

NOTES

(1) National Records of Scotland, 'Shipbuilding Records': https://www.nrscotland.gov.uk/research/guides/shipbuilding-records.

(2) James A. Pottinger, Wooden Fishing Boats of Scotland *(Stroud, The History Press, 2013), p. 124.*

(3) Thomas Armstrong, '70.8%: Chuck Paine's Frances', on 70point8percent blog: http://70point8percent.blogspot.com/2010/03/chuck-paines-frances.html.

11
ST AYLES SKIFF
– A ROWING REVIVAL

THIS TIME WE'LL START WITH a story. It happened in Shetland, so we are taking a detour, but then we'll return to the coast of Fife and look a bit closer at the south side of the Forth. A naval warship was visiting Lerwick. A rowing regatta was in full swing in the harbour. One officer said they should make an effort to meet the locals. They could surely get a fit team together. They did. It was all-male. They had a chat with the organisers. 'You'd be mighty welcome. Have your guys rowed together much before?'

The upshot was that the cream of the Royal Navy men lost to a local women's team. The officer might not have known that rowing was here approached with something like religious fervour. In the Faroe Islands, every district has its team and links were made with the neighbouring islanders. For some years communities all round Shetland had been competing with traditional clinker rowing craft very similar to the Faroese boats. Teams were selected and the international aspect of the Faroese–Shetlandic rowing regattas helped build up huge interest. Women were and are as involved as men. If we make an even bigger jump to the south-west and the Scilly Isles, there is also huge interest in competitive rowing of pilot gigs. I was lucky enough to be waiting for weather in St Mary's once while a regatta was on. It was the pitch of excitement that international football or rugby might generate, but this was different because there were as many participants as spectators.

That is now what has happened with the St Ayles skiff movement. The Scottish Coastal Rowing Association grew from meetings between boatbuilder Alec Jordan and the Scottish Fisheries Museum in Anstruther. The aim was to encourage members of Scotland's communities to become actively involved in coastal seafaring. This was to be inclusive and not dependent on having the means to own and maintain your own vessel. Iain Oughtred was approached. Iain has a deep interest in Scottish culture. He also has long experience of designing for building with glued plywood construction. His designs stipulate joining plywood planks with a suitable glue, such as epoxy resin, rather than traditional rivets or clenched nails on steamed ribs. Epoxy coating can also harden up the surface of softer veneers. His designs based on the timeless Norwegian faering are available in two versions, for traditional construction, or glued plywood planking.

The inherited form of vessel which is behind the very clean lines of Iain's drawing for a St Ayles skiff is the Fair Isle yole (or yoal). More of that later. The new craft was named after the medieval chapel which once stood on the site of the museum. A prototype was developed by Jordan Boats and trialled by enthusiasts gathered by the museum's membership and its active boat club. Maintenance of wooden vessels is often a huge issue for a boat club unless it has access to a suitable boatshed for work and storage. The four-oared boat, with a rudder for the cox, was light enough to be safely lifted on and off a trailer. It lent itself to a protective fitted cover. Its long shape and fine entry let her cut through the chop that will often stop a craft launched from the shore or at a slip. The skiff is 22 feet long (6.7 metres) with a beam of 5 feet 8 inches (1.7 metres) and fairly shallow draught.

Yet, like the vessels which inspired her, a fullness in her shape gives her enough buoyancy to give the lift required for seaworthiness. The factors that modified the shape of Norwegian originals for the

St Ayles skiff (Iain Oughtred design)

tide races in 'the hole' between Fair Isle and Mainland made for a design that would work for deeps or shallows all round Scotland. The Fifers were joined by a Robbie Wightman, a keen rower from North Berwick. The Fife miners had their rowing regattas as well as finely tuned lugsail boat racing. But there were remnants of once-vibrant rowing clubs, all around the coast, such as the boatshed at Portobello. From the beginning, the aim was to rekindle interest in a sport for all ages. This was not to be rowing in highly tuned sculls with moving seats, such as those used in many university rowing clubs.

The Scottish Coastal Rowing Association was formed on 29 May 2010 after a first regatta involving five boats. By 2013 a similar body was formed in New Zealand. The movement became especially strong in Northern Ireland, leading to the holding of the Skiff Worlds in Strangford Lough in 2016. Now there are also fleets in England, the Netherlands and Tasmania, just a few examples of the international distribution of this new take on an old concept. Because the vessel is sold (like its predecessors of timber planks) in kit form, it is bought at a very reasonable cost.

A fair measure of woodworking skill is needed for the initial construction, but then members, with a bit of care, can help with finishing and painting. Iain has deliberately left some scope for initiative with the finish of the construction, once the essential form is complete. You can see where perhaps a retired shipwright or even a cabinet-maker in a group has made laminations or sculpted hardwood trims to add some individual flair. Others are more utilitarian and no slower for that. The oars too are freestyle, within certain limits. For example, curved blades are not allowed as that might give an advantage to clubs with a higher budget or an ace joiner in their number. There is room for innovation in the design of fittings, such as the method of joining oars to securing pins. No metalwork is allowed, but ingenious fulcrums with nylon bushes have been invented. The concept is a development of the Faroese or Shetlandic pin and securing band (*kaeb* and *humlabund*), which adds efficiency by stopping the oar from sliding about between pins, thus losing some of the energy.

The skiff is a triumph of intermediate technology. Modern materials and innovation are encouraged, but only up to a point. In that respect this craft is more like a 'restricted class' of competitive sailing craft, like that built to an international set of rules or limits. It is not a 'one-design' where you could jump from boat to boat with no penalty or advantage.[1] Competition between clubs has been a strong stimulus from the beginning, perhaps learning from the racing fleets of like sailing craft which have driven boatbuilding in many areas. That seems to me similar to the way a competitive edge to 'taking your share' of a commercially successful fishery has prompted Scotland's boatbuilding on the much bigger scale.

If you look at the list of registered vessels, you will see the current number and distribution. At the time of writing (2021) there is still a noticeable cluster around the place of origin. The only areas where the scene has not taken off are those that already have a large number of people involved in their own small-craft scene, such as

Orkney and Shetland. Many coastal towns have more than one skiff. Sometimes this is to keep the element of competition to the fore and sometimes because there is a different emphasis. For some it is about fitness training. Practice for races and set-turns is part of that. Others are more interested in covering a few miles, perhaps to link with a neighbouring crew or make a landing on an island they could not otherwise reach.

It might all sound a bit sedate, but there are images of a light skiff being launched in significant surf, piling into Portobello. Safety issues are to the fore and most clubs have firm rules on equipment and procedures. I was to get a taste of both the seakeeping qualities of the skiff and the competitive edge, at the first Skiff World Championships, held at Ullapool in July 2013. Like nearly all the Stornoway team, I was there by accident. A skiff had been built, quite early on, driven by a dedicated father and daughter team. Sandy Macdonald (no relation to the Ardsligachan farmer-boatbuilder) nudged her dad, Kenny, who had already restored and built a boat or two, into taking the initiative. The club structure had not quite happened and the boat was little-used. Local sailors felt it was a bit of a disgrace if teams from the Netherlands and Tasmania took part but our own island could not manage to get the skiff and a few rowers across.

Our 'manager', Gerald, kept his own yacht in the harbour. He hailed a couple of us who also had our own boats and the plan was hatched. He would get the skiff across. We should get a couple of yachts over and that would be the accommodation sorted. Luckily some of us were quite old, so that was good for entering races where you needed over 50s and over 60s. Best bring a couple of tools over. He wasn't sure what the skiff might need. It had been lying for a while.

We had grand sailing through the Summer Isles in fresh breeze. The first impression at Ullapool was of colour. When we paddled ashore after picking up some harbour moorings, we were dazzled by the paint schemes. Some echoed the restrained black of fishing boats, with a yellow detail or an inscribed nameboard as the flourish. Then there was the Portsoy ladies' boat, lipstick pink. Other racers went for a yellow that was't very apologetic. That stood out even from the Ferrari reds. Some tillers were laminated in selected contrasting timbers. Others, like ours, didn't have a tiller at all but a couple of cords, Faroese style, with the luxury of a plastic fishing float at each end to gain a grip. 'Good,' I said. 'That saves weight, and if we're steering we're braking.' The others humoured me with a nod.

But the oars were a bit of an issue. Even with gloves, our hands weren't going to survive the first race, which was termed 'long-distance'. Gerald had reckoned the traditional set, made by the builder in larch, were just too heavy. A light set, in whitewood and ply, had been knocked up but the handle ends weren't quite complete. When was the first race? I'm no joiner but I do keep a little block plane in the boat's tool-box. I'd just emptied everything into the bag I'd taken ashore along with the oatcakes and cheese and bananas that would provide fuel. Others were throwing out heavy floorboards and improvising foot-rests. We got a lot of encouragement as the shavings flew. Dr Jim sanded as I moved on to the next handle. The spruce dust continued right up until the boat was in the water. 'Right,' said Gerald, who is quite heavy, taking the helming seat, 'we'd better get to the start.' I'm nudging 9 stone after a good Sunday dinner so I thought I might get asked to fill the cox's seat. Best get a banana down me.

I don't know who said it first, but we all thought it. We were the Jamaica bobsleigh team, on the water. The ferry hooted on its way out and then I recognised the funnel-red, the black and white trim of CalMac on our skiff. Wasn't the builder a bosun for a while? Gerald was on the VHF to find what lane we were in. These were all laid out and colour-coded. In the short races you had to remain in lane and pass your own post. The work gone into the logistics of this gathering was as huge as the goodwill and friendship in the air. None of this damped down the competitive edge. This was most visible in the local rivalry between the host boats and those from the other side of the headland. The word on the water was you had to eat nothing but beetroot for a week and abstain from sex forever to get a place in a Coigach skiff. We also gained a sense of creative frisson between teams either side of the Forth. The shouts across our deck, if we'd had one, were a clue. They were a bit over our Hebridean heads though, in pretty broad Forthspeak.

We lagged a lot in the sheltered harbour area. Our neighbours/enemies seemed to do some kind of quarter-stroke, followed by a half-stroke, then a full pull as a ritualistic thing. This was to help overcome inertia from a sitting start. Jim broke into heresy first. 'You don't think we should have done some practising first, Gerald?' he gasped, but our leader just smiled. The strange thing was, when we got into a good, friendly, short jabble, with winds sweeping down between Rhue Point and Isle Martin, we were well up the field. That was fine, but the flat water the rest of the weekend and the non-gassy real ale at the waterside dulled our keenness.

We were beginning to realise some folk did this as a means of exercise. There was a bit more to getting the skiff moving than the tweaking of a sail now and then. The full-length 'short' races were taking their toll on us. Then came the breakthrough. We could run a mixed male and female team. We got youth on our side when broad-shouldered young Martin, who worked for the harbour trust, let it slip that his grandpa was from Lewis. He qualified. Then we got a much-needed rest when Gerald found a real-live squad of actual female rowers from Essex. They had come to spectate but we could be twinned with these folks due to a century of herring trade. All our grandparents had been down that coast. Hell, we might even be related. We had a fresh women's team at one bold sweep.

Then came the evening 'sprints'. We were paired with some powerful-looking guys who had trailed their own boats from the Netherlands. Then I made a mistake. I know Iain Oughtred from the storytelling scene, so hailed him over. 'You haven't coxed one of your own boats yet, mate.' He was definitely lighter than Gerald. Once he sat down, I saw the evening light stall as it tried to penetrate his glasses. Oh, Oh. That was why we played such a tactical game, weaving a creative course to find the turning buoy as one of our squad did a commentary for a cox who couldn't see where we were going. Maybe the Dutch team thought we knew what we were doing and tried to follow us. Somehow, we crossed the finish line first. Sadly, this led to the dismantling of the best boat joinery in the whole fleet. Next day they weighed their skiff then took their tools out and took half of it apart. I think I know the Dutch for 'We don't need this.' It was like a chorus as the bits flew to the sand, 12 coats of varnish on each.

NOTES

(1) Note on 'one-design' aspect provided by Iain Oughtred in email to author, October 2022: 'The vital bit of the craft, the hull, really is one-design. This was reckoned to be essential, given the varying levels of experience of the builders; this was why the builders were restricted to using the plywood kits. And one-off building from plans was not permitted, likewise traditional construction. I am very aware of the difficulties experienced with one-design sailing dinghies: Jack Chippendale said that most classes were affected by builders tweaking the tolerances just a wee bit here and there, and making plainly faster boats. Jack gave up on building one-designs for this reason. But the skiffs seem to be so nearly the same that 'foreign' crews can come from far away and borrow a boat that they can race competitively. Only the oars might be a little different from their own.'

12
THE BALDIE OF LEITH

BEFORE WE LEAVE THE DOUBLE-ENDERS to be found from the Tay to the Forth, I would invite you to rest your eyes on one particular example. This vessel has several distinctive qualities. It also has a memorable name. The Baldie is not called that because of a sparse rig up top. Like the currant biscuit, it takes its name from the Italian patriot, Garibaldi. A clear explanation is provided by the Scottish Fisheries Museum, who maintain a surviving example in commission:

> The reason for this name dates back to the 1860s, when the first of these small boats were being built at a time when Scots were sympathetic to the unification of Italy being led by Garibaldi: this new class of small boats was named in tribute to him, with the 'Gari' bit later dropped! This outward-looking perspective is also responsible for those bigger herring drifters with raked sterns being called 'Zulus', after the South African wars of the time.[1]

The Scottish National Dictionary adds some notes on the craft, adding a spelling variation of 'bauldie': 'A carvel-built fishing-boat with the mast far forward, rigged with a lug sail and sometimes a jib.'

There are many archived photographs which show groups

of similar boats huddling behind the stone walls of small havens, often tidal, all down Scotland's east coast. Once more, an accurate model helps keep the shape alive. George Macleod's version is in the collection of the National Maritime Museum, Greenwich. It represents *Refuge*, registered LH1139, at 1:12 scale. That would put the 1885 original at about 9.6 metres or just over 31 foot on deck. And it does indeed have a deck, as this design was at least partially a response to the Washington Report (see pp. 21–2).[2]

You can also see a restored example, and even sail one if you join the boat club linked to the Scottish Fisheries Museum. Their *White Wing* was built in Gardenstown in 1917 at the yard of one Jas Cadger. She was last working as ME113, out of Montrose. Now restored by the museum, she joins the flagship *Reaper* to visit festivals and reach some places the larger vessel cannot access. Her modest draught allows her to transit Scotland's restored southern canal system, the Forth and Clyde and the Union. Like *Refuge*, she carries a single mast. Variations in the baldies' rig are a reminder that different options would be preferred by different skippers and in different areas, in the same way that the large-class Fifie, *Swan*, was gaff-rigged in Shetland. The range of locations is a reminder that designs have seldom been limited to one area, even if they are most closely associated with a particular port, in this case Leith. Peter Anson, author of several works on the vessels and lore of Scotland's east-coast fishing communities, also refers to the 'Leith Baldy'.[3] *White Wing* now carries a single dipping lug, tacked at the bow. Her mast and yard are of moderate height and length. At a glance, everything is geared to seaworthiness. She might need a bit of a breeze to get moving, but she has the look of a boat that could withstand a bit of a blow.

If she looks familiar to you, that could be because she starred in a film made for TV. The BBC 2 version of *The Shutter Falls*, by Norman Malcolm Macdonald, was screened in 1987. The script catches the contrast of voices and cultures of Scotland as the Hebridean herring

A baldie (based on White Wing*)*

girls travel to gut and pack the catches on east-coast quaysides. There is a brilliant poetic motif in the playscript carried forward into other forms of the work. A comparison is made between the pink gut of the herring and the bulb the photographer will press to still a moment in time.

The rig of George Macleod's *Refuge* is very different. She carries a long bowsprit, so there is a fair bit of sail forward in her foresail triangle. That seems to be flying free without a fixed forestay – a usual arrangement so that the lance of a sprit out front can be taken inboard before entering harbour. Nearly all the mainsail area is aft of the mast, so it would be used as a 'standing lug'. This has the huge advantage, in tight corners, of not needing lowering and dipping when you turn to take the wind on the other side. This is a rig you could work efficiently with only two souls, so it was ideal for working handlines or creels. You could even work single-handed if you needed to. Because the sprit sets a good proportion of the sail area forward, the boat would probably be very well balanced. I would imagine the jib would help you turn that long keel through the wind and water. You might have to let it 'back' with the wind pressure on it, to help. Controls for the rig could be set up so that it would be possible to raise sail, lower it and tack or gybe without leaving the comparative security of the well in the fish-hold, midships or the smaller cockpit at the helming position.

The hulls under these rigs are very similar in shape. This is best appreciated in the model. There is a very slight rake at both bow and stern. She is of moderate draught, which is good for extending the times she can enter tidal harbours. She is fairly sharp at the bow, and her stern comes in to a neat curve but with less fullness than would be usual on most west-coast or Orcadian inshore boats. Most significant is the fullness that is carried above her waterline from aft of the mast to about two-thirds of her length. My guess is that this shape has been refined until it is about the most perfect compromise between speed, directional stability and load-carrying. If I were working a small craft under sail, short-handed, she'd be close to my first choice. No wonder a contemporary designer like Chuck Paine sees sense in borrowing from that collective experience.

Surviving records show that these hulls could be from about 23 to 40 feet. The larger ones would carry the dipping lug forward with a standing-lug mizzen, like most of the larger sailing drifters. At the larger sizes they would also be likely to be flush skins composed of carvel planking, rather than built in overlapping clinker. *White Wing* is clinker-built, but records reveal that she carried the two-masted rig when first launched. She also carried a Kelvin 26/30-horsepower motor, regarded as an 'auxiliary' propulsion rather than the main power source. This was already a growing trend. In the same year a new vessel, registered in Methil, Fife, as *Perseverance* (ML456) and built by James Weatherhead of Eyemouth for a Buckhaven skipper, had the same model of motor installed. The choices give a clue to the uses the working boat was set to. That motor would not have provided enough power to tow a trawl or dredge so she would have most likely been longlining for quality inshore fish most of her working life. In season, that was likely to alternate with setting drift nets for herring and creels for crab and lobster.

The stoutness of her method of construction is revealed by images of restoration work undertaken by the Scottish Fisheries Museum. If you move from that to studying the shore-based collection, you can observe a sharp contrast. The museum has *Jim*, one of the Dysart racing fleet, as an example. She is of course pared back to be just strong enough to carry her rig and the strains from keen competition. There is no tolerance for wear and tear from hauling gear and transporting the catch.

The 'courtyard collection' also shows examples of the scaffie, Fifie and Zulu yawls or yoles which carry the essentials of the shape of the former great working vessels in their scaled-down inshore versions. You can also see an example of a salmon coble, now that so few are in active use. An example of a Fair Isle skiff is there too, so a comparison can be made between the craft in its traditional construction and the contemporary rowing vessels it inspired.

NOTES

(1) *Virtual tour of the Scottish Fisheries Museum: https://www.scotfishmuseum.org/ explore-the-museum.php.*

(2) *Captain John Washington, 'Fishing Boats (Scotland): Copy of Captain Washington's Report on the Loss of Life and on the Damage Caused to Fishing Boats on the East Coast of Scotland, in the Gale of the 19th August 1848', London, House of Commons, 1849.*

(3) *Peter Anson,* Fishing Boats and Fisherfolks on the East Coast of Scotland *(Boston, MA: E.P. Dutton & Co., 1930; reprinted J.M. Dent, 1971). Artist and author Anson turned his attention from the cathedrals of Europe (1929–36) to the fishing communities of Scotland.*

13
CRAFT OF THE EYEMOUTH DISASTER

AS I WRITE, I'M CONSULTING a detailed electronic chart for the approaches to Eyemouth harbour. It has depth contours for areas which should never be exposed even when there is an exceptional tidal range, and it has the underlined 'drying heights' of many reefs and stoney shores which certainly will be revealed when the sea falls back. This also means that for some periods in the ebb and flow of tide many reefs will be 'awash'. With seas rushing in, driven by both wind and tide, it will then be impossible to distinguish between the spray from a breaking wave and that created by water crashing against stone.

These days, a sailor approaching Eyemouth harbour, day or night, can refer to a screen, fixed in a suitable position on board or even hand-held. The navigator may also have a detailed paper chart or a detail from a pilot book, in clear graphics, all summarising the research and experience of others. A north cardinal mark with distinguishing features, day and night, will direct you to the safe side of another reef. Any combination of these aids will help you clear the line of hazards projecting out into the North Sea. You might be tired. There are very few refuges along this coast. A cruising sailor may have departed from Hull or Hartlepool or broken his journey at Scarborough. In previous days, a sailor would have had his compass, any local guiding lights working at the time, and the handed-down

Ariel Gazelle *(the original boat that survived the storm)*

knowledge of where the dangers lay. Fathoms charts, with their lines of soundings taken by lead-line from small boats, often had good detail. The rocks don't move but the banks of sand and shingle do. The difficulties of establishing and maintaining a safe harbour in this strategic location for fishing vessels, traders and transiting yachts are neatly summarised by the Eyemouth Harbour Trust: 'The two problems of shelter from wind and sea, and the restricted entrance due to the build-up of sand, have been the major concern of the Harbour Trustees over the decades. The original 1882 proposals put forward by Messrs Meek & Son might have gone a long way to solve them had the funds been available. A new breakwater and deep harbour entrance were eventually constructed in 1963/64. This involved the closure of the harbour with a coffer dam.'[1]

The 1882 proposals were part of a response to losses suffered in a great storm the previous year. It was not the first blast to wreak havoc in this vulnerable place. In 1767 the old pier was destroyed and ships driven so far inland they could not be refloated. The breakwater of Smeaton pier, which replaced it, stands yet, though it needed major repairs at different times. It did not save many of the fishermen caught out on 14 October 1881. Detailed studies on the Eyemouth disaster, including full-length books have been published.[2] Here, I can only attempt to convey something of the issues in running for a harbour, and compare factors affecting the losses in the Eyemouth area with those elsewhere on the Scottish coasts. There are strong similarities with devastation suffered at the north-east tip of Scotland at different times. Donald Campbell's powerful drama *The Widows of Clyth*, first produced by the Traverse Theatre in 1979 and described by the *Scotsman* as 'the major literary event of the Festival', explored the tragic effects of the 1876 storm on a small Caithness community. It is the sheer numbers lost which makes the Eyemouth disaster such a tragedy.

We are concerned here, first and foremost, with the boats which brought deaths as well as livelihoods. Judging from contemporary photographs of a packed harbour, those of Eyemouth and the near hamlets of Coldingham and Burnmouth were not radically different from the majority of craft of the time. The town has its own boatbuilding history. Its present boatyard, Eyemouth Marine, summarises this on its website. Other local records also reveal a history of building brigs to over 120 tons, by builders including Fergus Brown, from 1757 to 1812. Boats were simply built in the open, at the beach, before James Tait established his yard at Brownsbank. His first craft was launched in 1827. Thirty years later, the records show a succession of craft built by James Weatherhead and Sons. We can assume that individual skippers or owners would feed their requirements, based on experience, to the builder, so probably no two similar working craft would be completely identical. Many of these were lost in the disaster, along with even smaller craft, including inshore cobles or 'punts'.

Archived photographs show a fleet of 'summer boats' at Eyemouth, taken well up the burn and worked ashore on rollers. These are Fifie-type craft with plumb bows and sterns but with a very similar rounded stern to the Fife and Newhaven craft of the time. They are fairly deep in the planking shape which composes the 'wetted area' or keel, and they have a fullness which would give buoyancy as well as load-carrying capacity. They would have heavy supporting frames to brace the vessel for the knocks of a working life. These working boats would have good tracking qualities but would likely need skilful use of the oars to turn the tight corners into the tidal havens at both Burnmouth and Eyemouth. They would have worked herring nets in season, perhaps lining for mackerel and setting creels. Mainly they would work with handlines and set 'small lines', each with a hundred or so baited hooks, both for subsistence and for marketable catches like flatfish and haddock.

But the winter fishing required a fleet of larger craft. These were built to take the pounding from venturing out between gales to take a share of a valuable catch of haddock and cod. In season, they would also have fished herring. There are records of the larger Eyemouth boats, at over 50 feet overall, following the shoals down to Yarmouth. These were also of the Fifie type but still often open to the weather. Most were two-masted. The dipping lug would be dropped on the approach, but the standing-lug mizzen would usually be left to steady the boat for the turn into harbour. The usual crew was seven. At this stage the skipper would be on the tiller, with the crew putting out three oars on each side to lever that long keel into the tight turn. The photographs show this in light airs. Other images show craft rafted up at Eyemouth approaches, waiting for the tide to rise to allow entrance. Plans had been drawn up for extending the harbour to allow entry at all states of tide, but there were disputes and politics so these works had not been done by the morning of 14 October 1881.

We have to try to imagine attempting that entrance in conditions that devastated woodlands and brought huge waves surging over the outlying reefs. First, we have to ask why they were out at all. The winter fishing was a huge gamble. There had been a long period of gales when nothing was earned. Lines were baited with mussels and coiled by the fisherwives. The fish were there, if they could be reached. Grounds ranged from about 5 to 15 miles out into the North Sea. There would be an early parliament, by the barometer, installed in hope of improving the odds. The pressure reading on the 14th was the lowest recorded, but it was a fair morning after so many poor ones. It was a case of one out, all out.

Winds are seldom constant as a depression goes through. They tend to 'back' anticlockwise. Extreme low pressure would also cause a tidal surge. Perhaps some crews thought they were safe because the glass could not fall any further. But the strongest winds can come on the rise in barometric pressure as well as the fall, if that is extreme. The Eyemouth fishers were not the only ones to take the risk, but they had a reputation for venturing out when there were warning signs to be read. Maybe their long run of luck in gaining shelter gave them a false feeling of security. These were men under pressure. Many have argued that a local dispute with the Church of Scotland minister over Church tax or tithes added to this. A vessel was an investment, and costs needed to be paid from catches.

First they had to row until they found any breeze to take them to the grounds. Most boats had shot their lines by the time the sky changed. There was a sudden darkening. Most skippers abandoned their gear rather than make an attempt to recover it. The majority of the fleet simply ran for home. Qualities of these vessels, their long keel and steady tracking, would work to advantage at that point. You might assume a working boat would be much slower than a yacht, but these craft had long waterlines and powerful rigs. A turn of speed was needed to reach the grounds and to get the catch to market. But now we have to look to the chart of the approaches to study two of the possible places of refuge.

Burnmouth has the South Carr drying reefs to one side of the tight inlet and Ross Carrs to the north. You have to make good 241 degrees true to get your line between extending rocks. That leaves no room for error. The shoreline either side is hard and jagged. Even if there were good marks, these would be invisible in driving spray. Worse, there is the most sudden shallowing. A few cables out, you have 50 metres plus and then that halves in a very short space. If waves are being funnelled in from the North Sea – a huge open fetch – they will be forced up even higher when they meet the shallows. At this point the long keel would work against you if a surging wave carried you off and you needed to work back to that narrowest of tracks. With seven souls aboard as the average crew, and all used to working sail and oars on a daily basis, that strength could normally counter the type's natural resistance to turning. In seas as steep as these, it would be impossible to keep an oar in the water, far less row effectively. And many of the boats which did make the approach had already lost at least one crewman, swept over or carried away by a sail out of control. Many had their sails in tatters and gear strewn about.

Breaking waves would be likely to cause these vessels to surf out of control. That sudden increase of speed would not have helped steerage, if it was equal to the rate of the wave. At that point the rudder will do nothing to direct you. You must be slower or faster. Remember that there are high and jagged rocks, either side of the only line in. Some of the boats were overturned and others were lifted up only to be dropped on the reefs. If you ran on to the north, the foul ground extends even further out, with more rocks between the shore and the Ross Carrs. Let's say your skipper has decided against trying for Burnmouth for these reasons and kept her well out to make a try for Eyemouth.

You might have two options, but only if the wind direction at the time of approach allowed either. In winds from between the south and the north you might find the angle to come between Gunsgreen Point and the harbour mouth, but keeping south of the long chain of reefs which includes Hurker and Hinker. These small summits are charted as not covering, but they might take a lot of finding if you were staring through the mass of spray in storm-force winds. Recorded accounts describe vessels unable to beat a way in under sail. Many were wrecked in the eastern approach. There is always a huge measure of chance in the result of a decision that has to be made on factors you just do not know. All these skippers would have known the state of the tide at different times that day. But in these extreme conditions they could not have judged when they would reach the approach or exactly what the wind would be doing when they got there.

With wind from east to west quadrants you might have a chance of showing the smallest scrap of sail to drive you between that long line of reefs and the extending rocks around the normally visible Hard Luff Rock. It is a testament to the seamanship of the times that so many of the boats made it to the approaches, and astonishing that some did manage to negotiate all these hazards off both Eyemouth and Burnmouth to enter these possible havens.[3] These lug-rigged boats would have many reef points to reduce power in big winds. I have had the experience of helming a 33-foot dipping lug boat in gusts between 30 and 40 knots. This is of course beyond our operating conditions, but despite modern forecasting you can still get caught out.

A well-coordinated crew can use a tiny portion of sail effectively when it's simply become too much, even after all your reefs are in. You tend to use simple sign-language rather than try to shout above the wind noise. You want someone looking ahead and another set of eyes astern. Most of all, you must try to anticipate the gusts and the waves that might spin you out of control. Apply the rudder in time and get all cloth down in time. Nod for the person on the halyard to lift the yard just enough for the gale to catch a scrap of sailcloth. You need that power to drive you out of the troughs. At the helm, you have to catch the eye of the one at the bow to make sure they don't relax for a second but swing on the luff (front edge) of the sail to keep it in control. We found that the lugsail is very difficult to tack when all reefs are in. (A *sgoth* of 25 to 33 feet overall will carry a sail with six reefing points.) In fact, it had to be hauled back up a foot or two after the tack (lowest point on forward edge) was released. Then you could attempt to swing the yard to the other side.

These experiences were both in wide harbours with natural shelter and the few hazards well-marked. Doing that in storm surges in tight channels seems impossible. I believe every person who puts to sea has moments of the clearest empathy with those gone before without our contemporary safety equipment. As always, the most powerful commentary is based on a first-hand account from one of the survivors, in this case the skipper of *Onward*:

> They left the harbour about half past eight in the morning, and, with a fine breeze from the west, proceeded as fast as they could to the fishing ground. A portion of the boats went to the southward, but the bulk went right out from the harbour. When about 7 or 8 miles from the land, they commenced to shoot their lines, there being then a strong breeze from the west. All of a sudden the wind fell to a dead calm. They commenced pulling their lines as soon as they shot them; they did not let them stop in the water the usual time. Before they had got 300 or 400 fathoms out, that was 4 or 5 strings of lines, the sky turned dark in the north-east, and he said to his brother that they were going to have a change, and it would be better to take in the sail. They were then under full sail, and they proceeded to take in the sail before the gale overtook them. All in a moment it became as dark as darkness itself.
>
> They were at their wits' end; they did not know what to do. He had been at sea for 28 years, and all his past experience falls to the ground in comparison with that day. Some of the crew said one thing, and some another, but there were all men at

their wits' end. They let go their lines, put the buoy on them, and made for the shore. They had not left the shooting ground a few minutes when they lost a man overboard. They had taken the course for the harbour, when a heavy wind lifted the sail clean up out of the boat and carried the man overboard. He thought at the time he had also lost his son, but he was still in the boat. They brought the boat to northward, to see if they could save the man, but it was all in vain. They then made for St Abb's head, and when they had made St Abb's they took their course for the harbour of Eyemouth, and when near there they came in contact with another boat running straight for the harbour, and they had some suspicion that it afterwards made for the eastward. However, they determined to make the shore at all hazards, and after a great deal of trouble, for they could see nothing for wind and sea, they made the harbour all right.[4]

The fishery officer, John Doull, submitted a prompt report which captures the terror of helpless onlookers watching the vessels of their kin make their attempts to gain shelter. Only a handful of vessels gained Eyemouth, and a similar number ran into Burnmouth. About a week later he made an assessment which shows both insight and empathy. It includes this stark assessment:

It appears that the principal causes of the great loss of life and property arose from the fishermen not seeing the land when running for it in the thick of the storm until they were too close inshore and were then unable to work their boats into port, or out to sea again in the face of the gale. Some of the boats had their sails blown away or rendered utterly useless and were tossed about at the mercy of the waves and ultimately thrown on shore and lost with all hands.

It is also well-known that most of the boats carried their

ballast of stones not properly secured and that some of those saved had a narrow escape from destruction owing to it being thrown about in the hold by the heavy labouring they were subjected to in the storm . . .

Another very few ran on to find a way into a port much further from home. These were not old boats in poor repair. Among those driven onto the rocks was one first registered in 1881 and on her maiden voyage. The most cruel irony is that this vessel, broken on the rocks of the east approach to Eyemouth, was named *Press Home*. A few other craft gained the shore along the coast, with the vessels damaged or wrecked but at least some of their crews saved. David Stevenson was one of those dragged ashore in Goswick Bay from the remains of *Blossom*. His five crewmates perished. It is sadly typical of the consequences of that decision to put to sea that day – 189 lives lost in this area alone. Folk on the shore could do nothing.

A few skippers chose to try to ride it out at sea. One of them turned the *White Star* out to deep water. The vessel and her crew survived. The *Ariel Gazelle* held out longer. She was to be at sea for 45 hours before all seven of her crew reached shelter. After the blast had lost its power she did find her way in, past the wreckage of so many of their kith and kin. Often a photograph of *Ariel Gazelle* BK1082, with crew lined on deck, is used to show the boat which returned from the storm. This boat was a replacement vessel built by Weatherheads, first registered in 1884. The earlier boat of the same name was BK893, built for skipper Alex Burgeon in 1878. She was registered at 20 tons on a keel of 46 feet and so would have been in that larger class of about 50 feet overall. From the available photographs it would seem that some of the vessels were decked and some were not. Eyemouth is credited as being the first port to respond to the findings documented in the Washington Report by moving to decked craft. Decked or no, the seamanship, strength and courage in taking such a boat home from the North Sea inspires awe in a sailor of today. Even with the harbour improvements and navigation aids at last in place, this entry must still need great caution when seas are up.[5]

NOTES

(1) The current Eyemouth harbour website provides a summary of the port's history and an aerial view of the facilities now as a stark contrast: www.eyemouth-harbour. co.uk/brief-history/.

(2) Books on the disaster include: Peter Aitchison's Black Friday: The Eyemouth Fishing Disaster of 1881 *(Edinburgh, Birlinn, 2006) and his* Children of the Sea: The Story of the People of Eyemouth *(Edinburgh, Tuckwell Press, 2001).*

(3) For a full list of vessels, with those saved and lost, also a compilation of contemporary press accounts: https://www.geni.com/projects/Eyemouth-Disaster-Black-Friday-14th-October-1881/52638.

(4) For a concise compendium of contemporary records see the Scottish Archives for Schools website: www.scottisharchivesforschools.org/naturalscotland/ eyemouthdisaster.asp.

(5) Wider context of the storm can be found in Hubert Lamb and Knud Frydendahl, Historic Storms of the North Sea, British Isles and Northwest Europe *(Cambridge, Cambridge University Press, 1991).*

14
THE GABBERT AND
THE PUFFER

ACCORDING TO THE INSTITUTE OF Civil Engineers, the first person to describe his work with that term was John Smeaton (1724–92). His design for rebuilding the Eddystone Light after it was destroyed by fire was a major influence on the work of the Stevenson family in Scotland, and his plans for piers and breakwaters ranged from St Ives to Eyemouth. He was not the first to draw up plans for a massive canal-building project to link the Forth with the Clyde. In 1762 Robert McKell was commissioned by a group of Glasgow merchants to survey a route. Smeaton's later plan was adopted, with some alterations during construction. McKell was employed as assistant engineer when the project went ahead. The ambition was massive, as it would entail over 35 miles of construction with a section 150 feet above sea level to deal with.

Now reopened mainly for leisure purposes, it is difficult to imagine the scale of economic impact when a symbolic barrel of Forth water was emptied into the Clyde at Bowling in 1790. The industrial town of Grangemouth did not exist before the canal. Falkirk developed its manufacturing now that a means of transporting coal and the new manufactured goods to their markets existed. Exchanges of goods and produce between the south of Scotland's east and west coasts developed into trade on a scale as huge as the engineering feat which enabled it. New boats were needed. There were attempts to use coal – a main product of Scotland's Central Belt, to power its own transport. This took the form of a steam barge. That history is well-covered in the work of historical societies of such towns as Falkirk, which owe their development to the canal. The National Museum of Scotland has produced a series of publications which present 'key activities in the shaping of Scotland'. *Scotland's Inland Waterways*, by P.J.G. Ransom,summarises both work and pleasure craft, sail, horse-drawn and steam-driven.[1]

Despite the pace of technology, there was still a need to lay timber planks on keels of oak or elm. When we think of lost classes of vessel we tend to think of Viking longships entombed in peat; the great Saxon burial mound of Sutton Hoo with its mysterious imprint of a sophisticated ship, previously unknown. We will come later to the lost clan warships of the Lords of the Isles. But these were the load carriers which transported coal and other industrial cargoes. Of course, that was the oil of its day, driving transport and manufacturing. Once they were out into the wider Clyde channel, they were under their own power.

According to Arthur Young's *Nautical Dictionary*, these craft (sometimes listed as 'gabbart') were: 'A long narrow flat vessel or lighter with a hatchway extending almost the full length of the decks, sometimes fitted with masts that may be lowered to pass under bridges.'[2]

Their maximum size and draught were restricted by the canal to 70 feet (21.4 metres) in length and 20 feet (6.1 metres) in the beam, but the recorded dimensions of most were under 60 feet by 13 feet 6 inches. Existing photographs and drawings show a sloop rig (single-masted), though the Scottish Maritime Museum archive shows a ketch (two-masted) vessel. The distinguishing features are bow and stern. The bow looks Scandinavian, being fairly full but with a gradual curve to the stem-post, increasing below the waterline. The beam is carried

A gabbert (fully laden)

most of the way to a rising stern shape. That makes for load-carrying capacity. The rudder was hung on a sternpost with only a very slight rake. A bowsprit went through an iron hoop (gammon iron) so that it could be retracted back on deck during the canal transit. This allowed the vessel to set a flying jib outside the inner jib (staysail), which was tacked at the bow.

Sketches and photographs show a very handy craft. It had to be so, because the work was not over when she came through the sea-lock. These vessels would often carry coal to islands reached from the Clyde, such as Arran. Very often they would have a return cargo of grain. Although the Firth of Clyde is sheltered, there are often localised gusts of wind coming off the high ground which surrounds it. A blast will funnel between the islands to cause short, steep seas. And so the gabbert would have had to be a seaworthy craft as well as a load carrier which could be pulled by horse along the tow-paths. Drawings such as the author's own illustration in *Sailing Craft of the British Isles* by Roger Finch show a powerful rudder area and a stout tiller.[3] Freeboard is low, to allow for carrying ability below the waterline, and I would imagine long sweeps would have been carried to help swing her into tight corners or cover that last bit of water when the wind dropped.

Like many of the English coastal barges, the mainsail was gaff-rigged. In contrast, the large Thames barges carried a spritsail main. The word 'gaff' is borrowed from the Dutch language. The word names a spar which lifts the top or 'head' of the sail and stretches it out and up from the mast at an angle of around 45 degrees. A 'collar' holds the spar and therefore the sail close to the mast, and the whole assembly slides up and down with a system of hoops and beads to reduce friction. Many examples of diverse historic barges have been preserved in England and the Netherlands. The naval architect John Leather is author of a well-regarded work simply titled *Barges*.[4] There is no mention of the gabbert. However, a drawing of a sloop-rigged 'flat', also by Roger Finch, surely suggests some kinship with the Scottish craft. This is not surprising, as they worked the Mersey and the Weaver, not an enormous distance from the Clyde. Like the families of fishing craft we've been observing, these canal, river and coastal vessels developed their form from the functions they were built to carry out. The Mersey flat did not have the distinctive sheer of the gabbert, with that steep rise at the stern, but rig and shape have similar features. Neither type seems to have carried the leeboards used by most English and Dutch coastal barges to resist the leeway any flattish-bottomed craft is prone to.

We can only try to imagine what it must have been like to emerge from the shelter of the Clyde channel to feel a blow coming blasting down from the Kyles of Bute. Tidal interaction also becomes an issue here with a short, steep 'jabble' rising when the forces are in opposition. Though there would not usually be the height of seas which come from a long open fetch, an onward passage with your cargo would often have been nothing like a picnic. At that point, the load might well have worked to advantage as a steadying ballast, though it would also have slowed you down. A long boom on the mainsail would have been something to dodge in the high helming position, when you tacked or gybed. But it would have set a large low-aspect mainsail area without the need for the complications of a topsail. The two foresails would help the balance and the ability to turn but, without a keel or boards, they could not have been the best boats for beating to windward.

Roger Finch also summarises other aspects of the method of construction which led to recognisable features. Each second frame or rib was extended up above deck-level by about a foot. This gave strong support for a timber rail to provide at least a hold for a foot or arm without adding much windage. You could also imagine some items of gear or cargo being lashed to that.

It seems sad that there do not seem to be any surviving examples of this lost boat. There is still some very deep mud across from the rebuilt sea-lock where the canal enters the Clyde at Bowling. Many a timber bone or steel plate juts out from that when the range of tide exposes it. You cannot help but wonder if there is a preserved keel on which to lay a new form. The sailing barge did give way to another vessel which has become an icon in its own right. Experiments with steam propulsion on the canal eventually led to the coaster immortalised as the Clyde puffer.

Most people will think of Neil Munro's creation, *The Vital Spark*. The author was a journalist, critic and serious novelist who knew tragedy in his life, when one of his sons was killed in the First World War. The illegitimate son of a maid in Argyll, Neil Munro went on to champion Joseph Conrad and achieve his own reputation, mainly for *The New Road*,[5] though his output was derided by the poet and critic Chris Grieve, who himself wrote as Hugh MacDiarmid. The humour in Munro's stories,[6] which were first published in *The Glasgow Evening News* under the pen-name of Hugh Foulis, has been successfully translated into three different television series. They have also inspired what must be one of the most enduring of all Ealing comedies, *The Maggie*. Some might say there are stereotypes of the west-coast character as well as the patched-together surviving steam-vessel, but there is a wry quality in the writing that has been caught in the best of the productions.

It's worth turning the focus back on the short history of the steam-driven coaster which took over from the sailing gabbert. Some features were passed on. Shallow draught and a flattening-out, underwater shape allowed the puffer as well as the gabbert to be beached to discharge or take on cargo where there was neither pier nor derrick. When the puffer came to be built in riveted iron rather than the wooden gabbert's hull, it could be more forgiving of the grinding of shingle. They came to carry their own small derrick out on deck. There was not merely one type of puffer. Much depended on whether the vessel had to pass through the canal for its load and on the range it was expected to cover once it was back out on the west coast.

The name came from an early form of steam-powered propulsion. Prior to about 1870 the vessels were not expected to continue outwith the canal with their loads. Therefore fresh water could always be drawn from the canal and there was no need to condense the steam to reduce consumption. As the steam which drove the piston did its work it was expelled from the funnel, giving a characteristic puffing sound and sight. This simpler form of engine was in use up until around 1920. Long before then, vessels that went to sea from the canal had a more sophisticated form of steam-driven machinery installed. The name 'puffer' stuck and was also applied to vessels too long for the Forth and Clyde Canal. These could transit the Crinan Canal to avoid the open fetch around the Mull of Kintyre.

There were many builders, mainly along the canal and in the Firth of Clyde. One of the last is now a floating exhibit at the Scottish Maritime Museum in Irvine. *Spartan* was built by Hays of Kirkintilloch in 1942 for wartime use as a fleet tender, or VIC (victualling inshore craft). At 66 feet 6 inches, she was about the maximum length for a canal boat, though her wartime purpose was to provision warships in from the high seas. She was one of the last of the steam-driven craft, though with a compound engine to allow use at sea. Later vessels were built with diesel motors, though the name 'puffer' was still generally used for a small coaster on Scotland's west coast.

Munro's wonderful characters were never intended to ridicule the small crews who kept these workboats moving. Still, a reader might get the impression that the puffer skipper was coasting because the challenges of deep-water seamanship were not for him. If I can offer another personal experience, I would challenge that. These load carriers were piloted into some very tight channels to provide the essential service of supplying remote communities. They were indeed vital in keeping an economy going, though the range of goods carried might be picturesque. They would be beached in places like Islay where the distillery and farming trades were a mainstay of the island. One such location is the jetty along from the distillery at Ardbeg.

In a yacht drawing near 6 feet, I nosed a way in between reefs to a tight but protected anchorage. Our vessel had the benefit of updated notes published by the Clyde Cruising Club, as well as paper charts and an electronic plotter. We were soon in an area marked as 'no-go' on the most detailed paper chart available and hatched in red on our screen. We had to trust in the experience of a cruising community and use the clearing bearings passed on. Now that information is expanded into the excellent Antares system which overlays chart software with updated surveys of such anchorages. This is produced by enthusiasts, for no profit, so a user must sign a disclaimer that takes complete responsibility for any navigation. Most in the cruising community would agree that it is proving very helpful. But the original coaster skippers had no such aids. They must have had a vast knowledge of creeks and crannies in our complex coastal geography. Tides run fiercely in many of the sounds and channels. They would have had these heights and rates weighed-off too.

Whether they were true 'puffers' or not, these coastal load carriers performed a valuable service in peacetime as well as serving the warships that staved off invasion in wartime. But they have also provided us with stories, and Neil Munro's humour has well stood the test of time.

NOTES

(1) P.J.G. Ransom, Scotland's Inland Waterways: Canals, Rivers and Lochs (Edinburgh, NMS Publishing Ltd, 1988).

(2) Arthur Young, Nautical Dictionary (London, Longman and Roberts, 1863).

(3) Roger Finch, Sailing Craft of the British Isles (London, Collins, 1976), p. 101.

(4) John Leather, Barges (London, Adlard Coles, 1984).

(5) Neil Munro, The New Road, first published 1914 (new edition: Edinburgh, Black and White Publishing, 1999).

(6) Neil Munro, Para Handy – The Collected Stories (Edinburgh, Birlinn, 2015).

15
MAIDS OF THE LOCHS

PEOPLE DO GET ROMANTIC, WHEN it comes to boats, especially those built to elegant lines. Sometimes there is a conflict between keeping those clean looks and attending to practical matters such as sheltering the fare-paying passengers from the rain you do occasionally get in the Trossachs and Scotland's west coast.

In 2007, a large forward deck-cabin was fixed on the 1899 steamship *Sir Walter Scott*. This may have added to the comfort of passengers but there is some debate about how it might be seen as spoiling the clean lines of the craft. Perhaps it's completely appropriate that a number of vessels take their names from Sir Walter (1771–1832) or his characters, titles or prominent settings in his works. You might argue that many of Scott's strongest novels reveal a comparable tension between romantic swagger in the lush but wild settings of the stories, and a more hard-edged depiction of the politics and conflicts of the day.

Ever since Scott's long poem 'Lady of the Lake' brought torrents of visitors to Loch Katrine, generations of vessels have helped visitors from other lands (and Scots on their holidays) to experience both inland and coastal areas. The *Sir Walter Scott* took over from a steamship built a century earlier. Closer looks at the construction of the later vessel and the history of her builders, William Denny and Brothers, will reveal that ships like this were anything but toys. She is

110 feet long (34 metres) and her GRT is 115. There were challenges to overcome and innovations in design and manufacture. Other steam-driven craft operated on Loch Lomond. Even though they floated on fresh water, they had to be both safe and fast.

Scott's first novel, *Waverley*, gave its name to the vessel that turned out to be the world's last seagoing paddle steamer. From 1946, she plied the route from Craigendoran on the Clyde estuary to Arrochar on Loch Long. Probably more people have travelled on her, over recent years, than have read the novel. The book is often referred to as a romantic depiction of the 1745 Jacobite Rebellion. Yes, there is a euphoria in tartan as the Young Pretender takes Edinburgh and his Jacobites send Johnny Cope packing at Prestonpans. But there is also a sober and sustained description of the brutal aftermath. Scott had made his fortune on the much more lulling long poems 'Marmion' and 'Lady of the Lake'. He first published the novel under a pseudonym, just in case it damaged his reputation for pleasing verse. The inventor of the European historical novel had to think out his structures. In the same way, the designers of these ships that bear his name or those of his characters, had to innovate to solve the challenges which came from their own constructions. These continue as the ships age to become historic vessels. The challenge of keeping them alive by keeping them steaming also brings tensions. A conversation with a marine surveyor emphasised the challenge of ensuring that the passenger-carrying *Waverley* is safe to twenty-first-century standards. As this book is being prepared for print, in 2022, *Waverley* is back in commission. At Loch Katrine, *Sir Walter Scott* is not operating, but a funding campaign, to bring her back into service, is in progress.

As we emerge from the canal system at Bowling, we are very close to Dumbarton, the town where the yard of William Denny drew and built the 1899 *Sir Walter Scott*. Beauty must have been part of the remit because the function was to take visitors efficiently through Loch Katrine but in harmony with the varied woodland

SS Sir Walter Scott *on Loch Katrine*

hills and sheer rock-faces. She is long, slim and white-painted, with
varnished hardwood rails and plenty of non-ferrous fittings to polish.
Draught was a bit of an issue, and this is a clue that the sweet lines of
the ship were not easily won. In 1893, the company placed an advert
in the catalogue of the Chicago World Fair. It stressed the expertise
gained from developing river steamers for locations a long way east
of the Central Belt of Scotland. William Denny and Bros had already
developed successful steamers to operate on the Ganges and the
Irrawaddy. They had taken care to keep detailed records of the design
and testing processes. Correspondence between Denny Bros and their
customers, on this and other projects, can be consulted via University
of Glasgow Archive Services.[1]

Denny's combined compilation of practical experience with
a faith in the benefit of tank-testing. Again, the evidence is available
and so the scrupulous nature of the records can be judged. You can
visit a branch of the Scottish Maritime Museum in Dumbarton to
see displays housed in the former test site. In the same way as future

America's Cup yacht designers based their innovations on tank-testing, Denny's combined these findings with their manufacturing experience. Their steamers were shipped in sections, not-quite flatpacks but in dimensions which could be more easily transported and assembled on arrival at Rangoon. That is exactly how the *Sir Walter Scott* reached Loch Katrine. Rather than being riveted, sections were bolted together at the River Leven. The tested vessel was then taken apart. Sections and machinery were moved by barge as far as Loch Lomond. From there, the carters took over. That might explain why the cost of transportation came close to half the total cost of £4,269.

All this seems like a huge intrusion of technology into the fabled Trossachs landscape. But there was an element of fiction in the promotion of the area as one of completely natural beauty. There were already man-made interventions.

In 1859 Queen Victoria opened the Loch Katrine water system. This had been initiated in the 1840s and came to be seen as vital when about 4,000 deaths were caused by the cholera epidemic between 1848 and 1849. The proposal by John Frederick Bateman was to build a dam which would raise the level of Loch Katrine along the 8-mile stretch of its natural length. It would take 13 miles of tunnel through rock and 25 aqueduct bridges, built in iron and masonry, to convey the water to Glasgow. The scheme won the support of engineers of the stature of Robert Stephenson and Isambard Brunel.

And so, like Scott's masterpiece *Heart of Midlothian* and his dashing *Rob Roy* – which was placed in the very setting of the surrounds of Loch Katrine – it took considered structures to convey both the water and the stories. Scott and his unforgettable creation Jeanie Deans (the name given to another historic steamer) were to be thanked by the masters of the European novel from Balzac to Tolstoy. The engineering feat was also to be an international point of reference. The water itself and its surrounds provided the impetus for building more than one ship. It also continues to have a bearing on their form and workings. Recently replaced boilers at the heart of *Sir Walter Scott* have now been condemned. These were manufactured by the Annan firm of Cochran in 2007. They were designed to run on bio-fuel as an alternative to the coal combustion that is now unacceptable due to the emissions entering the water supply. The triple-expansion engine made by Mathew Paul and Co. of Dumbarton is still going strong.

Let's return to the sea at the Firth of Clyde. The huge influence of the now unfashionable Scott is also strong in this gateway to Scotland's west-coast islands and promontories. Current operators, the Paddle Steamer Preservation Society, list the current *Waverley* as the sixteenth Clyde-built one to bear the name of Scott's first novel. Like the *Sir Walter Scott*, her predecessor was also built in 1899. The ship, built by A. and J. Inglis of Glasgow to provide pleasure as well as transport, was sunk by aircraft during the evacuation of Dunkirk in 1940.

The current *Waverley* also has a triple-expansion steam engine, also Clyde-built, this time by Rankin and Blackmore. The machinery was constructed at Eagle Foundry, Greenock (across the river from Dumbarton). Some details of the works carried out since she changed hands for a token £1 give a clue as to the massive issues in maintaining such historic ships. Before a return to active use was possible, a further £7 million was spent in two stages of a Heritage Lottery project. Works were done at the yard of George Prior Engineering, Yarmouth. This included two new boilers and an upgrading of safety equipment to meet current standards. Her livery was also returned to her 1947 scheme. The two raked funnels are topped in black over white over red. Her black paddle-boxes are lit with gold stripes. The vessel cannot operate each paddle independently so her turning circle is wide. She is not slow, proving capable of over 18 knots. In terms of manoeuvrability, she must be challenging.

No matter what care is taken with repairs and maintenance, there is inherent risk in keeping a vessel in commission on salt or fresh water. In September 2020 her bow collided with Brodick Pier in the Isle of Arran. As well as repair costs, there was also the huge issue of loss of income due to the Coronavirus pandemic. This must have affected many vessels of historic importance, just as it has also put theatres, museums and galleries into crisis. Once more the relationship between the vessels named after Scott and his creations, and the author's own life can be compared. The great fortunes from being a literary superstar of the day were dissipated by Scott's attempt to live in the style of one of his historic heroes. Castles are nearly as expensive to run as ships.

Yet the romantic imagery associated with Scott continued. This remains despite the hard-edged nature of both subject and style in some of the novels. *Ivanhoe* is probably one which leans most to romance, though it also has its dilemmas. The title, like *Rob Roy*, has given its name to generations of vessels. Successive fleets of river, loch and seagoing steamer are celebrated by enthusiasts. In turn, a fleet of publications has been produced, often with reproductions of photographs of these craft in their heydays. Alistair Deayton's *Scottish Loch and Canal Steamers*[2] is an excellent example of a close study of a particular group, for those who would appreciate more detail on these genuine pleasure ships. The wider-ranging *Scotland's Inland Waterways* (P.J.G. Ransom) discusses the pleasure steamers as well as the history of canal-borne craft.[3]

Returning to the Clyde's meeting with the seaways, an 1880 article from the *Glasgow Herald* hints that there was a bit of an issue in holidaymakers having a bit too much pleasure as they went 'doon the watter'. The *Ivanhoe* was created, like the book which provided her name, more for escapism than serious voyaging but this was to be of the dry sort, according to *The Herald*:

LAUNCH OF A RIVER STEAMER.

Messrs D. & W. Henderson & Co. launched yesterday, April 25th 1880, from their shipbuilding yard, Partick, a handsome paddle steamer of the following dimensions: — Length, 255 feet; breadth, 22 feet; and depth, 8 feet.

The vessel is fitted with a pair of surface condensing diagonal oscillating engines, the cylinders being each 43 inches, and the stroke 5 feet 6 inches. She has also two haystack boilers, constructed entirely of steel, each 12 feet 9 inches diameter. The saloon, which will be very luxuriously furnished, is 190 feet long, and is on the upper deck. The smoking-room is forward, and the steerage aft. The dining saloon is below, and the galley, instead of being on deck, adjoins it. The route of the new vessel is to [steam] between Arran and Helensburgh via Kyles of Bute. She is owned by a few influential Glasgow gentlemen, with Capt. James Williamson as managing owner. The ceremony of naming the vessel *Ivanhoe* was performed by Mrs James Bell, Elmbank Crescent. The *Ivanhoe* will be conducted on temperance principles, and she is intended as the pioneer of a fleet of saloon temperance steamers.[4]

NOTES

(1) University of Glasgow Archive Services, 'Correspondence between Denny Bros and Irrawaddy Flotilla Co concerning the construction of two twin screw steam ships. Construction of hulls subcontracted to Robert Duncan & Co', Reference GB 248 UGD 003/39/37. Bookmark: https://archiveshub.jisc.ac.uk/data/gb248-ugd003andgb248ugd191/18/ugd003/39/37.

(2) Alistair Deayton, Scottish Loch and Canal Steamers *(Stroud, Tempus, 2004).*

(3) P.J.G. Ransom, Scotland's Inland Waterways: Canals, Rivers and Lochs *(Edinburgh, NMS Publishing Ltd, 1988).*

(4) Glasgow Herald, *quoted in the excellent Dalmadan online resource: https://www.dalmadan.com/?p=963. The Dalmadan site makes thorough research and archived photographs on Scotland's maritime history freely available online. It is particularly strong on steamships and shipbuilding outwith the scope of this book.*

16
YACHTS OF WATSON, MYLNE AND FIFE

WE ARE AT ONE OF the great maritime gateways when we work our way down the Clyde estuary. Depending on vessel and crew we could depart from this normally sheltered seaway to link with the world's sea routes. The oral history of Govan collects a story of two brothers.[1] One is on his way to work, crossing the river on the Renfrew ferry (a craft also documented in Ransom's *Scotland's Inland Waterways*). He looks up from the flat deck to see the bonnie stern of a seagoing liner, not long cast-off. She might be bound for India or some other part of the world that used to be coloured pink for Empire. It's close, probably too close. That's why he spots a hand, held up in the air for him. It's his brother, who has had enough of a dead-end job at home. Now he's coiling away the great mooring warps. He's just made a jump aboard to take the place of a seaman who didn't turn up.

In this tour we'll be in mainly coastal waters. As long as we gain some shelter from the open fetch to the west, we can harness breezes or even gales and race our dinghies or yachts through sounds and channels. In the early 1870s the son of a doctor was mesmerised by the shapes of sails and the craft under them. George Watson was to go on to serve his apprenticeship with the Clydeside engineering and shipbuilding firm Robert Napier and Son. At the age of 22 he set up his own firm with the sole aim of designing yachts.[2]

From 1873 his designs proved themselves in an increasingly competitive field. The rich came to him from the Continent as well as the UK. His clients included the then Prince of Wales, who commissioned a vessel of 122 feet (about 37.2 metres). She was of composite construction, timber on steel frames. This was not a new development – the clipper *Cutty Sark* was built of teak on iron, in Dumbarton, in 1869. But Watson was an innovator and drew what is now called a 'spoon bow'. At the time there was criticism that a young designer would dare try something not quite proven on the future king's yacht. Watson's design was realised by D. and W. Henderson alongside the very similar America's Cup challenger, *Valkyrie II*. She was launched on 20 April 1893 and proceeded to her base at Cowes, Isle of Wight, for the test of her first season.

Her first-year record of 33 wins from 43 starts was only the start of a career that made her perhaps the most successful racing yacht ever. George Lennox Watson's work was done in producing that shape, but continuing revision to sails and rig were needed to keep her competitive. She was passed from the king to his son. In a final incarnation, her rig was completely altered from the gaff-cutter standard of her day to the cloud-scraping height of the Bermudan (triangular) J Class. Her spruce pole, designed by Charles Nicholson, was hollow-sectioned but still came in at 3 tons or so. It was the highest tree in the forest for years to come. That rig was at least removed before the wishes of her last owner were carried out after his death: the shape that came off Watson's board and became actual at Partick was scuttled in deep water off St Catherine's Point, Isle of Wight on 10 July 1936. That shape is not lost. The drawings exist and a replica hull has been recently built, though not fitted out.

To me, this act of deliberate sinking does raise a nagging question. Spectators gathered by the Clyde and by the Solent to watch what was in effect the Grand Prix racing of the day. To that extent they shared in appreciation of the sheer beauty of constructions designed to move as efficiently through water as feasible within the rules. The audience was part of the challenge. Yet the number of human hours in moving from the plan to that moment when hull-speed is achieved is enormous. How can one person feel complete ownership of the results of all that labour, skill and imagination in the first place? *Britannia* was more than the pride of the Clyde.[3] On the last of three races, her near-sister, *Valkyrie II*, came within a hair's breadth of defeating the mighty America's Cup winner designed by Nathanael Greene Herreshoff, and that was after a tough sail across the Atlantic to meet the yacht of the host country.

On her return she had a similar racing record to *Britannia* before being accidentally sunk, following a collision. In recent times there has been a revival of racing the J class and other big yachts. What if *Britannia* had been handed to a charitable trust instead of being stripped and deliberately sunk? What if committed teachers had worked with the young of deprived parts of cities, say in Plymouth, Swansea, Belfast and Glasgow? Maybe the long decks of salt and sky-bleached timber could have carried a team to take on the millionaires of the day at their own game.[4]

Many G.L. Watson designs were on a more intimate scale. Sometimes these are built again, if an existing structure is not there to renew. In 1996 a hull form of under 25 feet (7.5 metres) was produced from Watson's plans of exactly a century earlier, this time in the south of France (Columbini yard). For less than 20 grand you could launch her again from her present shore-berth in Lancashire. That's less than the most basic of second-hand campers these days, but you'd have to be a diehard to sleep on this one. Like the great yachts of 100 feet or more she is gaff-cutter rigged. That is not really so different from many of the working boats of the time of her design. These too carried sufficient sail to power her up in all conditions but with a large number of reef points to reduce it when needed. Silhouettes would show similar shapes. The difference is the fineness of the hull. This

Valkyrie II *(G.L. Watson design)*

boat would not have to carry a ton or two of fish or a cargo of grain or coal. So what you have is a vertical bow (like on a Fifie or Zulu in fact) but the lowest and sharpest overhanging counter-stern. Her gradual sheer is disturbed only by the lowest of deck-roofs – a cuddie rather than a cabin. This is a 'day sailor' for no other purpose than going through the water with grace.

Let's now return to the office of her designer. One Alfred Mylne was in the team which worked on the lines of that cutter, produced for the man who would become known as King Edward VII. Mylne had served his apprenticeship in shipbuilding before that. In 1896 he established his own firm. It still exists and still carries his name. Even more than Watson, the firm (continuing through his nephew Alfred Mylne II and the racing sailor Ian Nicolson) has designed a wide range of craft, from the modest to the mighty. It first prospered with the establishment of an international set of rules for yacht racing known as the 'metre class'. Up until recently, America's Cup races were still run with 12-metre boats. That doesn't refer to the overall length but to a set of limitations (sail, rig and keel as well as hull form) which allowed for development and innovation within them. It sounds a bit like a game of chess, and the tactics of racing such powerful machines could be compared to that too. Mylne, like Watson, drew the most elegant hull forms. They also tended to win races. The designer and his apprentice Thomas Glen-Coats could sail – they took *Hera* (Glen-Coats' design) to gold medal place in the 12-metre class of the only Olympic races held in Scotland.

If we look over a shoulder to the working vessels discussed in previous chapters, it seems that admirers will want to see a vessel out of the water. They will lean back or even crawl to catch the run of her shape, whatever the finish and equipment. One might say, 'A good seaboat, that.' Just from the look of her. No matter the quality of the cut and cloth of the sails and the focus of the hand trimming them, it's the hull-form which must slide through the water. Maybe the technical need to make a shape streamlined to pass through air or water just happens to result in the most beautiful shape. Many would say that the aircraft Concorde was a fine form.

The money that kept staff in their jobs probably came from the big commissions like the 19-metre class cutter *Octavia*. But the firm didn't only draw boats for millionaires. Mylne's had their own boatyard, Bute Slip Dock Co., which built working boats as well as yachts, and also did contract work for the Royal Navy. Inshore yacht and dinghy racing often seeks to be affordable and fair by commissioning a 'one-design' fleet. Individuals or syndicates buy into a vessel to campaign. A fleet of a dozen alike Mylne craft returns us to the geography of waters accessed from the Clyde. In the 1920s and 1930s, each Scottish Islands class boat took the name of an island ending in 'a', like *Stroma* or *Hirta*. Most of these still race, though the majority now have auxiliary diesels and the rig is now a simpler Bermudan form. They are 28 feet (8.53 metres) overall but the waterline is a good bit shorter as they also have that famous 'spoon bow' and a stern that extends out over the water. I've heard contemporary sailors say how badly such boats are being sailed as they lean in the gusts. 'Too much mainsail,' they say. Yet they are designed to do just that to increase that waterline and so work the physics of speed. You might be over-canvassed in the gusts but you 'spill' a bit of wind then. If you carry too prudent an area of cloth for the conditions you will likely be underpowered in the lulls. I understand the principle from racing a powerful yacht of the next generation – Robert Clark's *El Vigo*. Well into the 1960s, Kim Holman gave his successful Stella design plenty of cloth for the same reason. This makes for spectacular images in the gusts when a fleet is vying for places.

Winning races was not the only motivation for commissioning a boat from Alfred Mylne. Many examples put comfort and ease of handling to the fore, and that is still the case as the firm adapts to the twenty-first century. At this time there is a revival of interest in restoring yachts seen as classics, and among these there is a third great Scottish designer: William Fife. There is much in common between his Clyde-based family firm and that of Mylne. Both continued through generations and both designed and sometimes built a range from 100-foot yachts to small craft. A shipwright or a winning sailor might tell us the distinctions say in sheer, fullness, 'entry' or 'tumblehome' which would distinguish a Watson, Mylne or Fife vessel, just by its lines. I'd guess these Clyde yacht designers could be seen as much a school as Colourist or Cubist in the art world.

All generations of the Fife dynasty's yachts are sought after now. Again, some are built new and some are detailed restorations. They are more likely to be seen at Antigua than Greenock, but there have been several recent Fife regattas on the Clyde, including one in June 2022. The canoe-sterned and yawl-rigged (small aft sail astern of steering gear) *Latifa* arrived from Italy for the 2013 event though her skipper was injured en route. She is a 1936 yacht from the pen of William Fife III. I recalled a former yachtbuilder (who has since become instructor in boatbuilding at the Scottish Maritime Museum, Irvine) saying, 'The only yacht you'll see in Fairlie now is the *Latifa* windvane on a spire over the town.' One of the world's great sailors, Éric Marcel Guy Tabarly (24 July 1931 – 13 June 1998), an ocean racer and circumnavigator loved to sail the Fife yacht that remained in his family. He was on his way from France in *Pen Duick* for an earlier gathering of Fife classics when he was lost overboard. It's not all glamour, because the sea is the sea.

Much has been written about Fife yachts. A video of *Pen Duick* leaning to the Brittany breeze says a lot.[5] Images of the clouds of sail, with their neat like-shirted crews lining their rails, are widespread. But let's give space for one short story. It's a wonder Ken Loach has not filmed this, but I hope he does. At the lead-up to the 2008 gathering, two elderly brothers took the time to hose down a dried-out wooden boat in their yard at Kilcreggan. The hull form had a slanting keel, sloping aft to a draught of 4 feet 3 inches (1.3 metres). Her length on deck was only 19 feet (5.8 metres) but most of that was carried to her waterline of 17 feet. No space for extravagant overhangs here. Her stern was stubby. It was not difficult to see where planking became keel, because there were streaks of rust and a join that could have been more smooth. Thus you could see that most of the boat was ballast. The length of her bowsprit and boom betrayed the fact that her sail area was more in proportion to the ballast than the hull.

As the large classes of Fife yachts were departing the Mediterranean or crossing the Atlantic, Ronnie and Ian McGrouther put in their entry form and scratched their heads. The word was out that they were racing time to relaunch the boat, then aged 114. 'What will she need?' The answer was something like, 'Nae that much. Did she no have a new transom just 50 years back?' I saw that boat in that yard as George Wylie, 'the scul?tor' (his term), had tipped me off that the owners of his former Yachting World dayboat would donate her to an island sailing club. I found her at Kilcreggan. Then I looked up from the clinker mahogany to an unusual carvel form. There was something about that shape. What I didn't know at the time was that *Hatasoo* was created to fight local battles as hard-fought as any America's Cup. Launched in 1894, not long after Watson's *Britannia*, she was William Fife's best shot to beat the designs of his friend and rival in the Clyde restricted class. His own design, *Hatasoo* had swept the boards then, but could she stay afloat now?

The brothers rigged her in time to enter as the smallest craft in Class II of the fleet. Some said the paint job might have been better. Others in the know said, never mind, the brothers were legends in their own racing days. It was good they had experience at pumping out wet boats. On 21 June the wind was fickle, but it often is around Cumbrae. The brothers could still sniff out the puffs. They thought they might have to quit while they were still afloat but there was no decision to make as the race was shortened to finish at the south-western tip of the island due to dropping wind. They completed the revised course. When the handicaps were applied and corrected times announced, *Hatasoo* proved she was still a winner in the right hands. This time she was not racing Watson's designs but the larger and shinier creations of the Fife family.

NOTES

(1) Collected by Cran theatre company in a collaboration with Fablevision, The GalGael Trust and Theatre Hebrides. Oral tradition shared with me by Frank Miller, 2008.

(2) Martin Black has written a full study of Watson's life and work: G.L. Watson – The Art and Science of Yacht Design *(Limerick, Peggy Bawn Press, 2011).*

(3) For good photographic documentation of Britannia, *see the Sail-World website: https://www.sail-world.com/news/232785/The-Best-of-Britannia. For a clear illustrated summary of the period of the large classes of Clyde yachts, the generous Dalmadan site shares research as a labour of love: https://www.dalmadan. com/?p=4755.*

(4) Charlotte Thomas, 'Britannia replica set to rule the waves again', SuperyachtNews. com, 26/9/2018: https://www.superyachtnews.com/owner/britannia-replica-to-rule-the-waves-again.

(5) 'William Fife III Pen Duick', on the Classic Sailboats website: http://classicsailboats.org/portfolio-view/william-fife-iii-pen-duick/.

17
YACHTS OF ROBERTSONS', McGRUERS' AND OTHERS

THE SUBJECT OF CLYDE-BUILT yachts has already generated volumes. In the same way, working craft are countless and generations of powered MFVs have their own literature. That said, let's evoke just a few more examples of the works of art that were built along the Clyde estuary to race or cruise, home or abroad.

The Fife yard at Fairlie was far from ideal for launching and recovering the big classes of yacht. Special cradles had to be built to bring them through shallows. Perhaps that was one reason significant commissions, often designed by the Fife dynasty, were built a fair bit up the estuary and over on the northern side at Sandbank, Argyll. From 1876 Alexander Robertson would repair yachts there. This led to new builds and the yard was well established by 1890. It was to continue, diversifying into production in GRP to survive into the 1980s.

In the early 1900s the firm of Alexander Robertson built several of the great 12-metre yachts. This led to the commission to build the first of the 15-metre class, the William Fife III design for *Shimna* in 1907. Clydeships list this vessel as 50 tons GRT and 62.7 by 13.9 feet beam (about 19 by 4.2 metres). She drew over 8 feet (2.4 metres) and was to mark the start of a new breed of big vessel built to take part in international regattas. Her chain of owners tells an international story: she went from a William Yates, of Shepperton on Thames, to subsequent home ports of Barcelona, Marseilles and Istanbul. In 1918 she was altered from her original cutter rig (two main headsails) to yawl rig. Unlike many of the classics of that period she has not been restored for another reincarnation on the luxury yacht scene but was damaged and broken up in Turkey in 1949.

It seems incredible that the intention of the 15-metre class was to become established as an Olympic class. These embodiments of elegance were not exactly available for all, though many a Highland family was glad of the seasonal income from a father or son working as a paid hand aboard a racing yacht. That was a bit more certain than the return from inshore fishing, but hard-won skills stood the sailors in good stead.[1] International competition of the 15s did set a total of 20 British, French, Spanish and German yachts in competition. It's a tragedy that all European issues were not resolved in such rivalries instead of in the arms race, land and sea. Fife and Mylne vied neck-and-neck for the commissions to design these, later joined by Charles Nicolson, working in England. Fife's own yard would build some. Mylne would alternate between the yards of Robert McAllister and Son and Robertson and Sons to lift his 15-metre designs from the plans. The overall length of a yacht built to the 1907 rule could be as much as 98 feet (30 metres). Surviving photographs show them as breathtakingly beautiful. You can understand why lines of people would watch from the shore or join in steamship excursions to watch them go through their paces.

A fairly long bowsprit would set a jib, usually with a high clew (aft lower point), often called a 'yankee'. Another flying jib could be set high above that. The inner staysail would be carried closer to the deck. The gaff mainsail was huge, extended way out aft, by a boom that stretched well over her stern. Up aloft, a significant topsail would fill the gap above the gaff and extend the area a good bit higher than the mast. All that power would put a heel on the vessel and thus use the extended waterline to accelerate. With subtle variations, the boats

McGruer 8CR (original fractional rig)

of the day still show that spoon-shaped curve at the bow and a long rounded counter which also extended way out over the water. *Mariska* (D1), *Tuiga* (D3), *Hispania* (D5) and *The Lady Anne* (D10), all built to the rules of the 15mR (15-metre) class, have all now been restored. A 2012 photograph shows them close-racing at St Tropez.

Euan Ross discusses the Scottish examples of metre-class yachts in great detail in a book as lively as its title suggests: *Highland Cowes.*[2] He emphasises the role of tank-testing, suggesting that Fifes of Fairlie were a bit more reluctant to admit the advantages this could provide. He also studies in detail the design of a 6mR (6-metre) from John G. Stephen. He notes, from details of the 'quite radical design' of *Maida* that the hull is likely to sail efficiently even when heeled to 35 degrees. Robertsons could not have provided employment for so many years if they had built only for this market for millionaires. Their history is probably typical of the adaptability needed to keep a yard going.[3] In both world wars, the yard built vessels for the Admiralty. In 1935 they built the first motor-powered lifeboat in Scotland, to be stationed at Port Askaig, Islay. There was to be a return to building for the international racing scene of the metres classes but for modern 12s. *Sceptre* was built by Robertson's in 1958 as the British challenger in the America's Cup. In 1963, Robertson's built the David Boyd design *Ikra* (12K3X), which went on to become an America's Cup training boat for some years before a later racing and cruising career in the Med.[4] The modern Bermudan-rigged 12mR still has overhangs fore and aft and a greyhound's build. She has a waterline length of close to 46 feet on a deck length near 70 (21.3 metres). It takes a draught of 8 feet 10 (2.7 metres) to carry a sail area of 1,972 square feet (174 square metres). A Genoa with significant overlap kisses the pristine timber side deck. The yard couldn't have done too bad a job because they went on to build the America's Cup challenger *Sovereign* in the following year. Tank-testing technology would have been a key part of the design and a composite of new age-materials such as carbon-fibre and kevlar would have been part of her spars and fittings.

Robertson's yard, under new ownership, had to adapt to building in GRP. First they fitted out the *Piper*, David Boyd's successful racing one-design keelboat, like a scaled-down version of his design for *Sovereign*.[5] Later they also laid-up the hulls but moved to moulding the American-designed Etchells class racing keelboats for the Clyde scene. The firm also designed some craft of their own, as well as building the designs of another generation who drew cruiser-racers such as the Ohlson 38. This was not the first time the firm had worked to their own drawings. *Elrhuna*, at 28 feet (8.5 metres), came from the founder's own pen and was built in 1904. A half-model reveals the overhangs of the day, especially at the drawn-out stern, but also a very useful-looking keel shape. Her current rig is Bermudan with a fair bit of roach (depth carried high instead of tapering into a narrow head) and an overlapping Genoa out on a sprit. She does not look slow. You can see this one would carry her cloth. And she still does.

By 1980, even that adaptability was not enough. Like so many boatbuilders, Robertson's just could not keep it going any longer. But they were by no means the only firm who managed to keep building yachts for a long period on the northern shore of the Clyde. I am indebted to many enthusiasts who have freely shared their research, but in this case mainly to Ewan G. Kennedy, who writes and edits contributions which amount to the varied but always interesting blog 'scottishboating'.[6] This is especially strong on the Scottish Islands class (Mylne design but many built at McGruers). The story once more implies that brilliant design and superb boatbuilding skills were not enough. To keep in business in a competitive field there had to be a willingness to adapt. In the same way, builders of commercial fishing boats had to change to working in the material of the day. It seems the McGruers moved from Tighnabruaich to Clynder due to the qualities of the site. A convenient burn could drive a mill that could generate electricity. Very early in the game, power-tools were used to make production more efficient. By building one-design fleets (Scottish Islands or the International Dragon), shaped planks could be cut in batches to save time. McGruers also developed a name for the quality of their hollow spruce spars. The dimensions of Mylne's Islands class reveal that McGruers, like Fifes, built quite small craft as well as the superyachts of the day:

> Tonnage 2.96 registered, 3.21 gross, 4 TM (about 3,200 k)
> Length OA 28.0 ft, WL 20.0 ft (8.53 m, 6.1 m)
> Breadth 7.0 ft, Draught 4.5 ft (2.1 m, 1.4 m)
> Sail Area 418 sq ft (39 sq m)[7]

At first, metalworking parts were jobbed out to local blacksmiths, but the yard again adapted to produce their own, so they could have control over selecting and forming compatible metals such as aluminium-bronze, used for keel-bolts because it did not react too strongly with lead. The keels themselves were still cast elsewhere, due to the specialised nature of the work and the dangers. Ewan Kennedy, in his blog, reports meeting many who benefited from apprenticeships and training run by the yard. I have heard, from Angus Smith, Lewis, assistant to John Murdo Macleod at the building of the full-sized *sgoth an Sulaire*, that the name McGruers had a magnetism for lads like him, growing up in the area. He had no wish to go on to further or higher education but instead 'got a start' as an apprentice. He learned to work with metal as well as wood.

Like Robertson's, the firm also thrived by offering slipping, storage and preparation of yachts of different sizes. But the mainstay was probably the reputation gained from design and build of yachts which were as fast as they were seaworthy. Postwar yachtbuilding at McGruers resumed in 1945 with a series of yachts built to a waterline length of 30 feet, beginning with the 17-ton sloop *Kelana* at just over 42 feet (12.8 metres) overall. These were cruiser-racers, many with yawl rig. They had a turn of speed that made them successful handicap racers, but they could keep driving in a choppy sea when the metre-class boats would be stalled. A higher sheer at the bow was another hallmark, and that helped make them dry seaboats. One of the most famous yawls, *Coigach*, might well have been crewed by seamen from the area that lent her her name. Such yachts tended to instil emotions. Laurie Douglas wrote, in 2016, of her father's job leading to a lasting family relationship:

> My dad's friend, Craig Downie, owned this yacht for many years. I can't remember how many. He brought her to Robertson's Yard Sandbank for her yearly winter makeover. My dad had the greatest yearly pleasure in this task. He worked on Mr Downie's previous yacht, *Carron*. My dad was foreman painter with Robertson's Yard Sandbank and he was there for many years. It was the most wonderful place for a young six-year-old girl whose dad loved and breathed the place, as I did, till the day it closed!!

We had many great trips on *Coigach*, as we as a family were invited out on day trips, but my dad went on many trips, regattas, races, and they were commodore, on many races round Scotland and Ireland. My dad's name was Daniel Douglas, and Craig wouldn't have anyone else painting her. Even when Robertson's closed down and they moved round to McGruers, Craig said he wanted his friend, and the only one that would do *Coigach* properly and proudly was my dad Danny, who sadly died August 1993. I am now 50 and we are still friends with Mr Downie, and the years of Robertson's and *Carron* and *Coigach* will remain, always . . .[8]

James McGruer is credited with drawing up the rule for a variation of the metre classes. His idea for an 8-metre CR (cruiser-racer) was to combine the qualities which made for fast, competitive sailing and the provision of simple but comfortable accommodation so a team or family could go on to cruise. This meant that a luxury yacht lived for more than the short periods of its life when her crew would be training or cruising. We are indebted again to the Peggy Bawn Press for its blog, which includes an atmospheric BBC film of the Tobermory Race.[9] The Robert Clark sloop *El Vigo* came with a logbook which showed several years of taking part. The son of a previous owner would talk of the metre-class boats out ahead on their own start but also the good nature and banter linked to the event. This film shows both the 8-metre racing fleets and a second start of very varied yachts racing on handicap. Many of the metre-class timber machines were built by McGruers. The trademark doghouse and windows can also be spotted among the cruisers.

Another classic boat forum run by enthusiasts sets out to list each one of the McGruer-built yachts that could be traced.[10] This is the website championing designs by the English enthusiast Harrison Butler, a GP who was passionate about yacht design and influential as the one who defined the 'megacentric' principle which put balance to the fore of the remit. I believe both Clark and James McGruer would score high in fulfilling that brief. There is a further link to documentation of the restoration of the McGruer 8-metre CR *Altricia* at Maylor Yacht Harbour, Cornwall. The vessel went, in shining new brightwork (varnish finish) to the 2016 London boat show before being offered for sale. Euan Ross is a bit critical of the sailing performance of the CR 8-metres but I think that has to be seen in comparison with the sleek though spartan all-out racing class.

The 1965 example built at Clynder is 41 feet 9 inches overall (12.7 metres), with quite a short waterline of 27 feet 3 inches (8.3 metres). Like Clark's designs of the period, she has a curve at the bow which continues to a 'cutaway' keel forward. Aft, her overhang to a short steeply raked transom is not as extreme as on the all-out racing 8-metres. Her beam of 9 feet 9 inches (about 3 metres) is quite narrow for a cruising yacht of that length and yet her hull shape looks fairly full. Rather than a compromise option, she has the look of a hard-won balance between performance, seakeeping and accommodation. This is 12 tons that can jockey for a windward position on a start-line or short-tack through a narrow channel into a west of Scotland anchorage. She inspired fidelity. Up until her move to Cornwall in 2013 all her owners are listed as basing her at Clynder.

The other hallmark feature is the raised after-cabin section usually called a 'doghouse' because it is seen as a bit of a distortion to her line for the sake of good standing room by chart table and galley. James McGruer drew a very simple shape here which looks neither modern nor retro. The windows let a good amount of light in, with the forward one being more angled to match the drop to a lower cabin area forward. We can get a nosy at the interior of another example, up for sale on a broker's website. Also about 41 feet, *Inismara* (1963) is still very original. There is excellent but simple joinery seen in a chart table with proper drawers and a basic galley area but with storage below. Berths and seating seem simple and also offer the stowage space vital for cruising with friends and family. Panelling is not ornate. You might call the aesthetic Scandinavian or international. From these two examples it is easy to see why 23 such yachts were built between 1951 and 1968. Even in the late 1990s *Inismara* was winning her class at West Highland Week and in the Scottish Series races.

The Lorne class from McGruers was a very handy cruising yacht of 28 feet. That was seen as quite a big family boat in the 1960s. Another 28-footer prompts mention of one more Clyde designer and one more boatbuilder. In 1958 Clyde Cruising Club and the *Glasgow Herald* launched a design competition for a four-berth boat suitable for cruising the west coast of Scotland. One of the judges happened to be a certain J. McGruer. A.K. Balfour's Honeybee design won from 52 sets of plans from nine countries. This went on to be built by William Boag, who had trained with Fifes of Fairlie. When you see her long-keeled, transom-sterned shape, it looks a bit familiar. Then you look up her dimensions of 28 feet (8.4 metres), 21 feet (6.4 metres) on the waterline and 5 feet (1.5 metres) draught. She displaced 4,318 kg, with 1,406 of that in her ballast keel.

Shape and dimensions are similar and very much in proportion to the slightly larger and now legendary Twister designed by Kim Holman, though the Honeybee was fractional rig (the foresail doesn't go to the top of the mast) like Holman's earlier Stella. Only thing is that A.K. Balfour's design was six years before Kim Holman's. In yachtbuilding, as in literature, it seems like fashions come and go, and proven examples influence later ones.

NOTES

(1) 'The Crofters who Raced Yachts for the Scottish Glitterati', The Scotsman, 22/9/2019: https://www.scotsman.com/heritage-and-retro/heritage/crofters-who-raced-yachts-scottish-glitterati-1401665.

(2) Euan Ross, Highland Cowes: A History of Sailing in Scotland through the Lens of Hunter's Quay, *independently published, 2020.*

(3) 'Robertson's Yard History', Classic Sailor, *9/4/2018: https://classicsailor. com/2018/04/robertsons-yard-history/.*

(4) 'David Boyd "12 Metre" IKRA', Classic Sailboats.org*: https://classicsailboats. org/portfolio-view/david-boyd-12-metre-ikra/.*

(5) Bob Donaldson, 'The Story of the Piper Class', Classic Yacht Info, *courtesy of The Piper Owners' Association: https://classicyachtinfo.com/yclass/piper/.*

(6) Ewan Kennedy, 'The McGruers of Clynder', scottishboating *(blog), 6/9/11: https://scottishboating.blogspot.com/2011/09/the-mcgruers-of-clynder.html.*

(7) As listed on Classic Yacht Info website: https://classicyachtinfo.com/yclass/ scottish-islands-class/.

(8) Laurie Douglas, 'Yacht: Coigach', Classic Yacht Info, *May 2016: https:// classicyachtinfo.com/yachts/coigach/.*

(9) 'Summer of '68 – The Tobermory Race', Peggy Bawn Press *(blog), 1/10/13: https://peggybawn.wordpress.com/2013/10/01/summer-of-68-the-tobermory- race/.*

(10) 'McGruer Designed or Built: The McGruer Boat List', The Harrison Butler Association *website, 16/5/21: http://harrisonbutlerassociation.com/Pages/McGruer. html.*

18
THE RING NETTERS
OF GIRVAN – WORKING
BOATS OF YACHT FINISH

THERE IS POETRY IN PROVENANCE. Following the dynasties of boatbuilders is a bit like what I remember of the begats in the Bible. Let's start at the Gareloch. In the early 1880s, one Peter R. Maclean established a boatbuilding yard at Rosneath. A former apprentice, James A. Silver, went on to make good in Glasgow, in partnership with his brother and with a designer of motor yachts. When the Rosneath yard came up for sale, Silvers Marine became established at that site. Through all the financial ups and downs, it still holds on. Its survival was helped by the role of John Bain, a respected designer of motor yachts but also a sound manager.

One shipwright who benefited from his time with Silvers was Alexander Noble. As the name suggests, he was of east-coast background. In fact, he already had boatbuilding in the blood, as one of the Nobles of Fraserburgh. He established his own firm in Girvan, Ayrshire, in 1946. Bronze plates with 'Alexander Noble & Sons Ltd, boatbuilders, Girvan' were fixed to about 90 vessels built in timber up until 1992. In the 1980s the yard also began to manufacture in steel and it still exists, mainly as an engineering yard. It was one of the few trusted to produce RNLI lifeboats before the charity moved to its own manufacturing process. The firm's website gallery hints of the range of craft as well as engineering solutions. Despite this proven ability for diversity, Nobles of Girvan still rings to many as the builder of fishing vessels with the sweet lines and bright finishes of yachts.

They were by no means the only builders of the ring netters. The prosperity of this stage of the herring industry (strong from the 1950s to the 1970s), prompted a steady stream of orders to boatyards east and west. And this method was not a new invention. A drift net is so called because it hangs in the water and waits. It could be secured to the vessel, also drifting or, in tighter corners such as narrow sea-lochs, anchored. The ring net was so called because there was a means of pulling it so it could (hopefully) encircle a shoal. Methods were developed to make that encircling more efficient, and that normally required two vessels working in partnership. In Loch Fyne and other areas there was tension between those who operated the different methods. The debate is mirrored whenever a more efficient use of a technology yields a greater harvest or makes production swifter. A finite stock can be decimated or a market flooded, or both. Those who invest in the new method and the vessels to operate it will say that the choice is open to all. Some who fish on the more modest scale might reply that the quality of their catch is better and they need to catch less as their haul would achieve a better price. In practice, once the expectations of larger yields are made, the market responds to that. Those who resist the change must then find a niche or give up.

In this case, the method resulted in as fine a line of commercial fishing craft as you could imagine. Most would say that the method did put smaller drift-netting vessels out of business and some medium-sized fortunes were made but the level of damage to stocks was nothing like that done by the purse-seiners that were to supplant them. The central concern of this book is to describe the vessels used to carry out the tasks. We will take a closer look at the hulls of the Girvan-built ring netters. But the method of fishing as well as the range they would cover are major influences in their form. Readers who wish more on the method and the cultural issues linked to the

Based on Ribhinn Donn II *(Nobles, Girvan)*

ring net fishery can now find resources that are both well-researched and clearly presented.

The history, principles and practical details of the methods are graphically laid out in the online 'Herripedia'. You could set up your own rig from the drawings. The ecological and political debates linked to the fishery are also set out in a direct and readable way. Best of all, the more technical drawings are augmented with examples of a first-hand oral history which allows natural communicators to speak for themselves. The author of 'Herripedia', Graeme Rigby, was put in touch with Jim Muir of Achiltibuie, Coigach, by Ullapool Folk Museum:

> You got a very, very good quality of fish by drift-netting, by catching them like that. When they began trawling, they sort of dragged them through the water and the herring got scaled and soft. The old herring, drift net-caught herring, was very, very superior. It would last longer.

Then, of course, there was the ring net herring, which originally was from the Clyde: that was circling the herring. You had two boats and one boat would set his net in a circle and then they would both haul it in. And that was the ring net herring. Again, the quality was not as good as the drift net herring, but they could catch bigger quantities: it was a more active form of fishing.[1]

'Herripedia' goes on to quote from the seminal study by Angus Martin, *The Ring-Net Fishermen*.[2] The author is a poet by trade and a postman by profession. Angus is from the Kintyre area and steeped in both its detailed history and its stories. The book is the result of a combination of meticulous research and intimacy with the people as well as the vessels. These boats took part in an industry which provided livelihoods for many, ashore as well as afloat. Angus is able to bring the sights and smells of the industry to your senses as you might expect from the author of poems like 'Always Boats and Men'.[3] In *The Ring-Net Fishermen*, stories, craic and statistics all serve to document swift-changing times.

Research by Angus was prompted when the artist Will Maclean engaged in a major study of the subject. The artist's main works were gathered in 'Will Maclean: Points of Departure' at the City Art Centre, Edinburgh (4 June to 2 October 2022), accompanied by a new publication. In Will's own words:

In 1973 I applied for and was granted an award by Scottish International Education Trust to make a visual record of the ring net herring fishing. I was able to take a year out of teaching and come and go as I liked on the Kyleakin BRD Ringers *Misty Isle* and *Fortitude*.

The resulting research was exhibited throughout Scotland (including An Lanntair) and was purchased by the Scottish

National Gallery of Modern Art. A group of drawings, plans and photographs will form part of the Edinburgh retrospective. In 1974 I met with Angus Martin, who knew my family in Kyleakin. Angus... agreed to contribute to the research and undertook the Campbeltown recordings and interviews and go on to publish *The Ring-Net Fishermen*. It is a testimony to Angus that not a word in that book has ever been challenged by anyone in the fishing community.

When I began the project it was something that I had known all my childhood days. The first 'Robertson'-varnished ringers came to Kyleakin just after the war. *Castle Moil* and *Misty Isle*. I had no idea that within a few years everything would change and the ring netting would be gone forever. How fortunate I was and how indebted to the Scottish International Education Trust.[4]

Although the vessels and the fishery were not at all restricted to south-west Scotland, Angus's book emphasises the pivotal role of skippers and boatbuilders working in that area. His introduction describes his process:

This book had its origins in a programme of tape-recording in the fishing communities of Tarbert, Campbeltown and Carradale, begun in April, 1974. The initial stimulus to activity was provided by the artist Will Maclean, who was then already engaged in researching the history of ring-netting. His concern was primarily with visual documentation, and the result was an exhibition of photographs, plans and drawings presented in Glasgow at the beginning of 1978 and now the property of the Scottish Gallery of Modern Art, Edinburgh.

My own fascination with ring-netting was fostered in early childhood within a family which had engaged with the method for four generations. When I finished with school in 1967, it was to ring-net fishing I went, thus representing the fifth – and probably the final – generation of my family active in the fishing.[5]

Angus maps the changes in boat-form and machinery as surely as an appendix details the local names for each bulge and bay in the coastline from Campeltown to the Mull of Kintyre. The combined effect of all these aspects of study is more elegy than nostalgia. Angus Martin's realism is lit with respect for his subjects. People come first. Thus his judicious summary of his own five years of research into the ring net fishery stands out all the more. His conclusion, back around 1980, has the urgency that many are only sensing now, as we are into the third decade of the 'new' millenium: 'The most profound and influential personal lesson of these five years of questioning and gathering has been this: that Western society, by its criminal contempt for the fellow creatures which share its corner of the planet, has brought itself to the edge of an ecological and moral crisis from which, without the exercise of immediate and unswerving restraint, there can be no withdrawal.'[6]

That summary could also help answer the question of why the vessels of one country are worthy of study. We are drawn to them because they are bonnie things but also because of the people linked to them and because they are evidence of the cultural and economic forces that helped to make them.

In the case of ring netters, like those of the Nobles of Girvan yard, the shape derived as the means to carry out that fishery must be just about perfect for its purpose. As with many of the other hull forms discussed in this book, a picture emerges where both east- and west-coast yards built similar craft for a purpose, in this case a developing fishery. Lessons learned from the proven shapes taken from other countries, often Scandinavian, are noted by experienced skippers and balanced with the distillation of their own years at sea with various craft. Angus relates how Robert Robertson, working out

149

of Campbeltown, Argyll, made an approach to the Millers yard at St Monans. He had already revealed a willingness to adapt by being one of the first in the area to accept motorised craft as inevitable. Robertson's observations of a craft in Norway had led him to approach the naval architect W.G. McBride of Glasgow for a drawing. Millers were to build two prototype vessels, each of over 50 feet (15 metres), longer but also beamier than the skiffs traditional to the area and with a completely different shape, most notable at the stern.

A trim canoe stern with a fairly modest sheer, seen mainly in a rise at the last few feet aft, became the hallmark of the craft most often associated with ring netting. Other developments included full-length decking, a neat aft cuddy to protect the helmsman and the use of a wheel linked to steering gear. In 1922 *Falcon* was launched, soon followed by *Frigate Bird*. The lines were admired but they were not an instant success. Even skippers of Robertson's experience had to get used to the speed and handling of the new craft. He was to find that the wheel steering made for a reliable turning circle, vital in accurate deployment of the ring net and recovery of the buoyed end, which could be pulled to form the killing circle. Everything has a trade-off. The greater length made for a faster boat. The higher freeboard, in proportion, made it more difficult to bring the catch aboard. Development of suitable capstans and winching-systems balanced that.

Again I'm indebted to Angus Martin for pointing out that the ring netters now regarded as typical Ayrshire boats, evolved through another stage. The Cockenzie yard, Weatherhead and Blackie, launched a near pair of vessels in 1926. These boats reveal how the lines became established. The Scottish Fisheries Museum cares for *Lively Hope* (LH432), a Weatherhead of Cockenzie build of 1936. Her shape reveals the Norwegian influence. There are the beginnings of a curve in the bow just above the waterline. The sheer is again gradual until very close to the sternpost. A canoe stern curves from just aft of the propellor to show its shape, yacht-like, well clear of the water. As in many yachts, this appears an extravagance when you are paying the builder by the foot. But that is buoyancy and a light aft end to rise to seas and a shape to part them and mitigate the power of a crashing wave. It also provides that bit more space for stowage. *Mary Sturgeon* has her wheelhouse well aft, probably nearly above the rudder. *Golden West* has hers further forward, no doubt in response to a directive from her future first skipper. Preferences of individuals were reflected the way they would be in the building of any custom-built object. This was bespoke tailoring in selected larch.

Millers continued to build vessels including ring netters for Clyde and Ayrshire skippers. As always, an individual skipper, commissioning the vessel on which the safety as well as the livelihood of all would depend, might have his input into the design. The 1950 *Mary McLean* is photographed at her stern-first launch, revealing her 'cruiser stern' variation to the world. The James Noble yard at Sandhaven, a short stretch northwards, along the coast from Fraserburgh, continued to build in timber. Ring netters were among their output. But many west-coast skippers would go to Alexander Noble of Girvan. This was the yard that owed its origin to the apprentice-training at the builders of Clyde motor yachts. You can get an immediate impression of the sweet lines in a fleet of these by returning to the 'casting the net' website.[7] As with many classes of Scottish working craft and many of the yards that built them, specialist studies of the subject are available. (A selection is listed in Further Reading.)

A wonderful BBC documentary with Billy Kay followed the building and working life of vessels, several built at Girvan for the fishing community of the Hebridean island of Scalpay, off Harris.[8] As always, the spirit of a type of vessel, something real but less visible than its frames or sheer-line, is revealed when you give scrutiny to a particular example. *Ribhinn Donn II* was built in Girvan for J. and A. MacLeod of the Isle of Scalpay, which is set in East Loch Tarbert,

Harris. Her 63 feet (9.3 metres) of deck length culminate in that trademark canoe stern. As SY141, she left the yard with the favoured Gardner 8L3B installed. She was a replacement for the first ring netter of that name, a 55-foot (16.8-metre) vessel, launched in 1966. She also had a Gardner, but of lower power. The progression in size and power hints of the prosperity that came from good hauls and a reasonably steady market.

That first *Ribhinn Donn* was sold on more than once and eventually found her way to the Irish Republic. She may well be still fishing. Her shape is preserved in the form of a detailed model by Jay Cresswell, an ex-trawler skipper and an expert on maritime history.[9] The hours of work in recreating the shape and materials in miniature is a tribute to the iconic form of the original. Once again, we can see how an experienced skipper would contribute his experience to influence the design of the vessel or its fitting out. In the case of the second *Ribhinn Donn*, this related to the comfort of a crew who were to spend long periods aboard: 'O yes, yes. But the second *Ribhinn Donn* . . . the last one we had . . . the engine was in her front . . . usually the engine is in the back of a boat . . . we asked for the engine to be in her front . . . For comfort. The cabins were in the back and the engine was a bit away from it and there was no noise you see . . . It worked well for us. In fact, the ones that built it in Girvan said they wished they had done it before.'[10]

On a personal note, I came very close to experiencing life in the foc'sle of a ring netter, not long after I left school. A friend living on the Isle of Mull had put in a word for me with a local skipper. Things were looking good, but these were boom days. By the time I reached Mull, the place was taken and so I was to work in the forestry, like many others. We looked down to see the herring fleet transit the Sound of Mull. At about that time Will Maclean was developing his project, which included sea-time aboard working boats. He contributed drawings and photographs to Angus's book. He was to go on, like the painter John Bellany from Port Seton and like my mother's brother Donald Smith from Lewis, to return again and again to the vessels of Scotland as a way into catching the visual poetry of the work. The vessels of Scotland are bound to be strongly represented, in drawings, prints, multimedia and three-dimensional works, in 'Points of Departure'.[11] The ring netters will be an element due to the artist's first-hand experience of the way of life bound to their shapes.

The oral poetry of the ring netters happens when you talk with someone who has memories of that fishing. Several of the creel-fishermen I met on Mull had gained sea-time aboard these boats. I was told a cloudy night was best. 'Too much moon wasn't so handy.' It seems the herring would not rise if the moon was bright.

NOTES

(1) Graeme Rigby, 'Muir, Jim (Herring Interview, Achiltibuie)', Herripedia (website), https://www.herripedia.com/muir-jim-herring-interview-achiltibuie/.

(2) Angus Martin, The Ring-Net Fishermen, *with drawings by Will Maclean (Edinburgh, John Donald, 1981, new edition 2001).*

(3) You can listen to the author read this poem: https://www.castingthenet.scot/ audio/angus-martin-reading-always-boats-and-men/. The title was also used for a collection of Angus's poems with paintings of vessels by Mark L'Anson, Always Boats and Men *(Catrine, Stenlake Publishing Ltd, 2010).*

(4) Email from Will Maclean to the author, 1991. Maclean's research, including time at sea, led to a series of visual works and the invitation to involve Angus Martin. This led in turn to Martin's book, The Ring-Net Fishermen, *now regarded as a seminal study.*

(5) Martin, The Ring-Net Fishermen, *p. v (1981 edition).*

(6) Ibid., p. 243 (1981 edition).

(7) 'Ring Netters in Girvan Harbour, c. 1956–1960', on Casting the Net website: https://www.castingthenet.scot/image/ring-netters-in-girvan-harbour-c-1956-1960/.

(8) 'Social History with Billy Kay', History Zone, BBC Archive, https://www.bbc.co.uk/ programmes/b00vc5cg (not currently available). See also Billy Kay's 'Odyssey' series.

(9) Gavin Atkin, 'A beautiful model of a ring-netter', intheboatshed.net, 5/1/2010: https://intheboatshed.net/2010/01/05/a-beautiful-model-of-a-ring-netter-made-by-jay-cresswell/?subscribe=success#blog_subscription-3.

(10) Interview with Alasdair Macleod (by Jo Macdonald – transcript Harris Development).

(11) Duncan MacMillan, The Art of Will Maclean – Symbols of Survival *(London, Transworld, first published 1992, updated 2002).*

19

THE WHAMMEL OF THE
SOLWAY FIRTH –
FIT FOR PURPOSE

FROM GIRVAN OF AYR, WE can proceed southwards to access the Solway Firth, that wide bight of shallows and tidal mudflats where there was not only boatbuilding but shipbuilding, despite the inconvenience of tidal havens. Cochrans the boilermakers and engineers had their works in Annan. The same town hosted the major shipbuilding firm of John Nicholson and Co. Timber from Canada was imported directly until the last of the great tea-clippers had her keel laid here. In 1865 the *Sarah Nicholson*, at over 194 feet (59 metres), was launched, and that was the end of that.[1] The workforce moved on as production ceased.

A coastal walk from such tide-served harbours as Gatehouse of Fleet will show old stonework and scars of once-dredged channels. These conditions amounted to yet another demanding set of requirements for the boatbuilders of previous years. At that time the flats formed the habitat of a range of species of fish of commercial importance. Migratory salmon and sea-trout could be trapped before they ran the rivers which empty into this wide basin. A form of ring net was used, with one end fixed ashore and the other run by one small flattish-bottomed craft, to circle a shoal. A form of coble was deployed but the Solway Firth whammel developed to prove itself as a multipurpose craft, well-adapted to the conditions. She could not survive if she could not take the ground and resist the thumping that

155

must happen as she was being refloated by tide. The designer and writer John Leather is mainly concerned with rig in his *Spritsails and Lugsails* but he does outline the boatbuilder's scantlings for the whammel.[2] Her ¾-inch carvel (flush) planking went into a hefty oak keel. That was sheathed in iron, which provided ballast as well as a buffer against the inevitable chafe from rubbing on pebbles and shingle.

This is now another craft known by name only as there are no extant examples. But there is a drawing and line plans of sufficient detail to make it all anew, if the impetus were there. A Solway Firth whammel net boat of 1900 was studied and her lines drawn by one Philip Jesse Oke in 1936. Her provenance is handwritten on the plans. She was built by James Wilson at Annan Waterfoot and previously owned by one J.W. Robinson of Annan. She was 19 feet 3 inches overall by 6 feet 3½ inches beam (5.85 by 1.9 metres). She drew under 3 feet. These drawings are preserved as part of the Philip J. Oke collection currently held at Royal Museums Greenwich.

They are the basis of a perfect case-study of a vessel, superbly adapted to work in challenging conditions. The tidal ports were established where miles of sand and grit and mud are exposed. These elements of course limit access to the fishing grounds. However, these same conditions make a good habitat for flatfish and also for the mud-dwelling species such as the skate, the rays, the dogfish.

The estuaries are freshened by the run of several rivers sniffed out by returning migratory species. That huge stretch from the high to the low water marks made it impossible to drag a working boat above the tideline. If you returned only at high water, the fishing time would have been impossibly restricted. The only solution was to build craft that were tough enough to withstand taking the ground.

The whammel boats were named after the fishing method but the distinctions of the type were mainly due to the tidal conditions. You have a plump bow and a raked stern to give that hard-won balance of tracking and turning ability. In this respect, the shape is similar to so many west-coast craft developed for inshore fishing, including those which worked in the Clyde estuary. It is also detail in rig, build and gear which become established to define a class of boat. The best analysis of why working craft developed the way they did, to my knowledge, is that of Eric McKee. The purpose, say trawling or longlining, has a bearing on layout, load-carrying, strength and weight. Geographical factors such as tidal range are also significant. Coastal geography, including tidal currents and prevailing winds, were part of the knowledge that drove the shipwright's adze, even if there were no plans to follow.

Michael Smylie retells the story of fishermen from Morecambe being driven to shelter in the firth but then finding rich grounds.[3] He outlines four fishing families who then chose to move, lock, stock and vessel, up the coast to re-establish themselves in Annan. Over the years the two types of imported vessel (a larger breed for trawling and a smaller one for setting a whammel net) gave way to one distinctive type. Distinctions in the craft favoured in different areas seem a bit like those observed in the beaks or plumage of birds or in fins and lateral lines of distinct species of fish. Of course, these variations are inventions when it comes to boats, but it still seems a bit sad that many can only now be seen in line plans or photographs. The emotional quality of sepia photographs can only be because we sense the whiff of past lives, the way we do in oral histories or folk songs. Despite the phrase often used by a shipwright friend, it's not the devil that's in the detail but evidence of human adaptation. His phrase is a reminder against complacency in reproducing the form of boats of similar shape. For many, the fascination is in probing the sheer creativity of the folk who made all these craft, and the gear and machinery which enabled so many to make their living.

Let's return to that very detail as captured in drawings of *Dora* to typify the lost class of Solway Firth wherry. As the rudder couldn't go deep, it is made wide, to give enough power. The sail plan reveals a

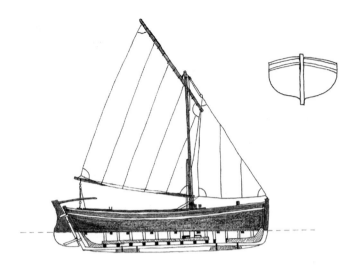

Solway Firth whammel (lost type)

similar smartness in problem-solving. The mast is short, so all could be shipped and carried within, to reduce rolling when the boat took the ground. But a decent-sized jib goes from just forward of the mast (about a third of the way aft) all the way to the stem-post. The foot of a handy standing lugsail is stretched out close to the sternpost by a long boom. It's not a huge area, but it is carried low so would provide power without much heeling. The sheet tackle is rigged above the tiller, so it could be controlled by the helmsman.

Records quoted by both John Leather and Michael Smylie reveal no fewer than four boatbuilders working in Annan in the 1870s. Thus the provision of inshore fishing craft continued as the ocean-going clippers were also created in the larger yards. McCubbin, Neilson, Shaw and Wilson produced and fitted out countless small craft. The 20-footers are described as being mainly decked. Though there was no cabin structure, the foredeck provided some shelter, necessary for those who would have to wait for tide. A basic stove could make this tight space more comfortable in winter. In comparison to the stripped-out craft of those who had to launch their boats from island boulder-beaches, this was a more civilised way of putting food on the table.

This type of craft could now be termed 'extinct', but perhaps the hard-won solutions have been carried forward into the design of shallow-draughted pleasure boats. Maybe an enterprising company will 'create' a dayboat which borrows on the Annan boatbuilders' variations on the whammel theme. It does seem sad that you cannot now watch one work the Solway tides in the same way, as the days of racing tea-clippers are over. The lines of the more modest craft, more local in range, also seem to want to speak of the lives of those who worked them.

NOTES

(1) *'Sailing Vessel Sarah Nicholson', Scottish Built Ships website,* *http://www.clydeships.co.uk/view.php?a1PageSize=75&ship_* *listPage=13&a1Page=89&ref=26438&vessel=SARAH+NICHOLSON.*
(2) John Leather, Spritsails and Lugsails *(London, Adlard Coles,1979).*
(3) Michael Smylie, Traditional Fishing Boats of Britain & Ireland: Design, History and Evolution *(Shrewsbury, Waterline Books, 1999).*

20
THE LINE-SKIFFS
AND THE DRONTHEIM –
THE NORTH CHANNEL

THE GABBERT AND THE WHAMMEL boat both developed a shape that was probably due more to function than anything else. We return to Norse influence when we look to two examples of historic craft from both sides of the North Channel. These bring contrasts in the solutions found in hull-shape and rig for a very similar set of issues. One form has been kept alive but the other is once more preserved only in photography and in drawings and measurements. Can we assume that the surviving example is the better solution, or do we have to look at other reasons for why some boats lived on and others died out?

Let's look at the dead one first. Michael Smylie draws a simple and helpful sketch which also shows a variation in rig for working close to a downwind angle. Once more, his primary source is the Maritime Museum in Greenwich.[1] *Brothers* was registered BA (Ballantrae) 318 and is described as a 'Portpatrick line boat'. One drawing is catalogued (available online) and described as: 'Scale 1:12. A plan showing the longitudinal half-breadth, longitudinal half-plan view, body, midships section and inboard profile of the *Brothers* BA318 (1898), a Portpatrick line boat. The plan has been signed "P.J. Oke, Plymouth" and is dated August 1936.'

As Michael points out, the resemblance in hull-shape to the

yoles built to work in the Pentland Firth area is striking. Coasters would often take a 'Southern Isles' yole on board as a deck cargo. It would be the ship's boat for the trip but then sold for profit before its return. Thus yoles were exported and you find surviving ones a long way up the sea-lochs of the Western Isles. Yet there is at least an equal chance that the boats built for line-fishing in the Portpatrick area developed that shape because they had to cope with very similar conditions – the ability to venture out into exposed waters where a significant tidal current can meet contrary seas. Freeboard had to be relatively high and a buoyant stern was the key feature. As with the whammel boats and so many variations of inshore skiff found from Largs to Lochinver, the rake is very slight at the bow and much more pronounced at the stern. This gives an underwater shape that gives a good grip on the water while still being able to turn without having to dip an oar. The wide beam allows for sufficient sail to drive that shape through steep seas.

A second catalogued drawing refers to the sail plan. The rig also has strong similarities with the yoles of Orkney's southern isles. A dipping lug forward, standing lug aft, are shown. Many of the northern yoles carried two spritsails, where one spar is set diagonally from the peak (top aft edge) of the sail to a point low down at the mast. Yet the principle is similar. The twin masts make the sail area manageable. Because that considerable amount of cloth is carried low, there is less tendency to heel. The wide beam also helps resist that tendency, but makes the vessel a good load carrier.

We have to try to read between these outlines just as we have to tune in to what is unsaid when someone tells their story. Strong currents passing over reefs, or parted by islands, or disturbed by headlands, all make for a build-up of plankton, crustaceans and the species of fish which feed on them. In turn, demersal species will shoal to feed there. Historically, cod and haddock were the most important at market, though whiting, coalfish and gurnard would be found

Drontheim (spritsail to left; standing lug to right)

among them, feeding within a fathom of the seabed. 'Greatlines' of hundreds of palm-sized hooks would be set by larger craft, but these 20-footers (about 16 feet in the keel) would be setting baskets of 'small lines', each with about a hundred hooks. In scale, these would be not much more than the stretch from a knuckle to a finger-tip in size. Each had to be laid out in sequence or a *bùrach* of impossibly tangled gear would result. A snood of twisted horsehair (latterly nylon) would connect the hook to the coiled main line. That would be of a softer and thicker cordage, easier to haul.

As this is labour-intensive fishing there might be three or four souls aboard, but sails and gear could be set by two or maybe one man and a boy when times were lean. I have set small lines but for subsistence rather than on a commercial scale. Even a couple of baskets of gear takes a bit of handling when there is any sea running. Now imagine multiple baskets. The baited hooks fly out, in their order, as the weighted line plummets down. The first line would probably be hauled as soon as the last was shot. There might be a live fish on every other hook or so, maybe even close to a full-house when shoals were thick. All these wriggling fish would have to be dealt with and sailing gear kept clear of the lively hooks. Maybe one line would have nothing but heavy dogfish and the slime and broken snoods which suggested conger or tope. This all happens at that confluence we call the North Channel with diving gannets and scudding waves all about. You can see why the sailing rig would be kept as simple as possible. And yet sufficient area had to be carried to drive vessel, crew and half a ton of fish through the chop and back home.

There has been a recent revival of the other craft developed for working the western edges of these waters. The origins are not in much doubt, as the name 'Drontheim' is derived from Trondheim, Norway. Originally, these boats which took a hold from the Isle of Islay to Rathlin and on around the coasts of Ireland as far as South Donegal were imported, either as finished craft, carried as a deck cargo or, more usually, as planking to be assembled. Once the form was proven, they were built by local craftsmen. Then, only the timber was imported in slab form. Normally ranging from about 20 to 27 feet overall, these craft are an entirely different shape to the Portpatrick line boat.

The Drontheim is long, narrow and shallow-draughted. She has a slight curvature at bow and stern so her length is carried over most of her waterline. There's not that much planking below that but the shallow keel is carried over most of her length. Freeboard is moderate. As a load carrier, the area would be similar to that of the shorter but beamier craft working the other side of the North Channel. But the Drontheim would be a much handier vessel to row. That length and a relatively small rudder area would make her tricky to turn but she would hold her line well and expert oarsmen would help with her steering. Her shallow draught made her easier to launch and recover on tight shores between rocky outcrops. She was also comparatively light for her length, so a village squad could haul up the craft vital to their subsistence.

As there has been a revival, the characteristics, under oars and sail, can be described without guesswork. Her slimness helps her cut the waves and yet there is sufficient buoyancy in her shape to ride them too. She will tend to roll a bit more than a beamy boat but her crew will be spaced out to lessen that risk. There are several variations of rig, with the 20-footers carrying a single mast and those of about 25 feet or over carrying two. Lugsails were and are still carried, but the spritsail rig was favoured. As Islay and Gigha are in reach of Rathlin and the northern coast of Ireland, the type was established there and so is within the scope of this book. The geographical reach is emphasised by Robin Ruddock, educator in outdoor sports and a key figure in the re-establishment of the class. The vessel has become a focal point of inter-community gatherings in coastal locations.

The website of the Causeway Coast Kayak Association reveals how like-minded people with an interest in both maritime heritage and outdoor education combined to bring a new vibrancy to coastal gatherings such as the Rathlin Sound Maritime Festival. Sailors make the passage from Gigha, Jura or Islay, as well as the harbours and bays of the mainland coast of Northern Ireland. A small fleet of the spritsailed craft is as much a distinctive feature of these gatherings as the expedition *curagh* or the smaller racing *curagh* which also find a way through the rips of Rathlin Sound. Yet the Drontheim very nearly died out. It was back in the 1960s when some examples were restored, most of them in Greencastle, Inishowen. The Maritime Heritage Group of the Causeway Coast worked with McDonalds Boatbuilders, to restore good examples. The commissioning of a new 25-foot Drontheim, in traditional clinker construction, larch on oak, was a key step. Robin had the *James Kelly* built for use in a wider project which combines sail-training with exploration of the rich coastal geography.

I was invited aboard at Rathlin. Christine Morrison, my wife, was handed the tiller and trusted to get on with that. As she had arrived in our wooden, long-keeled yacht, it was assumed she knew where to point the bow. Robin talked me through the rig as this was my first experience of a spritsail craft. The considerable sail area was stretched by the sprit, which was located in a reinforced pocket at the sail's peak. A band of cordage held it close to the mast, a couple of feet above the thwart. We found that the slim shape was easily driven. As you'd expect, the turning circle was fairly wide, even with a jib tacked right on the bow. As with many vessels, it helped if you let the jib back for a moment as the bow came through the eye of the wind in the turn or 'tack'.

On our return, we kept the sail powered up to follow the dogleg turn, avoiding the shallows as we neared the pontoon berths within the breakwater of this harbour. In our yacht, or in the traditional craft I was used to, we would have de-powered the sail a lot sooner. I knew Robin was demonstrating something unique to the rig. Not far from the pontoon he simply slipped the sprit from the band so the sail folded. At once the power was off. The slim hull had sufficient way to give Christine steerage as we glided in.

The *James Kelly* is a pleasure to look at. Her combination of painted and oiled timbers and her tan cloth are pleasing. She carries nothing unnecessary. But traditional boatbuilding is expensive in materials and in time. In 2002 Robin had a mould taken from a 22-foot example. About a dozen bare, GRP hulls were distributed around coastal communities. Each has been finished to either a basic or a more elaborate standard, as with coastal rowing skiffs. Similarly, a sail-kit is provided so costs can be saved by home-finishing. The result is a vessel that can race and cruise, under both oars and sail, to bring coastal communities together. I've also been fortunate in experiencing an example of this type, the Drontheim fitted out by Rathlin islanders.

Our crew found her better in light winds than some other examples with heavier sails of a cloth designed to replicate traditional heavy canvas. When it came to heavier breeze, things were different. This is the first and only time I've sailed to a funeral. My friend Fergus

McFaul, one of the usual skippers, asked me if I'd be happy to take the helm and take part in a group sail. The group of Drontheim were to sail-by the churchyard as the funeral of an islander was taking place. Fergus and the rest of the usual team were needed ashore. The person who had passed was an enthusiast of both full-size craft and a complementary scene of racing model vessels in a lough, up the road. You could see those who attended lining up their racing models along the route of the 'lift'. Robin guided the *James Kelly* around the bay as the procession began. We followed, along with the Ballycastle Drontheim, which had been taken over by members of the town community across the bay. Gusts were strong and I elected to carry foresail only as we were light in crew for the conditions. We could not venture too far downwind or it would be a hard row back against the chop. I could see no way of reefing the mainsail. But then I saw how it was done. Robin dropped the sprit again to make a fold which reduced the area by almost half. The rig was then manageable.

I could see how those imports from Trondheim served as versatile craft, perhaps in the way many Shetland and Faroese craft are also a compromise between sailing and rowing ability. I hope the communities of Islay, Jura and Gigha will also consider fitting out a craft from that mould to restore the tradition along a route that easily crosses any conceptual dotted line on the sea. The experiences of many communities from Rathlin to Unst show that rowing and sailing traditions can work together to mutual benefit.

NOTES

(1) Part of the P.J. Oke collection. Plans can be viewed at Royal Museums Greenwich. Catalogue reference: https://www.rmg.co.uk/collections/objects/rmgc-object-388638. See also list of references to articles on vessels, including references to the work of P.J. Oke: https://snr.org.uk/wp-content/uploads/2018/05/Topmasts-26-Supplement.pdf.

21
THE *CURACH*
– A SKIN ON
TIMBER BONES

WHEN IT COMES TO BOATS, it seems to me there are two main ways of doing it. You can build a frame, then stretch a skin around it. The other way is to lay planks from the keel up, overlapping, to form a shell. The *curach* is of the first type. Both the Portpatrick line boat and the Drontheim are examples of the second.

The *curach* is usually thought of as an Irish craft where the spelling is normally *curagh*, *curragh* or *currach*. As we are concerned with vessels linked to Scottish coasts here, the most usual Scottish Gaelic version of the name will be used from now on. Examples of the craft survived in areas of Ireland, especially the Atlantic islands of Aran and Blasket, at a time when more modern (and more expensive) solutions were adopted in most places. However, accounts of voyaging monks reveal that the vessel was central to communications between Ireland and Scotland, including the founding of monasteries such as Iona. Even the most distant monastic settlements out at Flannan Isles or North Rona must have been reached by seagoing versions of these skin boats. Alistair Moffat's *In Search of Angels* maps the routes and imagines the settlements and culture of these voyagers in an early Scotland.[1]

These were vessels of skin, but something has to give a craft a shape. Think of a lattice of light and flexible woods, lashed into compression. An overlaid material is stretched to cover that. Then that outer surface is proofed with fat or oil, tar or some other concoction, till it glistens. Materials were available or relatively cheap. The craft also had the advantage that it could be simply upturned and carried on the shoulders of her rowers, to safety up from the tides. The complementary disadvantage is that the light skin is vulnerable. If that is caught by a rock or chafed in abrasive sand, it will rip. The skin boats used to run tideways and ocean currents must have been robust, as re-created in Tim Severin's inspiring project to test if the 'stepping stones' route through the Hebrides and on to the Faroes, Iceland and the Labrador coast in *Brendan* was feasible in an oxhide craft. Smaller and lighter *curach* were in general use on routes between Scottish islands but we owe this knowledge to folklore and composed verses rather than archaeology. Materials did not favour the chances of long-term survival if the form was not renewed.

So we have to look down the ebbing tide to see and experience handed-down forms of the *curach*. Accounts of life on the Blasket Islands reveal the centrality of this type of vessel to the communities of Atlantic Ireland. Tomás O'Crohan's *The Islandman* was written in Gaelic and published in 1929 but available in English translation since 1934.[2] At one stage the islanders' craft of timber and nails are impounded in lieu of unpaid rent but they return to their home-made vessels of tarred canvas over lashed timbers. This is a memoir told with great craft and skill but the techniques are not flourished. In the same way, the *curach* looks primitive at first glance.

Robert Flaherty's film, *Man of Aran*, purports to be a documentary but there is strong dramatic contrast in the telling as well as the superb cinematography. The scene where two small *curach* make landfall in an Atlantic storm is heart-stopping to watch. The skills are humbling for any mariner to observe and you are left wondering if any other craft could have delivered its occupants ashore. An Inuit kayak certainly, but that is another result of the same concept – skin over bones.

Thus the *curach* has an unbroken line of continuity from prehistory. Its essentials remain unchanged though its skin might be ballistic nylon, in present times. Modern recreations have been used to restore links between international seafaring communities. The poet and broadcaster Danny Sheehy (Domhnall Mac Síthigh) had already taken part in a circumnavigation of Ireland in a *naomhóg* or Kerry *currach*. He had also been on an expedition to Iona in a larger seagoing craft. In June 2017 the *naomhóg* capsized in waters close to the Spanish and Portugese border. All aboard gained the shore but Mr Sheehy was taken ill and did not recover. The sad incident is a reminder that risk is always a part of voyaging, whatever the vessel and whether the purpose is to earn a living from the sea or to bring people together in a community joined by seas.

As there has not yet been a similar revival of interest in Scottish communities, it was to take a voyage to Rathlin Island to experience, first-hand, the behaviour of this vessel of stretched material, tough and fragile at the same time. At Rathlin Sound Maritime Festival, a small fleet of the very slim three-person *curach* was made ready to practise and race. I experienced the euphoria of whitewood blades crashing in close quarters. This did not seem to cause any cries of 'foul', just wider grins on both rowers and spectators. On rounding the buoys, spray was shedding from the shining nylon of her tilted-up bow. There is no hint of a keel and the forward oars do the steering. They are so narrow that your pair of oar handles will clash and rap your knuckles if you let them. You have to develop a curious, hand-over-hand technique. One clumsy stroke by one of the three rowers and she'll spin in a circle.

Another year, I helped take one of the pair of the small racing *curach* along the rips and shifts of one of the complex tidal systems down the south tip of Rathlin. We were to sneak into a protective geo by the squat and black-banded South Light. There was an 'oh, oh' moment when a standing wave caught up with us. As we held our breath, our light craft just shrugged her way through it. Next day,

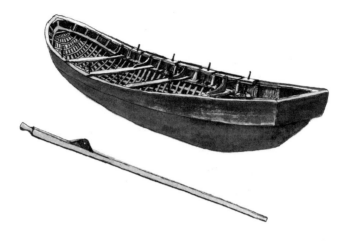

Naomhóg of Kerry and Cork (see also currach/curach*)*

Rathlin friends and visiting sailors took the ferry across to help launch the newly proofed and glistening *Colmcille* at Ballycastle. This is an example of the expedition craft and she was to cross to Rathlin for the festival to join another expedition *curach* on a similar scale.

With six oars a side and a heavier steering oar stationed aft, the 40-foot *Colmcille* is a powerful craft. This is a vessel built to emulate the type which would join communities on Scottish islands, and especially Iona. In fact, I first heard of her when there was a call for Scottish island mariners to join with Irish ones and row and sail together to mark the anniversary of the founding of Iona Abbey. Since that maiden adventure, the *Colmcille* has proved herself on that route several times. She and similar craft have also recently undertaken astonishing coastal adventures such as voyaging the jagged fringes of the Basque country in short and long hops. As the sad accident of the *naomhóg* capsize at the mouth of the River Minho reminds us, they are not invincible.[3]

On boarding *Colmcille*, I found that the vessel is still narrow in proportion to her length, but there is space for one of her crew to handle each oar. Like the smaller versions, she has not a hint of keel. Our red and green blades began to find that rhythm as our cool and mustachioed skipper, Ivor Neill, encouraged us on with his stories. He didn't look worried as the roar of the race came closer, so why should we. But it did seem loud. 'Just keep them going when we're in it now. Keep them driving.' High walls of white appeared from nowhere to lift us up in the air and drop us again. Another big sea would surge from a different angle. Our craft bucked but rose like a black salmon. I could see why her seafaring history was already so impressive.

Next day, two teams of local people raced the two small *curach* through the broth of thrashing waters to the mainland. Michael Cecil, chair of the festival and RNLI volunteer, reckoned that the crossing was about the distance many refugees had braved, before landing on a very different island in Greece. He had assisted at Lesbos, on rescue boats, back in the winter and now the aim was to raise awareness of the plight of those whose homes had been destroyed. The histories of Rathlin or the Outer Hebrides should help us find affinity with seaborne migrants.

At times it did not seem possible that the flimsy vessels could survive in the high jabble of the main sound. Seas pile back and fore between the North Channel and open Atlantic. Heavier displacement craft, powered with steady diesel engines, had been commandeered as safety boats. My friend Ken Linklater was one of the skippers. He told me his presence in a long-keeled yacht of 35 feet or so was not really required. 'I thought they'd had it when we went into the tide-rips,' he said. 'But these wee slight things just lifted like feathers. It was us who got a bit of a hammering.'

You cannot underestimate the work involved in preserving or reviving a type of craft. Expeditions and races help with motivation. Scottish communities could build from the success of the Coastal Rowing Movement in St Ayles skiffs to build their own voyaging *curach*. Again, it was at Rathlin Sound Maritime Festival where a route to this was suggested. One year of dodgy weather there were simply not enough folk available to get the racing *curach* out at the same time. I recently found the recorded times and names of crews, noted in our own boat's log, for stopwatched runs on a chosen route in a single racing craft. As our *El Vigo* was alongside on the pontoons we were nominated the committee boat. Niamh Scullion joined sculptor Paddy Bloomer and his brother Tim to record the fastest time of the weekend.

Niamh was already engaged in a project to bring the concept of a 10-metre community-run *curach* to the Lagan River, Belfast. The project, 'Lagan Currachs', involved over 80 volunteers in the building of the craft. Like the GalGael community boatbuilding project in Glasgow, this has an aspect of urban community renewal and an aim of involving disadvantaged people. It was emotional territory indeed to be aboard *Colmcille* again in 2018, but neck-and-neck with the newly completed vessel, crossing Rathlin Sound at speed, propelled by an all-woman crew. We can surely hope that the community fostered by the coastal rowing revival in Scotland might also look to recreating our own expedition craft of skin.

In 2021 Fergus McFaul shared images of the two layers of nylon skin being renewed. The coordination of hands and minds of willing helpers is exceptional. These images were soon followed by others showing a vessel at sea again in a post-lockdown row. Then the call came, in July. Once more, an expedition linked the northern coast of Ireland and Rathlin Island with communities on Gigha, Islay, Jura and Iona. The material of the new skin may be synthetic, but the principle of the vessel would be unchanged from that used by the monks who learned to run the tides to advantage. It would be even better if a Scottish community-built vessel would work the tides to return these visits.

Maybe the recreation of a vessel such as the voyaging *curach* is like a translation. Scotland's first Makar, Edwin Morgan, translated verse attributed to the saint Colmcille (St Columba). In his wide-ranging 2016 anthology of writing relating to the Isle of Iona, Robert Crawford reproduces two different translations of a well-known verse of celebration. Here is the one which aims to convey the music of the original:

> Isle of my heart, Isle that it loveth so,
> Where chaunts the monk, only the kine shall low;
> Yet before Heaven shall wax and Earth shall wane,
> Iona, as she was, shall be again![4]

NOTES

(1) Alistair Moffat, In Search of Angels *(Edinburgh, Birlinn, 2020).*

(2) *Tomás O'Crohan,* An t-Oileánach *'Tomás Ó Criomhthain, first published in 1929. An unabridged English translation was published in 2013:* The Islandman, *translated by Garry Bannister and David Sowby (Dublin, Gill & Macmillan, 2013).*

(3) *Report of the accident in Spain on the* Irish Times *website: https://www.irishtimes. com/news/ireland/irish-news/poet-domhnall-mac-s%C3%ADthigh-dies-after-boat-capsizes-off-spain-1.3115509.*

(4) *Mosse Macdonald, 'Iona' (Newdigate Prize Poem, Oxford, 1879), translation in Robert Crawford (ed.),* The Book of Iona – an Anthology *(Edinburgh, Birlinn, 2016, p. 203. Edwin Morgan,* The Maker on High *(Edinburgh, Mariscat Press, n.d.) is a limited edition of the Makar's translations of verse attributed to Colm Cille.*

22

THE LOCH FYNE SKIFF – SAILING FOR WORK AND FOR PLEASURE

WHEN IT COMES TO THE vessels known as the Loch Fyne skiff we find yet again that the story is not as simple as it seems. The location which gives the name is a long inlet that takes you out of the fierce tidal run from the North Channel. The long stretch of the Mull of Kintyre and the hammerhead of Dumfries and Galloway are like protective arms that tend to keep the Firth of Clyde and its offshoots fairly manageable for navigation. The Isle of Arran, with its high ground, can also help, though of course you may also meet cats' paws of squalls sent down from lochside heights.

You can reach Loch Fyne by rounding the Mull or you can coast by the Isle of Arran or beat through the narrows at the Kyles of Bute. These are all grand routes for the cruising sailor, but creel boats and scallop-dredgers still ply their trades in the area. As you take a breather in Campbeltown, moor off Carradale or hold off for entry to the Crinan Canal at Ardrishaig, there is little hint of the scale of herring fishing that made these waters some of the busiest. The methods and vessels changed but the herring fishing continued for centuries rather than years.

The name 'Loch Fyne skiff' only tells a part of the story. These were built by several Scottish yards, some on the east coast as well as those closer to the waters where they first worked. Once more, there is not a clear dividing line between vessels used for the sheer joy of sailing and those built for work. Archived photographs suggest that the shape did not appear out of the blue, either from a shipwright's adze or a draughtsman's pen.

An image of the nineteenth-century trawl skiffs of Loch Fyne[1] shows a fleet beached at Dalintober beach across from Campbeltown harbour. These were powered by oars. A fairly narrow beam and low freeboard were requirements. But they also had to be strong enough to take the stresses of towing heavy loads and they had to be buoyant enough to carry a weight of herring. There is a distinctive rise towards the stern. As the fishing method changed, through drift netting to ring netting, the vessels also altered. Elements of the type, proven for working in the area, were carried forward. That trend was not unique to any one area. When we come to look at the vernacular craft of Shetland, we'll see how there is a finely graded spectrum of shapes from those best suited to working under oars to those built for offshore work where sailing performance, seaworthiness and load-carrying ability were all essential to carry out the work.

The difference in scale from the trawl skiffs to the lug-rigged sailing skiffs was the shift from about 20 feet, bow to stern, to about 30, on average. Fishermen were to remain at sea for longer periods and fish through all seasons. Later, they would recoup their investment in the ever-larger vessels by following the shoals around the coasts. Decking made the formerly open craft safer, but also gave the opportunity for shelter. Angus Martin's research indicates that the first of these part-decked skiffs with a small cuddy forward were built at Girvan and launched in 1882. By 1893 the feature was expected in a new-built vessel such as the 32 foot 5 inch (nearly 10 metres) *Britannia*, built for the McFarlane family by James Fyfe at Port Bannatyne on the Isle of Bute. The accommodation provided was cramped and basic but it was shelter, and there was the possibility of a stove to make nights at sea more bearable.

However, it is the shape and rig which make this type of vessel

The Loch Fyne skiff (sloped keel)

as distinctive as the east-coast scaffie, Fifie and Zulu. Roger Finch's drawing in his *Sailing Craft of the British Isles*[2] does not show the sloping keel as an extreme feature in the same way as Michael Smylie draws the shape in his *Traditional Fishing Boats of Britain & Ireland*.[3] I'd say Mr Smylie was closer to the mark, when you compare the steep rake at the stern and the pronounced slant of her keel to that revealed in a photograph of a beached skiff – another Fyfe of Port Bannatyne boat, *Pscyhe*, of 1915 build (Smylie, p. 65). The photograph also confirms the more extreme shape drawn by Will Maclean. As part of the artist's research project, it also includes detailing on such practical concerns as the placing of stone ballast. A print is included in his 2022 exhibition. The shallower bow section would allow a skiff to nudge up close to a shelving beach to land a catch or take on stores, while the depth up to the rudder would give her grip and steerage as well as resistance to leeway.

Angus Martin provides excellent detail on particularities of the standing-lug rig carried by this type. I would direct a reader who wishes to know more on the contribution of blacksmith, rigger and sailmaker to that section of his *The Ring-Net Fishermen* (pp. 83–7). Let's just say here that this was a 'handy' solution because the yard that carried the lugsail did not require to be 'dipped' around the mast on tacking. Only a small part of the sail area was carried forward of the mast and the lower point (tack) was secured at the forward edge of the mast thwart. Eric McKee draws a detail to illustrate a typical iron horse designed for an efficient set of sail.[4] That sail was traditionally hoisted from the starboard side, perhaps due to prevailing winds, so there was a single fixed stay but the halyard, tensioned with a block and tackle, in effect became the second stay when secured. On the port side, two fixed stays could be permanently secured to support the mast.

Moving forward, the gap in sail area was filled by a jib or jibs. As the mast was situated or 'stepped' so far forward, one was run out on a 'traveller' of iron hooped around the bowsprit, which could be up to 14 feet long. A mainsail drives a boat up towards the wind and a foresail balances that by tending to push the bow back again. Thus the rig was easy to work, but all made for a very balanced sail plan. This is not just a matter of aesthetics, though it did look elegant. Without the foresails the boat would have weather-helm, so the tiller would be working to keep the boat from rounding up towards the wind. Every time you put pressure on the rudder you would also be braking the progress through the water. These fishers who made their living by working breeze to advantage day by day, night by night, developed a near-instinctive understanding of these principles.

There is at least one more refinement visible in the rig of the Loch Fyne skiff. This reveals knowledge of a principle that is still used in contemporary racing craft to optimise performance, whether the course takes the boat hard on the wind or running before it. The mast was stepped with a pronounced 'rake', but this was not for show. In effect, this brought more of the sail area aft, which helped drive the boat to windward. But when they were close to a run before the wind, wedges could lessen that rake as halyard tension was reduced. Most racing yachts or fast cruisers will now have a backstay tensioning device so that a similar process can use that same principle.

A detailed drawing with a sail plan held at the Science Museum, London, shows five reef points in the main and three different sizes of jib to hoist according to wind strength. All these elements point to a sophisticated approach to sailing these working craft. If further proof were needed, there are detailed records of the competitive regattas held annually. Trophies and prize money were fiercely contested. A skipper with a lead, gone through the beat and reach and running for the line, might be tempted to ask for the quiet release of some of his ballast of sand and shingle, but the rules were clear. You must finish the race with the same weight you carried at the start, else you would be disqualified.

The qualities of both the hull shape and the rig were noticed by those who would design or build sail boats for pleasure rather than as a means of pursuing the herring. The mention of Fyfe of Port Bannatyne leads us to a small number of seagoing yachts which were directly based on the working boats of Loch Fyne. These Fyfes were relatives of the family (or dynasty) who ran the Fairlie yard. Skills in producing a fair hull shape from boatskin were as vital in working boats as they were in yachts. Speed was needed to reach the shoals and bring the catch to market in time to make the steamer for Glasgow. I have been able to take a close look at two of the yachts based on the form as it developed. I would say these were built and rigged more for the comfortable seakeeping qualities that would let them cover a distance. Yacht *Kirsty* turned 100 years of age in 2021. *Craignair*, built at Port Bannatyne a few years later, was patched up and towed over to Lewis, where she spent her latter years.

The stories of *Kirsty* and *Craignair* warrant more space (see next chapter), as their hull shapes were so closely related to those of the working craft. But we can't leave Loch Fyne without mentioning at least two more works of literature which celebrate the bustle of the hunt for herring. John MacDougall Hay was the author of the novel *Gillespie*, first published in 1914.[5] It portrays the shoreside wheeling and dealing and the great gamble of the market for herring. The poetry of his son, George Campbell Hay (Deòrsa Mac Iain Deòrsa), reveals the deepest understanding of another type of trade – the international nature of the concerns which prompt poetry and the skills to make it as sound as a vessel. George's mastery of formal structures, in English, Scots, Gaelic or in translation from other European languages, is clear. It reveals a sense of how the necessity of structural integrity can help devise the most elegant of shapes. His poetry can be probing and challenging but it's not all difficult. 'Seeker Reaper' is a sea-poem, best sounded out loud, and many lively performances are available as sound recordings or videos.

NOTES

(1) Angus Martin, The Ring-Net Fishermen *(Edinburgh, John Donald, 1981, new edition 2001). From a photograph (plate 20, p. 93).*

(2) Roger Finch, Sailing Craft of the British Isles *(London, Collins, 1976), p. 99.*

(3) Michael Smylie, Traditional Fishing Boats of Britain & Ireland: Design, History and Evolution *(Shrewsbury, Waterline Books, 1999), p. 59.*

(4) Eric McKee, Working Boats of Britain: Their Shape and Purpose *(London, Conway Maritime Press, 1983), p. 207.*

(5) John MacDougall Hay, Gillespie, *first published 1914. Current edition introduced by Isobel Tait and Bob Murray (Edinburgh, Canongate Classics, 2001).*

23
A YACHT DERIVED FROM
A WORKING BOAT

DAY AND NIGHT FISHING MUST test a vessel and rig more than any tank-testing or occasional racing. Only the long-distance sailor can put a vessel through the combinations of weather and sea conditions which most working craft will meet all too often in their working life. Not for the first time, a shape and rig which were proven in a commercial fishery were adopted in yachtbuilding. Fyfes of Port Bannatyne continued to build both work and pleasure boats in the same way as the Silvers yard or that of McGruers on the Clyde, or Millers at St Monans could turn the hands of their boatbuilders to either. This family was related to the Fife yachtbuilders of Fairlie, though the spelling differs. Ewan Kennedy's interview with a descendant, Miss Jean M. Fife, outlines the family relationships and makes it clear that even Fifes of Fairlie built fishing boats in the nineteenth century.[1]

Based on this source and Ewan's additional research, two James Fyfes were building boats at Rothesay, Isle of Bute, in the mid 1850s. The Loch Fyne skiff, proven at regattas where there were only seconds between vessels after more than four hours of racing, was taken as the model for several yachts. In 1925, John Fyfe built a vessel of 11 tons gross at the Port Bannatyne yard. She came in at about 36 feet (11 metres) with about 10 feet (3 metres) in the beam and a maximum draught of 6 feet (1.83 metres). By this time the working skiffs were of carvel (flush-planked) construction, due to their larger size. The yachts were also carvel. Rather than larch, this skiff's planking was cut from the even more durable species of pitch-pine, then the preferred but more expensive material for yachts. Thus the construction of a commissioned yacht, to plans, was not a radical departure. Instead of internal ballast of selected boulders (or cobles), the design called for a cast-iron keel, bolted through the oak with forged ironwork. Instead of a cuddy, the yacht was flush-decked overall, with raised hatches. Decklights and portholes brought light into compact forecabin, saloon and galley areas below. Due to the greater aft draught, carried over from the working skiffs, there was good standing room when you descended from the small cockpit. The underwater shape granted that space without the need for a high deckhouse that would spoil her clean lines and add windage.

She would have to work, most times, with less than a fishing-boat crew. Her rig was modified to take that into account. The sail area was distributed over a main and a smaller mizzen aft (ketch-rig). A bowsprit was fixed on deck but did not extend as far out as that carried by the larger of the working boats. The owner's preference was for a gaff-cutter rig. Instead of one large foresail, the area was shared between two smaller jibs, again just like on most of the working boats. A gaff is like a lugsail yard except it locates onto the mast with a collar. Some form of anti-friction devices such as a greased leather gasket and cordage with parrel beads allow it to slide up and down. A second halyard then lifts the aft end of that gaff. Usually there is a gap above that. In light weather that can be filled with a topsail run up a topmast section. The most clear depiction of that rig I have seen is a repeated icon in the work of the artist Graham Rich. He is also a sailor. He lives in Topsham, at the estuary of the Exe, but he often exhibits in Scotland, including shows at the Pittenweem Festival, Cairn Gallery and at the Fine Art Society, Edinburgh.

Graham etches out that shape as a vessel discovered, often

Kirsty *(Port Bannatyne, 1921)*

among the distressed surface of a weathered material. The impression is of a brave small ship working its way on through cloud and waves. From the history of John Fyfe's *Craignair*, that would be an appropriate depiction of a hard-sailed yacht. The records of the RNLI record an incident from 1 June 1938. Berry Head Coastguard informed the lifeboat station at Torbay that a yacht called *Craignair* was showing a distress signal. She was caught out in a strong south-westerly gale in a position about a mile and a half east of Oddicombe. Two of her crew had already been taken aboard a small craft launched by members of a local sailing club, joined by sea-scouts. *Craignair* was at anchor but in an exposed position. She was towed into Brixham harbour to survive and go on further adventures.

I came across this vessel first when she was towed into Stornoway harbour in the late 1980s. She had been holed while lying at drying-out posts on the mainland and a locally based man, Bill Evans, had patched her and taken her across the North Minch. Bill made a sound job of making her safe and secure again. He improvised new masts and found a rig that would suit. The wing-engine was soon running and I did see her sailing with a reduced rig, and going very sweetly through the water. Bill saw my interest and filled in a bit of what lay between her launch at the Isle of Bute and her arrival in the Outer Hebrides. The story of her life under her second owner stuck in the mind. Roger Fothergill gave up on her engine and converted that into part of a mooring. Instead, he rigged a transverse yard to mount a small squaresail. His plan was to venture southwards to where the trade winds prevailed. According to his account, written for a bound *Yachting Monthly* annual, he found them. *Craignair* cruised the Caribbean before returning to home waters.

It was more like being in the doldrums after that. Photos show her moored by Tower Bridge. Then came an owner from overseas who altered her rig but did not seem to do much else. The damage, it seems, was done by a coaster gone astray and hitting her while she was on the posts for work. The story of boat renovations is not always a smooth one with a happy ending. Bill did attempt to sell on the boat, now black-hulled, from her permanent mooring off the Goat Island causeway in Stornoway. No deal was done and she came through storm after storm. Her galvanised rigging looked rusty but must have still been plenty strong. His hand-hewn masts also held up. Finally he found some gribble worm had entered at her sternpost, behind the rudder. She was propped up on stout posts again. This time she stayed. Nothing hit her but the tide and storm after storm. Still her masts stood. Once, one prop gave way but Bill and his friends succeeded in standing her on her keel again.

To some, she might have been an eyesore. To most, her hull shape remained to be admired. It was when you came close you could really appreciate why the family of one of the world's best-acknowledged yacht designers would want to build a yacht based on a working boat. More than once, a near-sister visited at Stornoway. Yacht *Kirsty* was also built by John Fyfe at Port Bannatyne and is also gaff ketch-rigged. In 1921 her ballast keel of 6 tons was bolted in place. She had also gone far afield, if you can say that about water. She also cruised the Caribbean, and other territories explored included France and the Baltic. Her current owners are the Borders-based architect Andy Law and his artist wife Pat Law. Like *Craignair*, she has inspired arts projects and writing. *Kirsty* does still have an interior, and a cosy but functional one too. I did my best to describe that while writing about helping Andy on a previous delivery trip to the Hebrides.[2] We came hard on the wind close by Hyskeir, south of Coll, where big seas bounced up from the shallow banks as 30 knots blew from the north. The vessel was comfortable and we made good speed at about 50 degrees off the wind, making Lochboisdale from our starting point at Oban that morning.

Kirsty survived a sinking under previous ownership when caught in a gale at an Isle of Wight harbour. In 2021 she reached her hundredth year. She has taken part in several arts projects devised by co-custodian Pat Law. A detailed photographic record can be found on Pat's Heriot Toun Studio website.[3] Pat shared a local newspaper clipping documenting a return to Bute under previous owners: 'She was built in 1921 for a Mr John Mowat and was a local yacht for many years. Now owned by Peter and Fran Flutter of Falmouth for the last 15 years, during which she has sailed thousands of miles to the West Indies and Barbados via the Canary Islands. She went up the American coast as far as New York, returning to Falmouth via the Azores. Also voyages to Norway.'

Craignair was broken up as part of clearing abandoned projects from a shoreline which is now part of Goat Island marina. Yet, in a sense, she has also survived. In this transition from working boat to ocean-going yacht it seems to me that shape is the most important element. Bill Evans brought some of the pitch-pine planking, still smelling of resin and as sound as when it was milled, to retired shipwright Dick Stenhouse. As in so many instances cited in this book, it is a meticulous model which best carries the shape of the vessel forward. In this case it is revealed and held by the very timber which was once part of that far-reaching hull.

Colin Myers, a retired rigger and onetime international competitive sailor (in Tornado class catamarans) is fascinated by the form of *Craignair*. He knew the vessel itself and her history before settling on the Isle of Lewis. Colin did his apprenticeship as a shipwright (like his father before him) and has very refined woodworking skills. To date he has made accurate half models of the Robert Clark sloop *El Vigo* and the traditional North Lewis *sgoth Niseach*. He is gathering more detail on *Craignair*, and I wonder if another take on her shape will further help secure the essential form of a boat that was translated from workboat to deep-sea cruising yacht.

At the other side of the North Minch one of the Loch Fyne skiffs built as a working boat is being restored. The *Clan Gordon* could be seen, varnished hull, raked mast and all, riding out the blasts which came down Loch Broom. Names sometimes form a series. Angus Martin quotes records of a *Clan MacDougall* and a *Clan Matheson* built at Carradale by fisherman turned boatbuilder Matthew MacDougall. Her keel was first laid by A. Munro of Ardrishaig in 1911. One time *Clan Gordon* dragged her moorings. Temporary repairs were made and she could be seen ashore at Ullapool. At the time of writing she is undergoing a complete restoration at Isle Ewe Boats in Aultbea. The current owner of one of the Summer Islands, Tanera Mor, is giving work to Alasdair Grant as well as Loftus and Johnson. Like *St Vincent* and like the two skiff-based yachts, the *Clan Gordon* is of smooth carvel construction. That shape, which has survived bumps, spills and groundings, is now being brought back to life.

Back in Tarbert, Argyll, an example of the smaller, inshore Loch Fyne skiff lies on posts in the harbour area. Her oiled planks, darkened in a few years since her build, show the deep aft draft on her sloping keel. Adam, of A and R Way (Argyll-based boatbuilders), involved local school students in a recreation of a typical small craft. Her mast spars and rig also show the typical steeply raked standing lug which also helps define the type.

NOTES

(1) Ewan Kennedy, 'The Other Fyfes', scottishboating (blog), 15/10/11: https:// scottishboating.blogspot.com/2011/10/other-fyfes.html.
(2)Ian Stephen, Waypoints *(London, Adlard Coles Nautical/Bloomsbury, 2017).*
(3) 'Kirsty Loch Fyne Skiff ... 2021: 100 years afloat', Heriot Toun Studio website: http://heriot-toun.co.uk/studio-log/kirsty.php.

24

RACING SKIFFS – MULL, OBAN AND TIREE

IT WAS ONLY A SMALL STEP from investing in a special set of regatta sails to keeping a boat for the purpose of racing rather than working. From the Faroe Islands to Antigua, examples of vernacular boats have continued because a competitive racing scene prompted boatbuilding when such craft were no longer viable as commercial fishing craft or even a vital part of subsistence. As with the highly developed sailing craft of the Loch Fyne area, localised skiff-racing became a popular sport all through the twentieth century. You could get a sense of the keen competition when you met anyone who remembered their place crewing or helming. The butcher's shop in Tobermory was well worth visiting anyway, for the craic as well as the meat. But if things were quiet, Richard Hughes would talk you through the photographs. Those taken from a pierhead showed open vessels with pointed noses and rounded sterns. There seemed to be some variations in the rig, though most carried a standing lug and a jib out on a bowsprit, like the Loch Fyne skiffs. The boats were from more than one builder and dimensions were not constant. If this was a class, it was 'restricted' rather than a 'one-design', which would ensure measurements and weights were within tight tolerances.

We were told that the Sound of Mull fleet also worked to the rule that you could not jettison ballast over the side during a race.

187

However, there was nothing to say that a sandbag or two could not be sneaked aboard another boat in a close-quarters situation. By the grin on the teller's face, reliving it, you got a sense there was room for mischief as well as a test of skills. It was later we found that the sailor and butcher and ace yarner also had a good grasp of the rhythms needed to be drummer in the local dance band.

I learned that there was a circuit of regattas in the Sound of Mull, island and mainland, but there was also at least one annual race on the west side. Topher Dawson, then a boatbuilder working in a wind-powered workshop on the Scoraig peninsula, Dundonnel, visited the Ross of Mull often. Among the matted pink granite, the sea-pinks and clover, lay the intact frame of *Argo*. Topher responded by email to my quest for more information: 'She was 20 feet and reputed to be very fast in races. I still have the original lines and also a redrawn version by Iain Oughtred which would have been gorgeous.'

A bow-iron showed that she had carried a bowsprit. Reminiscences of the lugsail-rigged racing have also been recorded and transcribed on the west side of the island. In the Sound of Iona, detailed knowledge of localised currents was often the deciding factor. Even from the printed page, you could sense that the informant was experiencing once more the thrill of picking up light airs to ghost a way ahead of a rival. There might be an inshore eddy of tide to work or a slight sweep around a point. Sailing through the landscapes which continued to inspire the Scottish Colourists is inspiring in itself. You would need to keep a focus on the shape of the sail and the ripples on the water rather than look out to the white sands and veins of green in the granite.

Topher thought the form of *Argo* so sweet he took her lines. So far he has not had a chance to make her anew, but we did collaborate on an art project which included making half a boat, scaled-down slightly. This was a commission for a public artwork on the occasion of the completion of *an Tobar*, the multi-arts space created from the old school. There was great interest in displaying a three-dimensional form of the type of craft still on display in the butcher's collection of photographs. But there was no budget to make a new community-owned craft. To me, it seemed as if a builder's half-model was, to use Topher's engineering term, 'necessary and sufficient' to preserve and communicate the essential shape of the craft. But if this could be made, like an actual boat, as a shell and sited outside, it could also provide seating. We looked from many angles and found a site where the shape would be seen as you came up the steep walking path from the main street. We devised a way of displaying the rig with rope outlines of the sail plan in synthetic hemp. My main part was to devise and inscribe a text which explored how that attractive shape combined the needs for buoyancy and resistance to drift.

A 'boat soup' of natural oils, turpentine and a dash of Stockholm tar preserves the boatskin larch. The stem is nearly plumb. You can see that the keel slopes, though not in the extreme way of the Loch Fyne skiff. That uptilt and rounding of the stern is similar though. Since that time there has been something of a revival of the west-coast skiff of this type, with the Oban skiff being perhaps best known. Several builders have made recent versions. A and R Way have recently built four vessels, but with some variations including a centreboard of cast iron, which would certainly give that example an advantage, beating to windward. It might also prompt endless discussion on handicaps when such a boat is on a race or rally with one that does not have the feature. The mast is high and the mainsail of a size which suggest the first of her three reefs has to go in early. One of his customers, Stan Reeve, researched the origins of the type of craft. He found she is also represented by line drawings, preserved in the National Maritime Museum. As reported in a feature in the *Oban Times*, he traced the history of *Gylen*, which came in at just over 18 feet (5.5 metres) without her sprit. She was built in 1886 by the Macdonald family, who had been forced off the fertile island of Lismore.

An Oban skiff (centreboard, A and R Way)

Iain Oughtred comments on the shape of the Oban skiff as created by Adam:

> The west-coast skiffs are broadly of similar form; the boats from Loch Fyne to around the Clyde. There is a profile reminiscent to the Zulu's, with straight stem and raked stern post, though shallower draught, and considerable drag to the keel. Fishermen and boatbuilders can recognise local variations, and on seeing any boat can quickly pin down where she comes from, and probably the builder. The Oban skiffs have extraordinarily full round stern, almost semi-circular sometimes. This stern is very buoyant and helps the boat when well-laden and running for home before a hard breeze. I found it difficult to imagine planking up the stern of Adam's boat, with its severe bending and twisting of the planks into the stern.[1]

The comments on the group of craft are very much in line with those of Mike Smylie and with the drawings of an Oban skiff, a Largs line skiff and a Girvan line skiff in his *Traditional Fishing Boats of Britain & Ireland*. These are certainly a family, in rig as in hull shape. I have heard very similar comments to Iain's as regards achieving that stern shape, from many boatbuilders, including John Murdo Macleod of the Ness boatbuilding family, Isle of Lewis. John Murdo wrote of achieving that curvature in the stern and the twist and tuck which allows the planking to sweep out until very close to the stern post. This is a sought-after feature, for the buoyancy it provides, especially in a following sea and when running before the breeze. I'd suggest it is not unique to the Oban skiff or even the larger family grouping of similar craft of about 18 feet overall. From Westray to Portpatrick, that twist and tuck required clear timber, plenty of steam and steady nerves.

Rather than rounding Ardnamurchan Point, let's set a course for Tiree. We leave the Treshnish Isles well to port and avoid the temptation to nip through Gunna Sound as a gate to the open west. One last glance at The Dutchman's Cap (Linga) and an imagining of the past lives between the fallen drystone forms still to be found on these offshore islands. That gap between Coll and Tiree may not be visible. When I was on a project documenting the work of inshore fishermen, I was out this way in a lobster boat working out from Ulva Sound. The skipper saw me sketching in a notebook, marking the silhouettes of the islands as a way of positively identifying each and remembering the visual relationship of similar low masses. 'Jist a flat line'll do for Tiree,' he said. But really it is a subtle skyline, often in haze.

If you do find a way, by one means or another, into Gott Bay, it would be good to time that visit to coincide with the regatta. I never have, but I've spoken to those who have and they did not have much option but to take part. Once more the regatta was born from a natural rivalry as a small fleet of similar boats returned from the fishing grounds. There have been attempts to classify the Tiree skiff and define her form and rig, most recently by Skye boatbuilder Malcolm Henry.

At present there does not seem to be a strong enough stock of like craft to ensure continuity of a tradition. A new build would certainly help. Photographs and models show a double-ended hull form but going quite deep and with fairly plumb ends, in fact more like a Fifie than a Zulu shape. This is a very different craft from the skiffs that raced in different parts of Mull, and very different in form and rig from the Oban skiff and its close cousins. To my eye, the double-ender is closer to a lean sailing skiff, *Lily*, found on the shores of Barra and drawn by Eric McKee.[2]

A glance at footage or stills tells you that they were primarily regatta boats, dependent on judicious shifting of crew weight as well as fixed ballast, to damp down the thrust from gusts when they caught a huge and high spread of canvas. They carried a single, dipping lugsail, tacked right on the bow. Some of the craft, possibly later ones, have transom sterns. Small craft could more easily carry an outboard motor when these became available, but Topher Dawson pointed out, in his email, that transom sterns were in use long before outboards, especially on a tender to be taken aboard a larger ship: 'The transom allowed a reduction of overall length without a loss of carrying capacity. [That part] was only above the water and the boat had a sweet wineglass stern below the water.'

It would be interesting to see how the Tiree transom-sterned boats compare with double-enders if other factors such as waterline length and sail area are equal. As someone who spends a fair bit of time on boats rigged with a dipping lug, I've heard countless suggestions about clever ways to avoid the necessity of dipping that tack around the mast. I'm afraid such commentators are missing the fun. This is an elegant and powerful rig, but it requires close coordination of actions by the crew. In short, you really do have to work as a team. In a race of comparable boats, that is the main skill on test because a poor tack will lose any advantage gained, even by careful sail trim. A pronounced rake on the mast can also help with tacking.

The relevance in teaching teamwork is not a new discovery. Both Merchant and Royal Navy cadets spent time on 'whalers' rigged with dipping lugs. You have to look as well as listen and really, telepathy is by far the best method of winning races. Tiree, like so many coastal communities now, has its own home-built St Ayles skiff. I would not see that as a distraction. Propulsion of these also depends on working in harmony. A similar set of skills is required in coxing these and skippering a sailing skiff. If the young folk have also been through nippy little sailing dinghies they are likely to have developed wind-awareness. The next step could be pulling all the skills together in like lugsail craft. Tiree now has a suitable boatshed, which is a meeting place as well as protection for the fleet. It is difficult to let any boat with a history go, or even to allow it to become a museum piece. However, the maintenance and repair of several small craft can get on top of a small community.

I'd guess you need two rather than one vessel in good repair to rekindle a competitive sailing scene, though timed runs round a course can also work. If you have three or four similar enough to be competitive round a course, then handicaps can be introduced, from experience in various conditions. Some vessels may prosper in heavy winds and others in light. Sport and heritage are combined. That is surely good value for funders and for club subscriptions. Malcolm's findings on surveying the survivors of the fleet on Tiree in 2004 are available online.[3] Of the larger double-enders, one *Gunna* at 17 feet 7 inches (5.4 metres) was 'salvageable' at the time. *Jessie* 19 feet (5.8 metres), typical but decked, was in excellent condition. *Isabella* at 18 feet (5.5 metres) and also judged typical, was in good condition. A 17-foot 5-inch double-ender, *Eilean Thiroid* (built 1998), was also excellent. Some transom-sterned vessels of different sizes were also measured. That would seem a strong enough basis to build on, with perhaps the smaller craft providing a stepping-stone to confidence in the larger. The Covid pandemic that started in 2020 has severely affected such borderline initiatives. The word on the tide is that the maritime tradition matters so much to both long-term and shorter-term residents on Tiree that the racing tradition and the vessels which continue it will not be allowed to die quietly.

Once more, participation in the Scottish Coastal Rowing Association can be complementary rather than in competition to a revival of local sailing craft. St Ayles skiffs seem to have found a niche nobody realised was there, with 210 in the UK, most in Scotland, and 51 elsewhere in the world (as of 2021). They are safe to race and cruise under oar, but because they have no built-in buoyancy or side decks, sailing is not officially encouraged.

NOTES

(1) See boatbuilder's website of A and R Way Ltd:
https://www.aandrwayboatbuilding.co.uk/new-range/oban-skiff/.
(2) Eric McKee, Working Boats of Britain: Their Shape and Purpose *(London, Conway Maritime Press, 1983), p. 40.*
(3) 'Boat Survey 2004', Tiree Maritime Trust website:
http://www.tireemaritimetrust.org.uk/boat-survey-2004/.

25
JACOBITE, DAWN TREADER AND OTHER CREEL BOATS

AS I'VE MENTIONED, I JUST missed out on working on a Mull ring netter shortly after I left school. I was, however, to get a taste of the work done from a Tobermory-based but Girvan-built craft, also finished in bright varnish, though some years were to pass first. This was part of a commission to document the life of inshore fisher folk working out of Mull and Iona in the last year of the previous millennium.

Almost every photo of Tobermory harbour up until a few years ago would show two varnished creel boats looking like they'd just come off the builder's slip. At first sight, the two vessels, normally moored at Tobermory Old Pier, were twins. They were indeed commissioned by twins but a closer look revealed the customising which comes from experience and individual preference. Each presented a high bow which would part and shed the seas. Each maintained its varnished finish on the hull 'topsides'. *Dawn Treader* had a longer and wider wheelhouse, while *Jacobite* opted for a more compact form. There are other variations too, most noticeably the lengths.

I'd suggest that a closer scrutiny of these two craft can show how they exemplify the way fishing boat designs have nearly always been tweaked by skippers' experience in a custom build. When I first became passionate about putting out to sea, a mentor was saving up for a creel-fishing boat, built to handle the much greater volume of traps needed to make a living as fishing intensified. His Stornoway-registered craft of 30 feet or so was built for him at Invergordon,[1] though he might have chosen McGaughey of Wick or one of the Orcadian builders, then producing very similar craft. Most had wide transom sterns and forward wheelhouses. The layout left a clear deck area for miles of ropes. On to Tobermory.

Dawn Treader (OB460) was built in 1988 by John Gaff and Sons of Girvan for Alasdair MacLean. She measures 32 feet (9.78 metres) by 15 feet beam (4.59 metres), a draught of 5 feet 7 (1.71 metres). *Jacobite* (OB560) was built in 1992 also by John Gaff, for Alasdair's brother Calum MacLean. She is a shade over 32 feet (9.82 metres) overall, by 14 feet 6 (4.42 metres) beam, with just over 6 feet (1.9 metres) draught. Both had Gardners to drive them, but *Dawn Treader* had a unit producing 180 horsepower installed while *Jacobite* was driven by an engine producing 150 horsepower.

I was to take notes and photograph Alasdair in his quest for the top-quality langoustines which were the mainstay of his small but steady business. It was late in the year and *Dawn Treader* was working 'wee corners' off the Sound of Mull. He would look over a shoulder to check a transit but I could see how the colour sonar was a vital tool for identifying likely ground. This fishing needed accurate pinpointing of the narrow runs of muddy ground left untrawled, very close to reefs sharp enough to claim most gear.

Alasdair, locally known as 'Steptoe', and his deckhand, made me very welcome aboard. He explained how he and fellow inshore skippers would agree to leave more sheltered pockets of ground for working when bad weather would rule out more distant areas. But all it would take was a skipper who ignored this common-sense pact and the informal insurance policy would be ripped apart. Such selective fishing is more sustainable than methods such as trawling and dredging. Unwanted species are returned alive from the traps, unlike the immature fish trawled to the surface each drag. The boat does not need to catch the same bulk of product to be viable. Faster boats consume more fuel and trawlers can't achieve the same premium price for a product which has been dragged under pressure. I sensed a respect for his targeted species: 'They're fancy wee buggers. They need to be. I've been at them thirty-odd year.'

The design of the creel-fishing vessels is very different from that of the varnished ring netters that used to work out of the Sound of Mull, but the chosen builder and the style of finishing and coating has been carried on to become something you might well call a style. The twins both worked craft which had to be capable of venturing out to the open Atlantic side of Mull. No matter how you studied forecasts, you'd get caught out sometimes. The draught of the boat is a big issue when working lobsters, because that will sometimes require dodging in as close as possible to the rocks. A decent amount of horsepower could also get you out of trouble, even though a creel boat doesn't need nearly the power of a trawler, which has to drag all that weight.

On the other hand, a deeper keel under the wide boat made for stability, seaworthiness and good tracking. These two comparatively deep-draughted boats were based on the commissioning skippers' individual judgements that the trade-off was worth it. Alasdair demonstrated his grasp of the state of tide at any time in the area. He took us through the Calve Island channel, which dries out but provides a short-cut home when there is sufficient rise of tidal level. I could see it was a bit borderline. This time his eye didn't go to the sounder but to his own marks. The tide has first to cover the 'drying height' then rise a further 2 metres or so. I'm looking at a fascimile of a 1959 chart (1836), remembering that depths are in fathoms. The Clyde Cruising Club sailing directions for Kintyre to Ardnamurchan, confirm that you can expect about 2 metres in the channel once the concrete supports of the channel markers are covered.[2] Most tides, you would want to be within 2 hours either side of high water.

Other features of the boats are now close to the default for

Jacobite *and* Dawn Treader *at Tobermory*

a modern creel-fishing vessel. The wheelhouse will often be offset to give room to work the heavy hauler and balance the weight of its installation. It now takes more and more gear to achieve the same catch. Long fleets of creels have to be laid out with care. Wide beam and a transom stern will also help provide the space to lay out the fleets. When the skipper gives the nod, the shooting will be swift. He may be weaving a course to keep lobster pots on the hard or prawn pots on the soft. As a former coastguard, I was all too aware of the risk of a crewman being carried over as the creels went over the side in their definite order. Prawn creels are not as heavy as the rubber-armoured pots which are designed to withstand a tumbling on rock as they lie in wait for lobster and crab. Still, all it would take would be a bight (loop) of the line round your boot and you'd be over the side and tangled in the gear. Shooting miles of long-lines must have been like this too. An anchor was taking these lines down. A hook in a hand and the crewman was going down with the gear.

The layout of the working area and the placing of machinery were driven by both efficiency and safety concerns. This is a fishing which is much more sustainable than more intensive methods, with lower overheads and in a craft which will not be outdated in a few years. *Dawn Treader* provided a good livelihood for Alasdair, but he had to say farewell to her in 2020. The occasion of her departure for a new Orcadian skipper was marked by the composition of a new tune from the band Skipinnish, who featured the boat on more than one album cover. The fact that she was sold to an area which is itself famous for the creel-fishing boats it produced speaks well of her design and build.

The days of a like group of craft of vernacular origins being used in an area for the pursuit of a task are already gone. We're going to jump from Tobermory harbour to Orkney, to take a closer look at variations of the commercial creel-fishing boat of about 10 to 12 metres or so. Eric McKee has also drawn a typical example, in comparison with other square-ended vessels such as some coracles and the salmon coble.[3] James Towers Anderson, known as 'Pia', returned to Orkney after his studies to become a principal teacher of technical subjects. His byname came from a grandfather who was skipper of the herring smack *Pioneer*. First he built 14-foot dinghies in mahogany, for local owners. Then this compulsion to build boats led to a commission for a new creel boat and a return to working full-time on the tools. An archive photograph (Orkney Historic Boat Society) shows a lean, tall man dressing heavy frames with an adze. Once again, the commissioning skipper's input was combined with the boatbuilder's instinct and consultation with a designer. Pia worked with plans drawn by Ewing McGruer, best known for his role in the family firm which produced so many Clyde-built yachts. Once more the line between workboat and pleasure craft is not so distinct, as the same team would turn their skills to both. The Orcadian collaboration produced *Mayflower*, a vessel with a forward cuddy and a deep well aft to work 150 creels – a fair number in 1964. The boatbuilder's ideas and skills met the skipper's requirements, and the designer's input helped achieve a seaworthy craft to carry out the stated functions. The result appears to be shallower-draughted than the John Gaff boats, perhaps due to the particular waters the craft was expected to work in.

A son of the same name who continued the trade for a time tells the story. In a few words, he describes the technical aspects of boat and propulsion but also the process of arriving at the found shape:

> Alan Pirie wanted a boat to carry a minimum of 150 creels so he could carry them and fish them on the north coast of the Scottish mainland and in the event of bad weather haul them aboard and run for shelter. My father took the remit and consulted his very good friend Ewing McGruer and between them they created what became known as the Mayflower design. The vessel was clinker-built on 10 sawn frames amidships and steamed timbers elsewhere, she had a very heavy 8" x 6" gunwale stringer and a shaped 8" x 6" external belting to create a very strong sheer strake and prevent the hull twisting in bad weather. Large open cockpit aft and accommodation for 3 crew in a forecastle complete with galley. Power was by a 36 HP air cooled Lister main engine. By today's standard a pretty basic set up.[4]

The photographs of the yard also show a pair of not-quite twin vessels built for owners from the Isle of Skye. Innovations continued, both in shape and materials. Iroko rather than oak was used for frames and there was a move from clinker to carvel construction. Perhaps the yard could have continued longer if there had also been a transition to working in GRP and aluminium, as several yards did, in order to keep competitive.

Before we leave the transom-sterned creel boats as a late form of boatbuilding in timber, let's swing back down the east coast to Invergordon. This is to describe one more example, similar but with distinctive features. For a time, fast-planing hulls seemed to be dominating the industry but fuel costs rose and the higher overheads led to an unsustainable demand for catching greater bulk. Other boatyards have survived by fitting out GRP hulls, but ones with remarkable similarities to the proven forms first developed in timber construction.

About the time I moved to Mull to plant trees rather than harvest fish, my fishing pal was taken on as a deckhand by our mentor Donald Morrison. The man who had shown us transits and the dark arts of anchoring was giving up deep-sea voyaging to go creel fishing close to home. He commissioned *Moraldie* from the Invergordon yard founded by John Mackenzie, who had trained at the Buckie firm of Herd and MacKenzie. Donald had told us how his own requirements were worked into a craft with a bow to part the seas, a forward wheelhouse and a wide, clear working space aft. From the notes contributed by Ed Malicki, a shipwright working at the yard at the time, we know that Donald's dream boat, 36 feet of larch on oak, provided six months of work for four men and two apprentices. He also reports that you could estimate the cost of such a vessel at the time as about £1,000 per foot.

Ed's excellent account gives detailed descriptions of the process of steaming planks, but also this succinct summary of the whole show:

It starts with the laying down of the keel, usually two pieces scarf jointed for length, on top of heavy built stools at the angle the keel would be when the boat is in the water. Next the hog is fixed on top of the keel (the frames will later be bolted right through the hog and keel); next is the stem and apron (fore end), then the stern post, this is a very large piece of solid oak that the propeller shaft will be drilled through. But before the stern post is fixed to the keel by a large mortise and tenon joint, a silver coin is placed into the mortise (tradition) usually just by the yard staff, sometimes owner and or management might be present. After the stern post, the outrigger and transom (above the propeller) are fixed. When that is complete, we have a small ceremony called the christening of the keel. All yard staff and management are usually present and owner if available – we need a bottle of best malt whisky for this, and usually the yard foreman gets the job of pouring the whisky gently over the length of the keel. I say gently because if there is any left it goes to the yard staff, more tradition! With that over, a shipwright would have been 'lofting out' the actual frame sizes and making half templates so we could mark out and cut the 3" oak slabs to make the frames. These were in two pieces joined by a bolted butt clamp. After all the frames were in place we started planking, on then to internal stringers, deck beams, engine fitting, decking, wheelhouse, fit out the fo'c'sle (i.e. line the inside of the frames and form bunks etc.), caulking, filling, plugging and painting, fitting of all ironmongery (i.e. gantry, winches, cleats, rudder, metal armouring to planking), all rigging wire and rope, fuel tanks, hydraulics and electrics . . . hope I got it all! . . . boat now ready for launching![5]

NOTES

(1) 'Invergordon Boat Yard History', The Invergordon Archive website: http://www.theinvergordonarchive.org/groups.asp?id=45.

(2) Clyde Cruising Club, Sailing Directions and Anchorages, Kintyre to Ardnamurchan (St Ives, Cambridgeshire, Imray and Clyde Cruising Club, 2008).

(3) Eric McKee, Working Boats of Britain: Their Shape and Purpose (London, Conway Maritime Press, 1983), p. 49.

(4) 'Orkney Boats', Orkney Historic Boat Society website: https://www.ohbs.net/orkney-boats/.

(5) Invergordon archive has a full list of vessels built and informative details of construction methods from shipwright Ed Malicki: http://www.theinvergordonarchive.org/groups.asp?id=45.

26

THE *BIRLINN* – LOST AND MAYBE FOUND

I GREW UP ON THE Isle of Lewis and still live there. The first boat I was trusted to steer was built in Stornoway in the clinker form. Most would accept that the technology is still recognisably Norse. The concept itself and the forms it has taken can be traced like genealogy. The extinct *birlinn*, documented in carvings and detailed in poetry, was the galley of the Lords of the Isles. The legend is that it played its part in defeating ship-borne Vikings. And yet you could argue that its construction was based on the same principle of overlapping planks for strength.

Now, the *birlinn* is a holy grail of maritime archaeology. Unlike the extant examples of various types of Viking craft, there is not even a skeleton to observe. The shipwright and researcher of boat forms John MacAulay makes the point that these are early days yet.[1] Viking ships were around much earlier, yet the preserved examples were unearthed in fairly recent history. Every time the sands and silt shift in a storm and the sea recedes for a short period below the mark of Lowest Astronomical Tide, there is hope of discovering the saturated oak members of her frame. Spoken, sung and written accounts celebrate these craft as the flagships of the Lords of the Isles. The art of the Outer Hebrides was historically stronger in language and melody than in visual form. Except for the shapes of boats. Sometimes these elements came together. The most detailed as well as the most resonant depiction of the lost craft is surely in *The Birlinn of Clanranald* by Alexander MacDonald (*Birlinn Chlann Raghnaill*, Alasdair mac Mhaighstir Alasdair). This poet lived in the turbulent political period from the 1690s to about 1770.

The narrative poem has sections which describe tackle and rig in detail sufficient to recreate it. It is a manual as well as a celebration and an account of what was probably an actual voyage, from South Uist to Carrickfergus. There are several translations, over a number of years, including one by Hugh MacDiarmid, guided by Sorley MacLean. Two iconic figures in the literature of Scots and of Scottish Gaelic have thus met in its recreation. Another Scottish poet, international in his outlook, Alan Riach, has recently published a new free translation printed alongside the original Gaelic in a publication from Kettilonia and illustrated by Sandy Moffat.[2] There is now a secondary culture of artefacts in response to the best available information of what a *birlinn* was really like.

In his study, from a boatbuilder's point of view, John MacAulay reproduced Alexander Nicolson's 1877 translation of the poem, parallel with the original Gaelic (*Birlinn – Longships of the Hebrides*). The implication is that the details of form, rig and sailing are the best information we have. John also listed details that can be gained from the bas relief of superb quality in Rodel Church. His years of working in the construction of craft of different scale bring his conclusion that the sculptor 'had more than just exalted praise in his mind'. Rather, '... he had intimate knowledge of the vessels to be able to furnish such accurate detail of boat and rigging . . .' From the depiction of 17 oar-ports along the side, John concludes that the *birlinn* was at least 75 feet in length (24 metres). He points out that this would make it comparable with the Viking burial ship excavated at Gokstad. Only eight strakes are shown in the carving, but John concludes that this is due to the scale of the work and the impossibility of carving an accurate representation of such a detail. The Gokstad ship had double that number. The rudder, however, can still be clearly seen in the Rodel carving, and it is this feature as well as associated deeper draught aft which makes the *birlinn* distinct from any known Norse form of the period. Many say that it was this feature that gave this craft a tactical advantage in close quarters over the Viking longship, which carried a steering oar. Hence the origins of the term 'starboard' for the side of the vessel where this was deployed.

Sadly, John MacAulay's book is now out of print. His intimate knowledge of both Scottish and Scandinavian boatbuilding illuminate his text. His drawings also clarify contrasting details and have something of the quality of the illustrations in the Dwelly Gaelic dictionary. As a native Gaelic speaker, he has access to the full tradition which illuminates this craft, in the absence of archaeological evidence. His knowledge and experience informed the GalGael Trust and their boatbuilding programmes which involve folk from the inner city of Glasgow. GalGael's 30-foot *Orcuan* (2001) is modestly and accurately described on the GalGael website as 'an interpretation of the historic galleys of the west coast'.[3]

I would suggest this is similar to the way Tim Severin's *Brendan*[4] was a designed attempt to recreate the type of craft feasible with the technology available at the time of the original narrative. There is a link between the recreation of the larger seagoing *curach* of voyaging monks and the building of a smaller form of the *birlinn*. Wallace Clark is known to most as the author of pilot books which circumnavigate the whole of Ireland and help make mariners of small craft bold enough to sneak into the crannies of a complex coast. He also navigated his carvel yacht to the Baltic, to explore Russian territory along with his elder son. He found common cause with George Macleod, who was a founder of the Iona community. They proposed the building of a large *curach* which could voyage between Lough Foyle and Iona, as Colmcille had. This was first accomplished in 1963, about 1,400 years after the historic event.

Aileach *(ashore, South Uist)*

In 1991 Clark was to skipper *Aileach*, the first *birlinn* to be at sea since the eighteenth century, on another voyage linking Northern Ireland and the Hebrides of Scotland.[5] In common with the vessel used to prove the possibility of St Brendan's crossing to the new world, the naval architect Colin Mudie was commissioned to propose building-drawings. The shape was suggested by stylised carvings, mainly the one in St Clement's Church. As I've had the pleasure of stepping aboard both the *Aileach* and the *curach Colmcille*, I would like to share impressions of their construction and of the way they take the water.

I first met with *Aileach* a year or so after her first voyage, which made, in stages, a safe passage through the waters associated with the history of the *birlinn*. As a serving Senior Watch Officer with the coastguard, stationed at Stornoway, I was intrigued by the passage plans passed to us on VHF radio from this open boat. At the time I sailed my own open boat, *Broad Bay*, so was eager to see her forerunner, complete with squaresail to supplement her 16 oars. (That is, eight per side as opposed to the 17 described by Alexander

MacDonald.) McDonalds shipwrights of Donegal worked in larch and oak to Mudie's plans as they had bent oak to construct the frame of *Brendan*. From the drawings supplied, the yard produced a vessel of 40 feet (12.2 metres) overall, 8 in the beam and 2 feet draught.

When I signed off, I walked straight to the harbour to take a close look at this piece of craftsmanship in oiled larch. The build quality was excellent and the timbers probably of far better quality than would have been available to the Clanranalds, Macleods or MacNeils, all in the Outer Hebrides. We discuss the shape of boats endlessly on the islands, the way you might discuss fine cattle or horses elsewhere. They are living things of course, and you develop a relationship. The principles of construction have not really changed since the Viking carpenters and smiths pooled their skills. Once the keel is laid, shaped planks are placed, edge on, then riveted together. You might think these would be straight-ish but they are cut in a complex series of concave and convex lines. It is the cut of the plank that forms the overall shape. Two would be cut to match then fastened by iron rivets, side by side, from the keel up. Later 'floors' bridge the keel, for stiffening and strengthening. Additional 'frames' or 'ribs' are installed later, usually in oak. In a boat built with rowing in mind, these are usually placed only where necessary, to save weight. These also stiffen the form but they cannot change the shape dictated by the planking.

A narrow craft with low freeboard will row well. But you also want buoyancy in a more full shape, so she will rise in big waters. That shape is yet again a compromise between the requirements of function and suitability for the conditions she may meet. If she sails the west coast of Scotland and the North Channel, she'll need to take the effects of strong tidal currents and she'll meet gales. To my eye, I was seeing a vessel built for fairly sheltered coastal areas. There are so many good anchorages and safe havens on the west coast of Scotland, it's possible to journey in shorter legs, working tide to advantage. You tend to wait for more settled weather to make the longer legs. These craft could be a flourish of wealth and skills as well as a mode of transport. But they also brought armed men to pursue endless feuds.

Scots may have defeated the Norse at the seaborne battle of Largs but the rudder-steered *birlinn*, deployed there, also came from this clear line of descent from Viking craft. John went on to supervise the build of smaller-scale versions of the lost vessel for the GalGael Trust in Glasgow. This charity involves city people recovering from addictions and other problems, in the building, rigging and sailing of these craft. To my eye, John's later versions – fuller, and deeper-keeled – looked more like seagoing vessels, though much smaller than *Aileach*.

Yet her skipper visited our Operations Room next day to plan his passage for the Faroe Islands. The forecast was not ideal. I asked him for a figure on leeway – the sideways drift a sailing craft will be subject to if the wind is not behind her. He was cagey.

'A lot,' he said finally.

'Oh well, you won't be sailing for Faroes on that wind,' I replied.

But they did sail, on a forecast which, from my plot, would take them to Orkney. As there was media coverage and sponsorship, it seemed to me that the skipper was under intolerable pressure. I passed details to our then neighbouring station. *Aileach* did drift eastwards and was caught in large and confused seas west of Orkney. Her steering gear broke under the strain and she was towed into Stromness by the RNLI lifeboat, with everyone safe. I thought it was unfortunate that the captain of the Search and Rescue helicopter sent to confirm her location passed comment in public. From the air, he thought the vessel unsuitable for the conditions likely to be encountered even in summer between the Scottish isles and Faroes. What he said was something like, 'She shouldn't be out on a duckpond.'

Since that incident I've sailed out west of Orkney in several different craft, including traditional Lewis open vessels (also of the family descended from Norse type). It is not always challenging, but conditions change fast and you can meet very steep seas even when there is not a huge amount of wind. Stromness is a good place to have troubles in. Boatbuilding and engineering skills are second to none. Once *Aileach* was seaworthy again, that same skipper bided his time. He must have realised that the light, long craft could only sail well if the wind was aft of the beam. And even the most powerful rowers could only be effective if seas were long enough or low enough to let them hit a rhythm. I was relieved to receive a message that they had arrived safely. Some time later, I was also on watch when I took a radio call to say that they had now cleared the Butt of Lewis and were re-entering the North Minch in good conditions. It was a notable achievement.

It seems to me now that this brave voyage was a triumph of pushing the vessel beyond the limits of its strengths. It was achieved by learning to wait for suitable conditions, with the aid of weather-forecasting and communications. This assistance was not an option for the skippers of earlier times. *Aileach* was to take part in an epic three-boat race round the Isle of Skye. From boatbuilder Malcolm Henry's perspective, this provides a valuable comparison of the performance of this guess at a *birlinn* against an actual *sgoth Niseach* and a proven Faroese craft, under sail and oar:

> The Faroese boat, *Svannen*, was superior under oars, by a significant margin. Whenever wind was in short supply she quickly took and held the lead. Only on the final leg, from Churchton Bay [Raasay] to Broadford, were we [*Oigh Niseach*] able to keep up with her, but that was only for a mile or so, and only because our makeshift crew had, by that time, had enough practice to make a decent fist of pulling reliably in time. Under sail, *Svannen* was, by some margin, the worst performer. Her small spritsails were very much auxiliaries to the oars.
>
> The only times that *Aileach* performed well were when there was a decent breeze from astern. Anything closer than a broad reach would tip her onto her very soft bilge and she

would slide sideways. Rowing her was a painful chore. There was insufficient spacing between the thwarts to work the oars properly, and the oars that they had were too short. In all of the rowing legs she came a distant third. The only leg that she won was Dunvegan to Staffin, and only because of a very favourable shift and strengthening of the breeze in the last half hour. Having trailed *Oigh Niseach* by a mile or two all day, she crossed the line a minute ahead of us.

Oigh Niseach came second in every leg of the race, proving to be the most adaptable to the wide variety of conditions that were experienced. On the epic leg from Isle Oronsay to Dunvegan the weather overnight turned nasty. The Faroese later told me that it was by far the worst they had ever been out in and they had to go ashore somewhere near Borreraig to recover from the trauma of rounding Dunvegan Head. *Aileach* couldn't make headway into Loch Dunvegan at all and had to be towed in. *Oigh Niseach* took it all in her stride. We came around Dunvegan Head doing c. 5kn under a bare pole and then beat our way to the pier without drama, using oars for only the final hundred yards.[6]

Sadly, *Aileach* is no longer in commission but exposed to the skin-drying winds of South Uist, as a static exhibit. There are hopes of combining her preservation in the wider context of an expanded museum project.[7] How many lost boats can we recover? Yet, if we in Scotland make comparisons with other countries with strong maritime traditions, we could be doing more.

Former shipwright Colin Myers became fascinated with vernacular craft after coming to live on Lewis. He is presently working on drawings for a half-model of the Clyde-built clipper *Sir Lancelot*. Colin met with another maker of models, Donald MacQueen, on a visit to the Uists. Research indicated that there was an oral history of a substantial wreck which revealed hints of its frames in extreme tidal conditions. A recorded sighting coincided with an exceptional tidal range due to barometric pressure as a storm went through. The location was at the heartland of the Clanranald clan culture, which has the strongest association with the *birlinn*. The goal of discovering the skeleton of such an important lost ship seemed to these experts as one which should meet more resources than they could summon as individuals.

Yes, we are fighting for our survival on this planet, still dependent on oil and gas. Entering 2022, a virus was still finding ever more forms to secure its own survival at our expense. Yet there is an argument that our survival would have a better chance if we put more effort into studying the collective experience of the past, as well as admitting that our current way of life is not sustainable. The shapes found by earlier shipwrights and the methods to achieve them are still worthy of study.

NOTES

(1) John MacAulay, Birlinn – Longships of the Hebrides *(Cambridge/Strond, White Horse Press, 1996).*

(2) Alasdair Mac Mhaighstir Alasdair (Alexander MacDonald), The Birlinn of Clanranald, *trans. Alan Riach (Newtyle, Angus, Kettilonia, 2015).*

(3) 'Boat building', GalGael website: https://www.galgael.org/boat-building.

(4) Tim Severin, The Brendan Voyage *(London, Hutchinson & Co., 1978; Arrow Books, 1979). See chapter 3 'Building' (p. 34 in the Arrow Books edition, and plates facing p. 50).*

(5) Wallace Clark, The Lord of the Isles Voyage: Western Ireland to the Scottish Hebrides in a Sixteen-Oar Galley *(Leinster, Leinster Leader Ltd, 1993).*

(6) Personal email from Malcom Henry, 2021.

(7) 'Aileach', The Lord of the Isles Galley Trust website: www.galleyaileach.co.uk.

27
THE ROLE OF THE LIGHTHOUSE-TENDER

TIREE ON A GOOD DAY can seem idyllic, especially if the blue and yellow are broken by a close-tacking flock of tan lugsails. In these conditions you have to remember that you will soon be sniffing the open Atlantic when you put your nose out from shelter. Even if you remain in the Sea of the Hebrides, you may be on a collision course with steep seas of short wavelength which have been squeezed down the North and Little Minches. If you're out of luck, you might have to deal with the residual effects of conflicting seas. Establishment of the great rock lighthouses, Dubh Artach (18 miles west of Colonsay), Skerryvore (11 miles south-west of Tiree) and Hyskeir (Oigh Sgeir, 5 miles south-west of Canna) did much to improve the safety of mariners. Even when the miracle of the Decca navigator enabled fishermen to fix their position on a dirty night, the confirmation of a light sequence was more than a comfort. Electronics do go wrong in the marine environment and that remains so in the days of the GPS (global positioning system). There are excellent studies of the Scottish lighthouses and their designers and builders (see Further Reading) so further discussion is outwith the scope of this tour, vessel by vessel. Yet we can't transit Gunna Sound and go on to the Outer Hebrides without mentioning at least some of the vessels that supplied these rock stations.

The ships of the Northern Lighthouse Board were always both powerful and fine. *Fingal* is alongside *Britannia* in Leith but fitted out as luxury accommodation. The old *Pole Star* was known in Orkney as 'Willy Tulloch's yat', after one of her masters but the new one is also both an elegant and practical ship. These are most certainly ships, not boats, and they have been well represented elsewhere. Let's now spare a thought for the humbler vessels which had to fight through severe conditions to relieve keepers and bring in supplies. The tenders which were lowered from *Fingal*, *Pharos* and *Pole Star* in the twentieth century were strong boats in their own right. They had to be buoyant load- and people-carriers but they also had to be able to withstand the strains of lowering and hoisting; nudging up to stone piers and steel ships. More than one could be seen in Lerwick or Stromness in a retirement job of setting a few creels. Some were double-ended and some were transom-sterned, but all were built to be able to work when other 19- or 20-footers would remain tied up.

Returning to the nineteenth century, a tender was launched in 1867 as No. 140 from the yard of Archibald McMillan in Dumbarton. She was a 50-footer (15.2 metres), of 16 feet beam (4.9 metres) and a draught of 8 feet (2.4 metres). At 29 registered tons, you get the impression of a vessel robust enough to be named *Skerryvore II,* as main tender to that offshore station.

The form of a twentieth-century tender which plied the Sea of the Hebrides is well documented, so can still be studied. *Bernera* was built by William Weatherhead and Sons at Cockenzie as relief tender for Barra Head lighthouse.[1] Launched in 1952, she was 45 feet (13.7 metres) overall, 13 feet 6 inches (4.1 metres) in beam, drawing 6 feet (1.8 metres). This is very much in the line of the more powerful MFVs, with a definite Scandinavian look to her uptilting canoe stern. She had a Kelvin V3 installed. When Barra Head lighthouse was automated, *Bernera* was deployed in transporting materials for the establishment of Vee lighthouse, off Orkney. That would indicate both

Pole Star III *(NLB, 1961–93)*

her seaworthiness and her ability to thump on with a load aboard.

It's perhaps not obvious that Barra Head lighthouse is not on Barra. The chain continues south of that island with its ferry port, Castlebay, through Vatersay, Sandray, Pabbay and the formerly populated Mingulay to the island usually charted as Berneray. There are of course several islands of this name in the Outer Hebrides, as there are several Pabbays. Once I was at anchor in my own vessel off the beach at Mingulay in a light westerly breeze, when the current NLB ship, *Pole Star*, dropped its heavy anchor gear a few cables out, in deeper water. Next day we could make out the stone landing jetty on the north side of Berneray. There are several local traditions relating to an early farm on the most southerly island of the chain and the legendary boat which supplied it and fished, in season, the length of the southern isles, east and west.[2]

Oral traditions relating to 'Shepherd Duncan' and his family are elusive in their detail on the craft which took over from smaller skiffs when the combination of crofting and fishing brought prosperity to the isolated family. As the family extended, so did the reach of their trade. Their own vessel could export their catches and their produce up to the north or down to Ireland. She was known simply as 'a trader with a white topsail'. At least one of the rowing craft used as tender to Barra Head lighthouse is documented in the form of a drawing by the author in Eric McKee's *Working Boats of Britain*.[3] It shows provision for four oars in a form which would balance pulling ability with load-carrying and seakeeping.

Historically, the tradition of great seamanship was controversial. Some legends have it that the MacNeils of Barra were pirates and there are tales of terrible deaths in Edinburgh for that crime. At least one local version takes a different slant. As I remember it, in a composite of several versions:

No, the MacNeils were not wreckers. This is what happened. A Spanish ship grounded on the west side in a bad storm. Everyone gathered on the shore to do what they could. It was a bad surf and so it would be impossible to get anyone safe ashore without a rope. But how could they get a hawser out to that high hull? Not even the strongest swimmer could punch through that. The chief's son secured a palm-sized pebble in a cradle of light line. There was a good length of that, all flaked out so it could not snag. That could be joined to a heavy line. The Spanish seamen were bound to have something suitable aboard.

MacNeil's son threw it well and the light line followed in an arc through the spray. Sure enough, they felt a tug or two. It seemed to take forever but then there was another pull. The shore party took that as a sign to haul. Sure enough, a ship's hawser came to them. Everyone stretched out along its length to put some tension to it. It would be secured to the stub of a broken mast at the seaward end. Living souls passed, one by one, along that rope and gained the shore. They were wrapped in warming cloth and cared for. But the last to come was clutching the lifeless body of a young boy. This was the skipper's son.

The same stone that had saved the others had struck him in the head. He did not survive and the skipper blamed the chief's son for the death of his own. When political alliances changed and a distant power wished to curry favour with the Spanish, the MacNeils were declared pirates and outlaws. The chief's son crossed to Mingulay. He would take refuge on a sea stack, out from the cliff, because no one else could make that leap. There was many a great chase under oars until a traitor replaced stout thole pins with sticks as weak as carrots. That's how young MacNeil was captured.

The reputation of seamen from the Barra group is second to none. Once when I was stranded in North Uist, a local AB (competent Merchant Seaman) voiced something that was between admiration and complaint. 'I was never bosun. You've got to be from Barra to reach bosun. I think they throw all their youth off the pier at Castlebay when they're about 12 years old and shout down to them – You don't get back here till you're at least a bosun.'

Despite this justified reputation for great skills at inshore work or deep-sea, there does not seem to be a specific example of a vessel you could say was unique to Barra. There was boatbuilding of course, but the type of craft favoured for inshore work tended to be a variant of either a west-coast skiff or the Fifie type, both deep enough in the planking to carry a powerful dipping lugsail. That would drive her through a chop and recover heavy creels. Similar craft would be seen all through the southern isles but it was in Grimsay, off Benbecula, where the form of the lobster boat was developed into its most admired shape. These will be described in some detail when we move a few islands up the chain.

The excellent archive at *Comunn Eachdraidh Bharraidh agus Bhatarsaidh* (Barra Heritage and Cultural Centre) includes photographs of many generations of working boats which worked the seas off Barra, Vatersay and Eriskay. Castlebay was a herring port, so Zulus and Fifies were well-known in the area. The surviving *St Vincent* was first registered CY (for Castlebay). Archived photographs reveal a classic Zulu hull but converted to work fleets of creels under power. Another shows a classic ring netter shape. Successive generations of MFV, in timber, in steel and in GRP have worked out of Castlebay, Acarsaidh Mhor, Eriskay and Lochboisdale.

A recent contemporary arts project by Stephen Hurrel and social ecologist Ruth Brennan, 'Mapping the Sea', linked recorded traditions to the coordinates of their settings.[4] The lively telling of Katie Douglas crosses centuries. For as long as anyone could remember, a headland in Barra was known by the Gaelic version of 'The Point where English is Spoken'. No one could say why. Mid twentieth century, a coastguard hut was built there. Bad weather watches were set and the folk from the nearby village would take turns to drop by a great pot of tea wrapped in a towel, fresh baking and all. No doubt there would be a good yarn, in Gaelic of course. One night the penny dropped for a woman who brought the provisions. As she approached the hut she heard the voices, speaking in English. When she opened the door she could see that the voices were coming from the speaker of the radio unit. And yet the Point had been given that name long before radio was invented.

The coastguard lookout was sited there for a reason. We have to avoid getting romantic on the subject of setting creels between reefs and skerries of spectacular coastline. There have always been losses. The positive side is affirmed in a ringing description of a confident man setting pots under sail, in the folklorist Margaret Fay Shaw's account of her time with the community of South Uist. A simple lugsail rig was favoured because there was little to snarl, little to go wrong.

217

There are several vivid descriptions of making a crossing, for example from Lochboisdale pier, in challenging conditions. These reveal expert handling of small craft and a cool manner even when there are snags such as the rudder fouling a creel marker set in mid-channel. The implication is that the simplicity of the single lugsail rig on that small scale allows for quickly adjusting the amount of sail hoisted, for the conditions.

Margaret Fay Shaw's autobiography is illustrated with her own strong photographs. Several of the local small craft are shown, including a shot of the 'lighthouse dinghy' off Mingulay, possibly the one later drawn by Eric McKee. Fay Shaw's earlier travels are illuminating, because there is a comparison between her perceptions of life in the Aran Islands and in the southern isles of the Outer Hebrides at the time. A 1930 photograph shows a well-laden *curragh* making the landing at Inishmaan.[5]

Despite training and improved safety equipment, risk is still ever-present in seafaring, and high in all forms of commercial fishing. Writing of Mingulay at this time is impossible without the tragic sinking of the *Louisa* coming to mind. This is a vessel launched in 2008, in steel, built for a contemporary shellfish industry, using fleets of creels (traps). At 32 tons (GRT) and under 15 metres, her design incorporated the experience of two brothers, with knowledge of both boatbuilding and commercial fishing. The vessel was built near Fowey, Cornwall, by 'The Boatyard' of C. Toms & Son. That would follow a trend where vessels commissioned to operate in an area of Scottish waters would not necessarily be constructed locally. *Louisa* was well-equipped with electronic navigation and safety devices. The vessel was designed to land live shellfish and so a large-volume tank with circulating seawater was integral. Valve failures in such systems have often caused accidents in modern fishing vessels, so bilge alarms are vital, as well as scrupulous checks and maintenance on the fittings which allow water to enter the boat.

When crews routinely work for periods of up to 20 hours, brief periods of sleep are precious. The skipper had judged it dangerous to work on until all had had some rest. Before hitting their bunks, there had been a tidy-up and deck-wash as a meal was prepared. All four persons on board were in their bunks in the same cabin. This is where one small and probably very common action was crucial:

> The bilge alarm float switches in the hold and engine room bilge wells were connected to an audible/visual alarm panel in the wheelhouse. Following a previous pipe failure, which had resulted in the engine room flooding, the owners had fitted a remote alarm sounder in the crew cabin to alert the skipper and crew that the bilge alarm had activated in the event the wheelhouse was unmanned.
>
> During the investigation, the alarm sounder in the crew cabin was found to have been disabled. It was reported that small quantities of melt water from the refrigerated bait storage lockers routinely collected in the hold bilge well, which caused the hold bilge alarm to sound when the vessel rolled. The alarm sounder in the crew cabin had regularly disturbed the skipper and crew, and consequently they had disabled it.[6]

The evidence pointed to the washer-pump running on and so filling the bilges. However, the finalised Fatal Accident Inquiry findings, published on 2 March 2022, stated that the exact cause of flooding could not be established without doubt. All woke as the bow was sinking. It was now too late to find the cause. The electronic distress beacon was activated. The life raft's inflation could be triggered by water pressure but they had time to pull the cord that would inflate it manually. The CO_2 cylinder was opened by that action but the life raft did not inflate. The crew thrust fenders into the raft, desperate to keep it afloat. All had their lifejackets on by this time. These should have had the power to turn a floating person if they were face-down.

One person attempted to swim ashore while the others followed normal guidelines by staying with the life raft even though it was not inflated. It was over two hours before the shivering survivor was recovered by crew from Barra Lifeboat, partly due to uncertainty over the initial satellite fix. The lifejackets failed to turn the two men who had followed sea-survival procedure and remained with the uninflated raft. One body was recovered but one drifted and was lost. A third body was discovered closer to the shore. Again it's best to go to the careful wording of the Marine Accident Investigation Branch (MAIB) report:

> In November 2011, Premium Liferaft Services had sub-contracted refurbishment of the cylinder to Thameside Fire Protection Company Limited. The cylinder was one of a batch of nine cylinders that had been sent for five-yearly refurbishment and refilling. The process included cleaning, inspection, pressure testing, painting and refilling of the cylinders. Prior to filling, the shoulder of the cylinder was date-stamped to indicate that pressure testing had taken place. A label was adhered to the cylinder showing its tare weight, gas charge (CO_2 and N_2) and full weight, which was 8.40kg (Figure 8). When the cylinder was weighed following the accident, its tare weight was 8.40kg. It was therefore concluded that, following refurbishment in 2011, the cylinder had not been refilled prior to its return to Premium Liferaft Services.
>
> Following this discovery, MAIB inspectors arranged for the remaining eight cylinders from the batch of nine to be recalled and weighed. All were found to have been correctly filled and labelled.[7]

One purpose of a Fatal Accident Inquiry (FAI, the Scottish equivalent of the English Coroner's Court) is to establish the cause of death, but there is also a remit to point to any actions which would help prevent a similar accident occurring. As the vessel was raised and transported to the Clyde for close scrutiny and tests, a forensic analysis of the investigation is now available to all. The hull itself was virtually undamaged and she is certified and fishing again, close to her place of build.

The thoughts of all go out to the families of the lost but also to the sole survivor, who must have suffered trauma as well as physical distress. With rising overheads and unstable markets, the pressures on commercial fishermen are enormous. Sleep deprivation has usually been considered part of the way of life. In this case it was not extreme weather but a tragic progression of circumstances which led to the loss of three lives. The findings of the FAI into the loss of crew members of *Louisa* are now public. These include a directive to owners: 'Sheriff Principal Pyle called on all owners of fishing vessels to closely follow the set rules on maintenance.'[8]

The most efficient of hulls and machinery can never be immune from risk. Annual checks, such as returning hired liferafts for inspection, are arduous, especially when the nearest testing station is a distance away. The accident is now part of the culture of the industry. It must now be to the fore when safety procedures and equipment checks are considered. You have to hope that it is also to the fore in staff training and checking procedures in firms which test safety equipment.

NOTES

(1) 'Bernera', National Historic Ships website: https://www.nationalhistoricships.org.uk/register/2781/berneray. See also the history section of the Northern Lighthouse Board website: https://www.nlb.org.uk/history/ships/.

(2) John MacPherson, Tales from Barra: Told by The Coddy (Edinburgh, W. &

A.K. Johnstone, 1961, reissued Edinburgh, Birlinn, 1991). See also transcription of local history from Calum MacNeil as downloadable PDF: https://www.ssns.org.uk/wp-content/uploads/2019/10/04_MacNeil_Barra_2006_pp_66-90.pdf.

(3) Eric McKee, Working Boats of Britain: Their Shape and Purpose (London, Conway Maritime Press, 1983), p. 205.

(4) Mapping the Sea website: http://mappingthesea.net.

(5) Margaret Fay Shaw, From the Alleghenies to the Hebrides: An Autobiography (first published Canongate, Edinburgh, 1993, current edition Birlinn, Edinburgh).

(6) 'Sinking of vivier creel boat Louisa with loss of 3 lives', Marine Accident Investigation Branch (MAIB) report, 27/7/2017, p. 11: https://www.gov.uk/maib-reports/sinking-of-vivier-creel-boat-louisa-with-loss-of-3-lives.

(7) Ibid., p. 19.

(8) 'FAI Determination Summary: The Sinking of the Louisa', Judiciary of Scotland website: https://www.judiciary.scot/home/sentences-judgments/fai-determination-summaries/2022/03/02/sinking-of-the-louisa.

28
CRAFT BY THE STEWARTS OF GRIMSAY

YOU'LL SEE THEM IN THE creeks and geos of Barra and Eriskay; in the snug one-boat nests tucked into shores in the bays of Harris and Scalpay. Double-ended forms prevail. These are load carriers, pretty much plumb at bow and stern and full in shape. Fifie-type yoles, with infinite variations, thrived on the west coast of Scotland and in the Outer Isles, just as they did on the east coast. Local builders had their following. They introduced their own small innovations, whether construction was clinker or carvel. Some builders, like a legend of a man from Uig (south-west Lewis) was famous for speed of build. If his customer had planking, oak for framing and the listed fastenings to hand, along with a pair of strapping helpers, the stout vessel would be formed in two weeks. If the craft could be moored, as in many bays on the east sides of Barra, the Uists and Harris, then lightness could be sacrificed for increased strength. So, I wondered, when told of efforts to preserve examples of the craft built by the Stewarts of Grimsay, what was so special about them?

Between about 1840 and 1994 four generations of the Stewarts built boats at Ceann na h-Àirigh (Kennary), a bay on the Minch side of Grimsay Island, near Benbecula. We are now about the middle of the long line of islands which comprise the Outer Hebrides group. The first Charles Stewart came from Argyll for carpentry work then married and remained in Grimsay, where the boatyard was set up. We've already admired the rounded sterns of the typical craft of Argyll, such as the Oban skiff. It would seem natural that this feature could be identified as a mark of continuity. Yet a boatbuilder, like a tailor, cuts his planking to the requirements and purse of his customer. These varied. Some would require an inshore craft to fish and carry stock and goods and peats in sheltered waters. This was a time before causeways connected islands. Other customers sniffed the west and looked for a boat capable of piloting the tidal fords which led out that way, from the Grimsay haven.

The very difficulties of navigating the shallows and the short, steep seas thrown up by banks and reefs made the waters around the Monach Islands (also called the Heisker Islands) rich grounds for lobsters. If a stout craft could punch her way out there, she could be moored in the pool at Siolaigh (Shillay), close to the tall brick lighthouse which was established by David and Thomas Stevenson in 1864. White-painted markers still guide a vessel in between the reefs. The lobster fishermen of Grimsay would sleep in simple bothies ashore for a night or three until they had a catch and the conditions to take it safely back home. There are alternative anchorages such as one on the northern shore of Ceann Ear off the beach named as Traigh Dhomhnuill. If the west wind blows there is shelter for a shallow-draughted craft in Port Ruadh, a bay on the east side of that same island. The way in is shallow and obscured by kelp-fringed rocks. If you approach from the north, you must first round Rubh a' nam Marbh, which reaches out in an untidy scattering of sharp reefs.

Once I was aboard a Grimsay boat aptly named *Sealladh* (Vision) as the son of the fisherman who commissioned her guided us in. It was then I understood the great sea tradition, usually told in Gaelic and translated as 'Black John of the Driven Snow':

Raiders from the north struck at the fertile townships of the Balranald machair of North Uist. They were not content with that as the grazings out at Heisker were legendary. One look at the seas breaking in the shallow sound between West Uist and the island group convinced the raiders they needed a pilot. Black John knew the waters best. They reminded the captive that the fate of all aboard was mutual. They were nervous, all except John, even before the weather turned bad. At least you could see some of the reefs and the boiling water.

When the blizzard came, John went right to the bow and pointed a way, rather than trying to shout above the wind and hail. The raiders had no option but to trust him. At last, a point appeared, black, out of the grey and white. 'Take her in close, a palm's width from that one,' said John. He had a hand up, holding to the taut luff of the reefed sail that was driving them. He pointed closer still but then he sprang from his forward position to get his feet on that rock. The boat drove on to hidden reefs and its destruction. In those conditions the raiders had no chance. John had got rid of a menace to the peace of the district. From then on it was *Rubh nam Marbh* – the Point of Death.[1]

Sealladh had been restored by a community association on the island of Berneray (now also connected to North Uist by causeway). She was powered by a dipping lugsail. Her mast was quite tall, as this was a harbour-moored boat and so it did not have to be dropped for beaching. The yard was shorter than those I was used to on Lewis. This made for easier sail-handling but we were still glad of the twin-cylinder Beta diesel aboard. This was installed new when *Sealladh* (formerly *Royal*) was renovated by the community in the early 2000s. The motor is based on a Kubota industrial engine and so is pretty much an international standard unit, taking much of the business that

Crystal Sea *(William Charles Stewart, 1963)*

the companies of Perkins or Lister Petter used to win.

The internal combustion engine was seen as a godsend by those who made their living by working as close to treacherous rocks as possible – the habitat of lobsters. The shape of Grimsay-built boats did of course change to accommodate engines when they became available. Construction was also affected. Lightness of weight, for sailing performance, was no longer so crucial. *Sealladh* has now been bought back into the original family and the money used to finance building of a community St Ayles skiff for Berneray. Looking back to our voyages together, I would say she is a motor boat with an auxiliary sail, for passage-making in suitable breeze, rather than a sailing boat with an auxiliary engine.

Typical examples of several variations of Grimsay-built boats are now displayed with clear interpretation material and an associated book at the Grimsay Boat Museum.[2] The building itself is minimal – a nod to the Nissan hut – but very suitable to a challenging environment with heavy salt-laden winds. In common with Unst Boat Museum,

Wick Heritage Museum, the Scottish Fisheries Museum and the Scottish Maritime Museum, Irvine, pertinent examples have been sourced, gathered and in some cases restored. At Grimsay, there is a curated approach which includes leaving recent repairs in oiled timber rather than painting them to disguise them. It took a bit of stooping and crawling, as well as walking away, to gain a sense of what really is unique about the main craft built by this family.

I had already done a trip in the *Morning Star*, painted up in a maroon and dark blue. She also now carries a Beta unit, by no means her first engine installation. This is a seminal vessel, because she was the first built for motor alone. That is recorded as the Kelvin Poppet, which was started on petrol before switching to the tank filled with cheaper paraffin. At close to 28 feet overall, she draws only 2 feet 3 inches, hinting of her history. She was commissioned by MacDonalds of Heisker, who were contracted to run supplies and mail to the lighthouse on Heisker. That might also explain why she has all sawn frames rather than the alternating sawn and steam-bent framing common in boats built by the Stewarts. I'd guess the time spent on substantial but very neat framing was influenced by the possibility of gaining a more steady return through the lighthouse service, rather than facing the uncertainties of marketing lobsters. Fishing boats were built to a tight price. I'd already heard some of her history on that trip to the anchorage at Port Ruadh in the later *Sealladh*.

Angus 'Moy' Macdonald came with us. He was born out at Heisker and did his first few years of schooling there. The old school was donated back to the community and has now also been renovated. We joined a group of contemporary school pupils, out for the day in a RIB, from the Uists, to hear, first-hand, what it was like to grow up in this place, now uninhabited. Among the stories (including 'Black John'), Angus told us that the boat now named *Morning Star* had been moored at Port Ruadh, as a big gale threatened. The families who lived nearby were preparing to take her ashore when the blast struck and it was no longer safe. She was driven ashore and her proud new Kelvin destroyed. Framing and planking were also shattered. Any other vessel would have been fenceposts and firewood, but this had been built to such a standard that the Stewarts considered her worth saving. She was towed to Ceann na h-Àirigh and the job done, not the last of her renovations.

She has a very fine 'entry', in that the planking at her stem is kept very narrow, even below the waterline. This shape only very gradually widens to her maximum beam of about 10 feet 6 inches. Now I was able to compare that shape with others in the museum. *Elm* is very different, as a double-ended example of a beamy multipurpose craft. She has a very fine form but is still fairly typical of an island load-carrying double-ender, just shy of 18 feet. The 23-foot *Silver Spray* shows that characteristic fine entry too, but has a bit more draught and beam in proportion than *Morning Star*. She appears to me a successful compromise between a motor boat and a sailing vessel.

But it was *Crystal Sea*, out of the water, which revealed to me just why the Stewart generations had such a reputation. She was built in 1963 by William Charles Stewart, but not for a customer. This fact reminded me of a story told in Shetland.[3] A son makes good in the Merchant Navy and commissions a boat for the father who first passed on boat-handling skills. Father and son travel to Norway to meet the builders and the new craft they will sail home is revealed.

'If this is the boat you build for your customers, I'd like to see the boat you'd build for yourselves,' says the son, astonished at the craftsmanship.

'We have no need of boats,' says the cryptic master-builder. This is the first hint that the tall, dark and quiet fellow and his sons are of course men ashore and great selkies at sea.

Crystal Sea is a shade over the 25 feet (7.6 metres), with a beam of 10 feet (3 metres). She is a double-ender with high freeboard and the comparatively deep draught of 4 feet 5 inches (1.3 metres). Several times, in oral history connected to the Grimsay boatbuilding, there is an account of the emphasis placed on the underwater shape by more than one of the Stewart craftsmen. Very few moulds or measurements were used. The emphasis was in building by eye. I was reminded of conversations with my late friend Archie Tyrrell. Archie was a nephew of the boatbuilders and picked up his own building skills, as well as a sense of structure and the need for sharp tools and sharper wit when he spent his summer holidays home from Glasgow.

'No, they didn't bother wi moulds or templates or suchlike. There wis a hell of a lot of standing back an jist lookin at the thing. An every wee bitty larch wis used. They used to get a lot of shite wood sent over. The yards kent it wis that difficult to send it back again. So they had to make do and make use o every decent bit. Long lengths wis difficult to get.'

Several commentators have judged that the Stewarts made a virtue out of this inescapable aspect of working on an island. They argue that it was easier to achieve the fine but complex underwater shape which gladdened the eye if you made the whole plank length from three parts, joined with scarphs (tapering simple joints), over a frame. These scarphs would of course be staggered so there was no line to introduce a possible weakness in the hull form. That hull would have to stand the hard bash through the shallows, the jolt of big seas and the strains of setting and hauling heavy creels. Once more, it is that fine entry, carried a daring distance aft, which, for me, is the defining feature. The beam then continues until it is taken into a pleasing rounded stern.

The close-up vision of the model-maker captures that shape best, for those who cannot travel to see the actual vessel. Donald MacQuarrie has made many model boats, often seen on display at Taigh Chearsabhagh museum, Lochmaddy, for example. The stern, often considered a hallmark of the boats of Argyll, is also invoked in the model-maker's comment, 'where Argyll meets the Norse'. Like

Fifie types, the keel continues over most of the length of the craft, with only the gentlest of rakes and a slight curve where post meets keel. From below, you get an impression of a high, buoyant sweep up to the rudder-top. I would say priority is given to directional stability. Perhaps there was trust in oar-craft at close quarters, nosing up to creels on lee shores. Skills would include giving bursts of propellor turbulence to the rudder to pull her in the direction you wanted. This one is listed as carrying only 'emergency sail', but I'd have thought she would have been an excellent passage-maker under sail, with the right rig.

The sails (often home-made) on display at Grimsay, indicate that the luff came down pretty plumb also and not far forward of the mast. There might be room for a jib, which would counter a tendency to weather-helm and also help her through the tack.

As to the sophistication of construction, framing can often seem fairly crude. A bent timber will be worked into a sawn floor. A section of a sawn frame will simply be butted to the next, maybe with an overlapping, joining-piece nailed or bolted through. Then you remember that these were built quickly for fishermen rather than rich recreational sailors. Like the great Zulus and Fifies before them, the vessel had to earn its keep in a few short years. The build was so strong that there was tolerance in scantlings of framing and other parts. A joint might not be constructed to yachtbuilding or cabinet-making quality, but it would still be sufficient to the purpose, done to a price and a timescale. If builders could achieve shapes as fine as those, they could have gone for finer finishes in the framing and fitting out, given time and coin.

Archie Tyrrell has left a few boats behind him. I was able to sail *Kennary*, one of these with him, through the tidal territories of the Sound of Shiants, to return to the bay where he picked up his awesome range of skills.[4] He never did quite complete her fitting-out. Still, the strong, seaworthy hull would be the basis of an excellent working craft or pocket-cruiser for someone who appreciates her lines. I took another look at her, now lying ashore in the village of Tong, Isle of Lewis. Her sheer and high bow seem part of Archie's own individual vision. Despite not having a huge amount of sea-time, he knew what would part seas and shed water. But that fine entry, carried on to become a gradual fullness – that's her pedigree showing.

NOTES

(1) This is a composite from many tellings. A strong version is transcribed in Bruford and Macdonald's Scottish Traditional Tales, *from the archives of the School of Scottish Studies, University of Edinburgh, current edition published by Birlinn (2007). My* Waypoints: Seascapes and Stories of Scotland's West Coast *(London, Adlard Coles Nautical/Bloomsbury, 2017) includes a transcription of a telling from Angus 'Moy' MacDonald, recorded live at the Monachs. Shipwright John MacAulay was aware of the tradition from nights spent ashore in the lobster fishers' bothies on Shillay.*

(2) Mary Norton (ed.), Never Broken in a Sea – Gun Fhaillin San Fhairge: The Hebridean Workboats of Grimsay, North Uist, Western Isles, Scotland *(Grimsay Boat Project, Grimsay, 2000). See also* Boats of the Grimsay Boat Haven, *a booklet produced by the Grimsay Boat Haven with a detailed history of the craft:* https://www.grimsay.org/centre/boat-haven.

(3) Heard first from Lawrence Tulloch but, as I remember, he attributed it to Jamsie Laurenson of Fetlar. Lawrence was a lightkeeper who wrote of that experience in On the Rocks – a Lightkeeper's Tale *(Lerwick, Shetland Times, 2010). Lawrence gathered the stories he told in* The Foy And Other Folk Tales *(Lerwick, Shetland Times, 2006). He also wrote* Shetland Folk Tales *(Stroud, The History Press, 2014).*

(4) A chapter of Ian Stephen, Waypoints *is devoted to the expedition in Kennary.*

29
SGOTH NISEACH
– THE SEABOAT OF
NORTH LEWIS

IT SEEMED A STRANGE TIME of the year to launch a boat. In December 1994, a huge group of local people of all ages turned out at Cuddy Point, across from Stornoway harbour. Many had been following a boatbuilding project by dropping in to the open workshop where a full-sized *sgoth Niseach* was taking shape. The design of hull and rig are unique to North Lewis, and this was the first of the large class to be built since early in the twentieth century. John Murdo Macleod had already constructed boats of this type at 17 feet and at 25. These were known as a 'half *sgoth*' and a 'three-quarter *sgoth*'. They had turned out to be both handy and seaworthy, with a surprising turn of speed. Being very beamy for their length and carrying a simple single sail, they did not at first look like fast craft. These new examples of a proven seaboat were built for use in outdoor education. As the rig is a dipping lug sail, coordination and good communication are required. These are skills which come in very handy whatever the vessel you go on to manage.

A word or two more on the dipping-lug and its variations, revisiting John Leather's wide-ranging study, *Spritsails and Lugsails*. I'm caught by his simple drawing of the hull and rig of a small craft from 'Bombay' (Mumbai). Her lateen sail also has a yard longer than the mast. A short luff falls, near vertical from that to be tacked at the bow. Like the *sgoth Niseach*, her halyard tackle also stays the mast, secured on the weather side. You have to look twice to see what is different. The mast is stepped in the aft section of the boat and has a steep rake forward. The hull form is much deeper forward and shallower aft, with a significant curve in her keel. The principles are like a Loch Fyne skiff in reverse. I wonder if these boats are pulled into beaches, going astern. Like the stories we tell, there are strong shared motifs across continents and endless variations. In the same chapter, Leather's drawing of a Somali coast *malapa* shows a rig incredibly similar to the Shetland version of a squaresail.[1]

Returning to the North Lewis craft, let's focus on the nearly lost class of bigger offshore boats. The jump from 27 to 33 feet does not seem enormous, but when you see *an Sulaire* alongside 'three-quarter *sgoth*' *Jubilee*, they have a completely different character. Out of the water, the internal volume of the full *sgoth* seems immense. It grows larger still when you start to paint the broad interior. John Murdo was not merely scaling up from the smaller vessels. There were photographs of a whole fleet of the big offshore boats, abandoned at Port Nis (Port of Ness). Two world wars took away most of the able young men who would have proved themselves on these craft. Some returned to the fishing, but markets for the dried cod and ling and for cured herring never completely recovered. The handier small craft were more suited for subsistence fishing, not far offshore. The full *sgoth* had been developed to set greatlines up to 40 miles into the Atlantic.

John Murdo wanted to build at least one example of the offshore boats last built by his father. Once more, a scale model proved a vital part of the development. Measurements taken from wreckage also helped. Like his brothers, he had done his share of time in the saw-pit at his father, John Finlay Macleod's workshop in Port Nis. All the boys had also been at an end of a riveting hammer. Memories could be checked in the notebooks which contained figures and keel-measurements. John Murdo had worked at the Clyde shipyards and he had also been at the Normandy landings. Then he made his career

Half sgoth Bluebird *off Arnish Point, Stornoway*

in education, teaching at the local technical college. He had often used boatbuilding projects to convey a sense of structure to his students.

BBC 2 collaborated with Eolas, a new Lewis-based film-making company founded by photographer Sam Maynard, to commission a documentary. Dialogue and narration were to be mainly in Gaelic, and support came from the EU's Leader fund. One of the aims was to show and document the transfer of knowledge from a master boatbuilder, John Murdo, to his assistant, Angus Smith, who had done his apprenticeship at McGruers but was also a Gaelic speaker. The film, shot with an artist's eye, has the most clear narrative of the process.[2] Subtitles in English catch the wit as well as the practicalities. Visitors are shown to engage with the process in the same way as when they called by at John Finlay Macleod's workshop, one generation back.

As *an Sulaire* (gannet) was growing, a three-quarter *sgoth*, *Jubilee*, built by John Finlay, was revitalised to serve as a training craft for new crews and skippers. It was found that a moderate amount of ballast helped her beat to windward. When used for sail-training, skippers had found that *Callicvol* at 17 feet and *Oigh Niseach* at 25 would sail well without internal ballast. The crew would learn to use their own weight, just as when sailing a dinghy. Now the boatbuilder judged that the full-sized *sgoth* would need about a ton of weight between her mast and the aft thwart. Rather than trust to placing boulders in the bilges after launching, lead ingots were handed aboard.

An Sgoth catches the shared pride as the oiled larch leans to the press of fresh breeze on tan sailcloth. Even with two of her six reefs secured, the sail area is significant. Angus, on the helm, grins. Unlike yachts of short waterline length, designed to lean, these boats like to sail on a fairly even keel. That's just as well, because they are completely open. There is no decked cuddy forward, no side deck to shed waves. She has close cousins in Scotland, especially in her neighbours up the searoad along the north coast and over on Orkney.

You will know a *sgoth Niseach* of any size from the shape of her sail. The single mast will fit inside the boat but can be hoisted on its own sailing tackle once she is afloat or to prepare her for beaching again. The only other spar (rounded timber) in her rig is the yard. The head (top length) of the sail is stretched along that to suspend the cloth. This yard crosses the mast but is hoisted on a hinged iron hoop (traveller) at a point about a third of the way from its leading edge. The full sail is carried over much of the length of the boat but the centre of effort is low.

Many of these vessels worked out of the tidal harbour at Port Nis, developed for the longline fishery. Others continued the village tradition of launching from exposed shores. I heard Nessman Peter Graham recall how, as a boy, he would join the line of villagers passing out round boulders to a boat in the surf. (Perhaps *sgoth Jubilee* at Borgh.) All would also help with the recovery. Even out of the harbour at Port Nis, they would usually have to punch through surf to find deeper water. The rig gives her power to do that without making her heel, or tilt steeply over.

The first time I really understood this was when helming 27-foot *Jubilee* through the dogleg at that breakwater. We had to negotiate a steep incoming swell, breaking just a few waves out. This is the last of the original working boats, built in 1935 by John Finlay Macleod. She was returned to sailing order in the late 1970s by a project led by another of his sons. John Murdo built the similar *Oigh Niseach* at about that time. Eric McKee's book includes drawings and notes which describe the two craft, by two generations, sailing together.[3] I might not have called it, that breezy day, but another son of the man who built her gave me a nudge. Norman (Gagan) Macleod said, 'You'll be fine today for another few hours of the tide. Just time it between the surges at the turn.'

Many have likened the iconic shape to the lateen sail seen in the Middle East. There are also craft with a similar rig in Portugal. Tack hooks, forged by a local blacksmith, are secured just back from her bow, at a reinforced point on either side. The lower, forward point of the sail (tack) is secured to the 'weather' one. The tackle which will help hoist stick and cloth is also hooked onto an eye on the side the wind is blowing on. The sail and the rope which controls it (sheet) are carried on the other (lee) side of the mast. As a fair proportion of the sail is forward of the mast, there is quite an area of sailcoth to 'dip' around that mast with the yard, as the boat is turning. The action introduces a twist into the wire strop (tie). Thus the heavy yard has to be lowered all the way down. It is unhooked from the hinged 'traveller' so that twist can be removed before hooking it on again. As this happens, the tackle, which is both halyard and stay, must be passed into the care of crew on the new weather side. The sheet, a single line with no tackle or purchase, must also be passed over. The tack will have been passed forward again so the person at the bow can place it on one of the row of eyes sewn into the forward edge (luff) of the great sail. All these items are heavy. Safe tacking needs care and consideration.

That is a fair number of actions to coordinate. A new crew will usually take a few tacks to get the sequence smooth. It is certainly easier to show rather than tell. At its best, it becomes a dance with very little spoken. Everything just described would have been done at speed when boats previously described, such as the Dysart yoles or Tiree skiffs, fought for position. The major differences are the length of the yard and the scale of the gear, in proportion to the overall length of the craft. Two people can just about manage a half *sgoth* such as the 17-foot *Callicvol* (1974), and three or four is an ideal crew. It takes four strong and handy people to sail a three-quarter *sgoth* such as *Jubilee*, and five or six make a stronger team. The scale of equipment on *an Sulaire* makes you wonder how five men and a boy could drive such a ship. Once *an Sulaire* powered up, glistening with saturation oil at that first launch, it was found that each position usually needed two people, doubling up, to work effectively. She can carry up to 12 people. The small and medium-sized craft row quite well, but the full *sgoth* is hard work.

The move from subsistence fishing with the handline or *dorgh* to setting miles of greatlines is discussed in a paper by John Murdo Macleod. His 'Loss of Boats and Crews at Ness, 1830–1920' was part of research that contributed to a memorial now sited at Port Nis. The boatbuilder's summary sheds light on the progression of boatbuilding linked to a developing commercial fishery. His analysis of the influence of these demands on the shape, construction and scale of vessel could surely be applied all around our coasts. Information passed down the family points to at least three boats being built by John Murdo's grandfather, Finlay, at the village of Fivepenny in the 1820s. These are described as 'long, narrow with little freeboard, very sparsely sewn and obviously for rowing'.[4] These would seem similar to the craft of Fair Isle and Shetland mainland, in fact closer to their Norse origins, though locally built. Finlay is also credited with introducing the more efficient greatline. Five boats were lost at Ness in the great storm of December 1862, though some craft survived by making for the mainland rather than risking the difficult waters of home shores.

First-hand sources suggest these were much smaller in volume than the later three-quarter *sgoth*, and with far less freeboard.

The commercial fishery was carried out mainly in the nineteenth century, with some large boats surviving into the twentieth. Boats became beamier, to carry greater loads, and with more freeboard they could carry more sail. These factors also made them better seaboats in the big waters they would face almost every working day. From photographic evidence, these were similar to vessels that were being built in Stornoway at the time. They have kinship with the north coast and South Orkney craft.

Breakwaters were improved at Port Nis as well as Tolsta. A new, larger class of offshore vessel, built to over 30 feet overall, was developed. According to John Murdo's research, the shift to larger craft for offshore work greatly improved the safety record. Accidents still happened. The writer describes how in 1889 two craft, probably the three-quarter size, were swamped west of the Butt of Lewis. One was observed from the shore to 'turn a complete somersault'. This is a sad reminder of the inherent dangers of these waters. In my coastguard career I can recall an ocean-going yacht which had made the passage from Greenland requiring assistance off the Butt.

I've been able to listen to first-hand accounts of the last days of these powerful craft. The half- and three-quarter *sgoth* was to work on for longer, between setting 'small lines' and, in season, herring nets. The historical society of the North Lewis district, *Comunn Eachdraidh Nis*, has done important work in collecting both artefacts and the oral history that gives them life and meaning. Any visitor to the island would do well to call in to the newly developed museum at North Dell. But it is the historian Donald MacDonald who really caught the oral history which brought both the challenge and the terror of that fishery to life.[5] The Tolsta Historical Society published his booklet on Tolsta townships, a substantial chapter of which is devoted to the history and stories of the line-fishing fleet.[6] Most of these were *sgoth*

Niseach built half a day's sail up the coast. There is celebration of the skills and courage, but many reminders that winter fishing from open boats is a gamble. Yet the boats could not have been decked, because weight was everything. A famous photograph of the *Brothers Delight* at Tolsta shows a crew putting their shoulders to a couple of tons of larch on oak. Boulders would be placed, as ballast, after launch and the rudder swung on its irons.

Mr Macdonald's account is filled with empathy as he also celebrates the legends. Transits are intoned like poems and the lore of 'escape routes' for different conditions is relayed. One slightly built skipper won the longest byname in the village. It went something like 'the one who tacked his *sgoth* six times in the breakers that bad day out off Traigh Ghearadha'. Another skipper had to dampen the enthusiasm of his youthful crew, who wanted him to let out the reefs so they could race to catch a *sgoth* which overtook them with more cloth up. Soon they were sailing through its wreckage. When a survivor was taken aboard he listened to how the bowman gave a commentary on the waters seen under the sail, up ahead. That is quietly passed down the boat so the helmsman responds. The man they've plucked from the sea comments that if they'd done that on his own boat, they might have come through it.

The best advice I've had on taking command of a *sgoth* was from a master mariner but also a first-hand tradition bearer. Alasdair Smith, now port pilot in Stornoway, relayed how there would always be a dialogue between different points of the boat, sheet, halyard and helm. No one would shout, but there would be a nudge, a sign or eye contact. The wide, buoyant stern – a point of pride in the boatbuilder according to John Murdo – will rise in a following sea which is taken on the quarter rather than the sternpost. The boat is then capable of speed beyond that which is possible in theory. (She has a curving bow and raked sternpost, so she is manoeuvrable but quite short in the waterline.) She will just 'lift up her skirts' and semi-plane. But that can bring her out of control. Thus the dialogue will lead to constant adjustments. She can be powered up and down as fine-tuning to ride big water. As the halyard lowers the sail, luff (front edge) and leach (aft edge) are held taut. An experienced team will use the same technique to control speed so she can be sailed alongside pier or pontoon. Alasdair now has his own beamy half *sgoth*, built new by Mark Stockl, who has put many hours into restoring and repairing *sgoth Niseach*.

Falmadair (tiller) – the North Lewis Maritime Trust – now look after an example of each of the three sizes of *sgoth*. The original working craft, *Jubilee*, has had at least three major renovations. This three-quarter *sgoth* has made the successful return passage to see the neighbours in Stromness, Orkney.[7] Now she is in need of another major refit. When Covid hit club activities, and so membership numbers, this was no easy matter. This crisis coincided with loss of revenue for local charities from community windfarm trusts due to failure of the power line which allows export of energy from wind. John Murdo once intimated to me that he felt his father had produced something exceptional in the shape of *Jubilee*. It so happens that John Finlay was the man who reached the shore of Holm with a rope from the grounded *Iolaire* on the first night of 1919. Most of the survivors of that tragedy owed their lives to that lifeline. Approaching the centenary of the disaster, Acair Books, Stornoway, published what must be the definitive study, *The Darkest Dawn – The Story of the Iolaire Tragedy*, by Malcolm Macdonald and Donald John MacLeod. Could it be that plans for a maritime museum in Stornoway, to be named after the *Iolaire* as a commemoration, could help save *Jubilee*? Perhaps the original vessel could be preserved but a replica built to be kept in active use?

The half *sgoth Callicvol* (the previous name for Port Nis township) started off in 1974 as she meant to go on. Simon Gray, who generously donated the craft to *Falmadair* Trust for restoration and use, recounts how his father and his father's crew took charge of the boat at the harbour in Ness. Her launch is captured on Super-8 film.

After a brief shakedown, they set off for Lochinver on a breezy day. In 2021 the boat, restored by Mark Stockl, was launched at East Loch Roag, Lewis, to take part in a combined rowing skiff and sailing *sgoth* expedition. Each day she took on some of the rowers to experience a different set of challenges. There was bright, strong breeze for most of the week. The rowers were amazed to see the distances covered, with long tacks, to achieve the angles that would allow each landfall. As a co-skipper that week, I can look at the log to see a good many miles covered in a significant Atlantic swell, but no anxious times.

Stunning images of the week from both skiffs and the half *sgoth* surely reveal a way forward. There is much to be gained by close cooperation between rowing groups and those who sail traditional craft.

NOTES

(1) John Leather, Spritsails and Lugsails *(London, Adlard Coles Ltd, 1979), pp. 26, 29.*

(2) Sam Maynard, An Sgoth *(Alba TV/BBC 2), is still shown from time to time on the Alba channel. It is available, new, on DVD from www.falmadair.org or on eBay. Profits are used to maintain sgoth Niseach.*

(3) Eric McKee, Working Boats of Britain: Their Shape and Purpose *(London, Conway Maritime Press, 1983). See p. 180 (facing page has drawings of sgoth Jubilee before and after first renovation).*

(4) John Murdo Macleod, 'Loss of Boats and Crews at Ness, 1830–1920', quoted courtesy of the family. Research by John Murdo is also published by the Stornoway Gazette *in the Eilean an Fhraoich Annual.*

(5) Donald Macdonald, A History of Lewis *(Edinburgh, Gordon Wright Publishing, 1978), p. 198.*

(6) Donald Macdonald, The Tolsta Townships *(Tolsta, Comann Eachdraidh Tholastaidh bho Thuath/North Tolsta Historical Society, 1984).*

(7) Ian Stephen, Waypoints: Seascapes and Stories of Scotland's West Coast *(London, Adlard Coles Nautical/Bloomsbury, 2017). See chapters on Jubilee and an Sulaire.*

30

THE RACING DINGHIES OF PLOCKTON

SOMETIMES ARDNAMAURCHAN POINT IS CALLED 'Scotland's Cape Horn'. The seas out from the headland are exposed to winds with anything of the west in them and completely exposed to the Atlantic, due west. Even in good weather, the high, brick lighthouse is a milestone: you know you're leaving the shelter of the Sound of Mull, northbound. There are nooks and crannies to give shelter and anchorage though some of these, like Loch Ailort, need very cautious pilotage to negotiate their reef-strewn entrances.[1] We are at the heart of challenging but rewarding cruising territory. With improved navigation aids, more and more yachts dare to explore. Among the great rewards are the harbours and bays of the Small Isles. All this territory is under the spellbinding Cuillin skyline and a lower but no less jagged echo on the skyline of Rum. I cannot sail this area without thinking of Neil M. Gunn's *Off in a Boat*. This is the wry and entertaining report of buying a motor vessel on Skye but one not very closely related to those of Silver and Bain mentioned before. This account was first published in 1938. Gunn describes rigging it with a much-needed auxiliary sail as a back-up. The report alternates with the stories of the area. Now the reader is conscious that this was just before a new hell came to Europe in the Second World War. The book has invited a musical suite and a performance as its creative echo from the musician Mike Vass.[2] Mike retraced the route in his own yacht by way of tuning in to the narrative.

I often return to Gunn's self-deprecating description of his entry into what is now called 'experiential learning' in sailing schools. He realises he has bought a motor launch which is in effect 'a shell':

> A floor board over the propellor shaft was missing, and I was told the owner would have put in a new one had I not been in such an inexplicable haste. I expressed my sorrow for that. Moreover, there had not been enough time to stow the ballast properly or quite finish the painting, while the engine throttle still needed a spring and one or two other things still needed adjustment. Besides that, the old magneto had been damaged by salt water, but there was a borrowed one in her and she was going well enough. By salt water? Had the boat's plug been left out? Hsh! said a shaken head.[3]

Most sailors or power-boaters now feel you need a bit more than a Primus stove, a chart and an oilskin to cover these miles. The exception is those who cruise in dinghies or dayboats such as the intrepid Wayfarer class, at 16 feet. These became most famous when Frank Dye was crazy enough to set out from Kinlochbervie to sail one for Faroes and Iceland in 1963 and for Norway in 1964. Scotland had its own classes of local dinghy. The clinker-built craft usually called a Plockton Boat was built mainly on Skye. This dayboat evolved to sail for the sake of sailing. In that respect they are a bit like the Loch Longs, from the Clyde, but these are not keelboats, and they are not built to one design. Instead there are more broad rules limiting dimensions: '. . . the club's rules do limit hull length (15 feet waterline length), keel depth (6 inches) and sail area (16.53m^2)'.[4]

A club was first established at Plockton in 1933. There were some variations in the vessels of around 16 feet. They mainly carried a

*Two Plockton boats (*Nancy *to left)*

gunter rig (like that of a Mirror dinghy). The yard sets as an extension of a short mast so, in effect, a standing lugsail becomes pretty much a triangular Bermudan form. This makes tacking a much simpler matter. By 1957 boats were being built with centreboards that could be lowered to act as a keel, resisting sideways movement (leeway) and so improving upwind performance. Sometimes handicapping is established to try to even out any advantage from such variations. When boats are of very different character, and there are enough of them, different races for each type are seen as a fairer competition. To this day, there are some controversies but the main distinction is between 'local boats', where the shape of the clinker planking provides the underwater form, and those built with a centreboard.

As time passes, different rigs are tried out. Like most sailing clubs, beginners start with a recognised single-handed dinghy like the Topper class or more recently the Laser Pico. Probably from this experience, aluminium masts and sophisticated sails began to appear on the local boats. These are allowed if they fit within the stated club rules, but of course are another matter for the handicap committee. In theory, one of the hundred-year-old boats should race with an equal chance as one just built. And they do continue to be built. Most of the original boats were built in Portree by John MacKenzie and Son. In the 1980s, it looked like no new craft were being built, but Skye-based builder Malcolm Henry was commissioned to make a few:

> On the Plockton boats . . . I believe the early ones were standard MacKenzie boats with an extra bit nailed onto the bottom of the keel. They were built at Heatherfield, Penifiler, which is across the loch from Portree. The early Plockton boats may have been built by John MacKenzie's father . . . I think I built five of them over a 20-year period from c. 1985, two in Portree and the rest after I had moved to Drynoch. Peter Matheson, who taught me the trade, built at least one in the 1990s when he was at Scarfskerry [Caithness]. He's still building boats at Clydebank.[5]

Since then, boatbuilder Mark Stockl has left his yard at Loch Broom to work with pupils at Plockton School on a regular basis. I met his students more than once. A group brought the new Plockton-type dinghy they had constructed, with Mark's supervision, to the popular event that was The Grimsay Boat Day. This time they resorted to trailer and ferry travel. Mark's easy relationship with his students allowed them to speak for themselves. It seems that the teamwork instilled by traditional craft can happen at their building as well as at their sailing. At least one student went on to do an apprenticeship with Mark. I was to meet him when he was working on further repairs to sgoth Jubilee. But all Mark's students shone with pride to match the sheen on the new planking. I hope they went on to race that boat. The project continues even at a time when funding is very tight, because of the proven benefits. The new builds and major repairs also undertaken have kept the fleet active and competitive.

At anchor in Plockton, I was to see and hear that. The bay was crowded with painted and varnished craft of similar type. This level of participation does not happen overnight. It was a good spectator sport, though any aboard our boat would have jumped-to if any dinghy had been short. There were just a few hair's breadths between the lead boats.

A sailor who did his share of dinghy-instructing at Plockton went on to prove the seaworthiness of the class, a fair bit outside that bay. I knew Peter McAlister as the man who cruised around the Faroe Islands in his Fastnet 34 (a cruiser-racer of the 1970s) along with a good friend of mine who was not in the best of health at the time. It turned out that Peter had his faulty engine lifted out at Suðuroy and collected it just before the return home. In between these events, Peter's *Seol na Mara* worked the huge tide races of the Faroes, entering havens under sail alone. He also managed with one of his crew undergoing a heart attack. Our pal, Ken Linklater, did not have his heart removed at any of the harbours they sailed into, but he did get an emergency operation on return to Scotland. Peter's log won the Clyde Cruising Club's trophy that year. So I was not too surprised to hear he was plotting another cruise with a difference, fundraising for the Sport Relief charity.

An architect by trade, Peter had applied his sense of form to more than one renovation of a traditionally built boat. While *Seol na Mara* was ashore for work, he put a lot of hours into 'bringing back' a Plockton dinghy. Here is his own description, elaborating on his 2010 blog in a 2021 email to me (you can also see photos of the return of *Nancy* on the website of Plockton Sailing Club).

The *Nancy* is a 15'6" open Plockton sailing dinghy built in 1934 by John McKenzie and Son, boat builders in Portree,

Skye. At the time she cost £1/foot to build (£3/m) and is built of larch with oak frames. Sadly, the years have not been too kind to her and she was fibreglass sheathed in 1994.

As with most of the current Plockton fleet she carries a Flying 15 rig and the only other means of propulsion are the oars. She has no centreboard or built-in ballast, just a 6" deep (150mm) wooden keel.[6]

I'm studying Peter's own photograph of the MacKenzie dinghy, after his work in preparing her for the voyage. There is a neat little forward cubby hole under a short foredeck with a camber to match the shape of the hull and timber 'cutting-boards' to shed spray. Up on a trailer before the launch into the Clyde, she shows the key feature of her stern. Although she is shallow in the forefoot, that timber keel shape deepens aft. Under her 'hourglass' transom you can see how the first four boards or so slant to the near-vertical in that area but round out to give buoyancy right at her stern. There is also a good area in her rudder. Without increasing her draught much, that would add to her resistance to leeway. I would say her distinguishing feature is where these planks or strakes come home to that stern. That shape is fairly wide at the top, to discourage a sea from 'pooping' her. But it fines away to help her streamlining, allowing the waters she has displaced to meet again at her sternwake. The images show how very little disturbance is left in the sea behind her. The logo on the sail betrays its origin. The rig of Uffa Fox's 'Flying Fifteen' keelboat design seems to have become the default option for converting a traditional rig to a Bermudan one. The mainsail is a substantial area, held out on a long boom. The smaller fractional foresail (not as high as the mast) overlaps. That's a pretty decent amount of cloth for the vessel under it, sailing without the benefit of the Flying Fifteen's bolted-on ballast keel. You can see how a boat like this will sail, without centreboard or other trickery, as long as her crew have a firm grasp of where to place their own weight at a given time.

Peter McAlister's log shows acute awareness of the route, gained over many years of cruising in different vessels. There is also a list of safety equipment, including dry suits and lifejackets, VHF radio and an electronic beacon for emergencies. Hand-bearing compasses, charts and flares are also listed, but the most vital equipment was two large buckets for bailing. He could have towed *Nancy* behind his yacht when he sailed up to do his next stint as instructor. Instead, he worked out a route for sailing the 16-footer from the Clyde to her natural home in Plockton, departing from the Clydebank yard where he'd prepared the dinghy. Dinghy-camping can involve sleeping under the sail, at anchor or beaching between tides to grab some sleep ashore. Peter knew well how to work tides to advantage along that way, as monks in a *curach* would have done centuries before. Even the skipper of a powerful *birlinn*, with oar and sail combined, would not fight these forces unless he had to.

But whatever the route, there was the outrun of Corrievreckan to ride, Ardnamurchan to round and the rollercoaster tidal rapid of Kylerhea to hit. As long as he could wait, if wind was in opposition to that tide, he was confident the dinghy could make it. Day one set the pattern. At times they had to row to avoid missing the tidal gate. Berthing at Rothesay brought relief from nine hours in a drysuit. The log noted 30 nautical miles under sail and a further five under oars. Next day a similar pattern of oar and sail took them in very changeable conditions through the Kyles of Bute. One more day, and they were in the sea-basin of the Crinan Canal. To get there they'd had to jury-rig the mainsheet after a laminated stern-knee disintegrated under the strain of strong gusts, swiftly following glass calm. Peter's photo shows them alongside an oiled *birlinn* which surely must be one of the GalGael boats. Under oars, usually propelled by his crew, Gordon, Peter reckoned the five-hour transit was the best he'd made in any craft.

There was a waiting game for tide, to take them to Seil Island. Then they were rewarded, covering 18 miles in three hours, in their deep-reefed charge. This took them up the Sound of Mull and through the Doirlinn Passage first shown to me by Steptoe. Deep sleep at Tobermory was followed by a hard fight to clear Ardnamurchan. They had come a long way since the keel of the Portree-built dinghy passed under the Erskine bridge. After rest on Eigg and a combination of hard rowing, hard sailing and riding tide, she went under the Skye bridge, close to the finale of Peter's adventure, as told in that 2010 blog: 'Off the wind now the *Nancy* surged up into Plockton bay with cars on the shore honking their horns and [...] taking snapshots of us as we sailed up harbour to tie up against the pontoons at 12.30.'

NOTES

(1) Martin Lawrence, The Yachtsman's Pilot: Skye and Northwest Scotland. *(A guide to passages, anchorages and harbours.) Also Edward Mason (ed.),* Ardnamurchan to Cape Wrath *(both published in St Ives, Cambridgeshire, by Imray, Laurie, Norie & Wilson Ltd, 2013).*

(2) Mike Vass, Notes from the Boat, see https://mikevass.bandcamp.com/album/ notes-from-the-boat.

(3) Neil M. Gunn, Off in a Boat *(London, Faber and Faber, 1938), pp. 51–2.*

(4) Plockton Small Boat Sailing Club website: http://www.plockton-sailing.com.

(5) Email to author from Malcolm Henry, 2021.

(6) Email to author from Peter McAlister (2021), with text of 'The Voyage of the Nancy'. See also his blog (6/5/2010), which includes photos: 'Taking "The Nancy" back to Plockton', http://mcalistersnancy.blogspot.com/.

31
BÀTA GHEÀRRLOCH AND THE LOCH BROOM POST BOAT

GEÀRRLOCH OR GAIRLOCH, THE HIGHLAND port, is not to be confused with the Gareloch on the Clyde. Here is a harbour which, like most in Scotland, has survived through boom and bust days in the fishing industry. It is not typical in that the military and naval presence, especially during the Second World War, had a strong effect on its economy. That was even stronger in Aultbea, Loch Ewe. The majority of commercial boats berthing and landing here are now working large fleets of creels. Variations of design are used to target prawns (nehrops, also marketed as langoustine); brown crab; velvet crab (red-eyed, nippy little green ones); and indigo lobsters. There has often been tension between those working trawlers and creel fishers, and that remains.

Judging from reports and underwater photography, undersea habitats as well as stocks are devastated by repetitive trawling and dredging in the same area. Politics can't be separated from commerce and rules from Brussels can no longer be blamed for everything. The Common Fisheries Policy of the EU was always deeply controversial. But maybe most will admit that there have to be binding measures, from some authority, to slow the decline of stocks from over-fishing. Land or sea, most people get greedy when there's big money rather than a living to be made. Regulation of the fishing industry from

Westminster, pre-1973 with the UK's accession to the European Communities (EC), was not very popular either.

Let's just say the ironies and complications are immense, but they do have a bearing on the viability of commercial fishing and so boatbuilding. For many years the long, refrigerated lorries from Spain have somehow found their way along narrow roads to load selected shellfish. Post-Brexit, that export has become complex and uncertain. Shellfish die if there are delays, and they are then unsaleable. It's difficult to see how restaurants in the UK, trying to recover from lengthy periods of closure while the pandemic was dominant, can provide an alternative market of sufficient buying power to keep the creel boats in business. As commercial fishing declines, for whatever reasons, more space is given in harbours for visiting yachts. Highland Council pontoons like those at Gairloch, Kyleakin and Lochinver aim to encourage cruising by providing infrastructure at reasonable cost. After a few nights at anchor many sailors will be happy to pay to berth alongside and have a meal ashore. Every little helps a small local economy in a Highland village.

And local leisure-sailing is revived and adapts. Across from Gairloch pier, in the lee of Eilean Horrisdale, anchorage can still be found among used and disused moorings off Badachro.[1] The shoreline was a bit of a ships' graveyard when I was last there. I spotted *Pivot*, a once-fine yacht, built in teak on mangrove, at the Cheoy Lee yard in Hong Kong. I know this because the folkboat-based craft was moored beside my own yole, *Broad Bay*, for some years at Stornoway. Her generous owner would wave me aboard and give me the tiller. When a wooden yacht becomes a project, costs escalate. More difficult to explain is why a couple of smaller open craft of traditional clinker construction were sinking into the mud. Sometimes a craft is neglected due to illness or bereavement. It can take a long time for a family to decide that it is time to part with a boat. Responsibility for a distinctive craft is maybe more a matter of being a custodian rather than an owner. The neglected small craft would locally have been considered of the *bàta Gheàrrloch* type. They have many similarities to the Oban skiffs or those used on the east and west coasts of Mull. They were the foundation of recreational sailing, often fired by competition, in Loch Broom as well as Loch Gairloch. The website of Loch Broom Sailing Club provides a potted history.[2]

The dipping lug-rigged craft, with origins as general-purpose fishing and transport boats, were of course adapted for racing. As with most scenes round Scotland's coasts, a standing lug and jib gave way first to gunter then Bermudan rigs. External ballast was added in a quest for further improvement. *Speireag* was built by Malcolm Henry. His comments, in a 2021 email to me, seem to confirm the very similar characteristics of a 'west-coast skiff', from the Clyde to Loch Broom. They are as seaworthy as they are nippy:

> *Speireag* was my second attempt at a double-ender of the west-coast style. The first, *Nereid*, I built for myself from basic measurements that I took from a boat that used to do the mail run from Lochaline to Craignure in the early part of the twentieth century. At the time, in the early 1980s, the only such double-ender that I know to be still working was used to carry sheep from Balmacqueen to Trodday. She was built by John MacKenzie's father (Bodach's grandfather). All of the other west-coast double-enders that I knew were lying ashore in various stages of disintegration. *Neried* appeared at the Museum of Island Life in Kilmuir a couple of years ago, having been donated by her owner, who was somewhere in the north of England. He had rescued her from Badachro, done some work to her, and sailed her for a few years until old age got the better of him. Both boats had the same rig – standing lug with jib on a short bowsprit – which was an approximate copy of the one on the Lochaline skiff. I built *Neried* at Scarfskerry and sailed

The boat that delivered the mail (see also bàta Gheàrrloch*)*

her home to Portree from Kinlochbervie, doing my fair share of running and hiding from the weather ... The final leg was an overnight row from Fladda to Portree.[3]

Speireag was to take part in a series of radio programmes made for Radio Scotland. I know this because I took part in one by accident. As I moored *Broad Bay* in the lee of Sober Island, across the Minch, in Stornoway harbour, *Speireag* sailed in. She had a very charming and chatty skipper aboard. Then along came the support boat and before long a microphone appeared. We soon forgot we were being recorded and just had a cross-Minch yarn. It was at that time that *Pivot* was my neighbour, and her oiled or varnished planking showed its quality in the evening light.

This is an irony I'd rather not be pointing out. *Pivot* and *Speireag* now appear to share the same resting place back over at Badachro. Why or how are other stories. Both of them could have had many more years' active use and it's possible that both could still be saved, given the will. *Pivot* was worth saving because of the exceptional quality of her build and materials. She had been seen as valuable enough to transport halfway round the world. But what of the little west-coast skiff? Eric McKee's *Working Boats of Britain* includes the author's own drawing of the typical semi-circular gunnel (gunwale) aft of a west-coast skiff. He also explains the practical reasons for the pleasing shape: 'Room aft gives space for the helmsman clear of those working forward, reserve of buoyancy to prevent swamping by overtaking waves and a wider sheeting base. All combine to give more boat for the same length and are an inducement to make a pointed stern full above the water.'[4]

I'd suggest the combination of simplicity of rig and hard-won shape combine to make an ideal sailing-club boat. The emphasis is on teamwork rather than high-tech and expensive sails and controls. A boat could use a dipping lug rig to foster teamwork but quickly shift to a standing lug and jib when short-handed. Two-handed racing is also a lot of fun.

Some years ago, Malcolm proposed a restricted class of vessels of about 25 feet or so for competitive racing under oars and sail. Such a concept allows for continuation of local types, best suited for local conditions, but also breeds comparison and companionship. I would argue that the same principle could be applied to examples of smaller craft such as similar skiffs up to around 18 feet or so. *Speireag* would be a fine template. A craft of similar shape was built by Topher Dawson, working from his windmill-powered boatshed on Scoraig at the time. The catch is that *Sgorr na Creag* was built in Tasmania for Alan Bush, a previous resident of Scoraig. Thus we have a recognisable west-coast skiff, Down Under. That seems to me a recent parallel to the way boats very similar to Orkney yoles were built in Canada by Orcadian employees of the Hudson Bay Company. Could these examples still be termed Scottish boats? Topher's own account (again in an email to me) adds to the picture of cross-influence by reproducing proven features of boat shape:

... lines ⌊of *Sgorr na Creag*⌋ were taken off a boat I bought in Ullapool. I was told it had been a kelp collecting boat from the west coast of Harris, which led to its shallow draught and great beam [20 feet long and 8 feet wide]. So the boat is a faithful copy of the original, except the keel and stem are blue gum and the planking and ribs the legendary Huon Pine. Alan's daughter Pippi, who lives in Margate, Tasmania, now has possession of the boat after I spotted it in a field looking rather derelict. I was on a 150 km rowing 'raid' up the D'Entrecasteaux Channel and back in 2019. Its previous owner had taken it on an epic voyage up the east coast of Tasmania to visit the native peoples of Flinders Island.[5]

Loch Broom Sailing Club now run a keen racing series between well-matched Flying Fifteens, but it's good the roots of the club are acknowledged in their literature. There is perhaps another lesson or route forward here because older plywood examples and GRP versions of the Uffa Fox classic weigh alike and are rigged alike to provoke fair competition without the need for complex handicapping. There is one example of a *bàta* of the Loch Broom area based directly on the lines of an older craft, *Mary*. The present skipper, Diyanne Ross, questions the idea that the Loch Broom skiffs were all *bàta Gheàrrloch*: 'It's debatable whether the Loch Broom *bàta* came from the Gairloch boats; personally I think the *bàta* was adapted from the generic kit builds coming over from Norway to Shetland in the 1700s. Loch Broom was where the herring was and Tanera, the herring processing station and the first stop from Shetland.'

This would tie in with Topher's comments and confirm the idea of very similar craft being developed, from Norse examples, for the task to be done and the conditions they would meet. Diyanne also describes the process which brought the recreation into being: '*Wee Hector* was commissioned by the Ullapool Business & Tourist

Association, built to commemorate the sailing of the *Hector* and launched during the "Fish Week" festival we had in Ullapool that year. The fundraising was interesting, you weren't just asked for money, people were asked to buy a rivet for 50p or a plank . . . that gave an added feeling of participation and ownership to the boat to those who put their money in. There would be bulletins in the *Ullapool News* to say "the mast is now fully paid for", etc.'[6]

The name is an ironic reference to the emigrant ship which decimated the population around Loch Broom. Descendants of the survivors of that voyage to Pictou, Nova Scotia, in 1773 now link up on Facebook and Twitter.[7] The first time I sailed *Wee Hector* was a happy accident. A team of us had crossed the Minch to recommission *Jubilee* following a refit. That involved replacement of about a third of her planking by Mark Stockl. We were of course to the wire in meeting a deadline for sailing her home to take part in the Sail Hebrides Festival. Mark proposed a job-swap. If club members who had volunteered to carry out painting works could also re-fix newly galvanised ironwork on sternpost and rudder and fashion a new tiller, he would cast lead to fit the shape of her bilges. This would make her safe for open sea passages as it would not shift, unless we were upside-down. He had already installed buoyancy, hidden in very traditional-seeming tongue-and-groove joinery under her thwarts. This appeared just like boards to separate catch from gear but it would compensate for that fixed ballast. She would then stay afloat if swamped. That is a lesson learned from painstaking histories of pretty much all traditional coastal craft around Scotland, including a list of Minch disasters in Donald Macdonald's *A History of Lewis*.[8]

But a huge advantage of the smaller-scale craft, including *Wee Hector*, at about 16 feet (4.9 metres), is that they sail well without ballast. In that case, buoyancy bags, fitted under thwarts, are usually sufficient to compensate for the weight of fastenings, tackle and gear aboard. If the idea is to instil the need for cooperation, then it's good to learn the importance of your own weight, modest though that may be. We found that installing the heavy blocks in *Jubilee* could not be done safely before the tide turned. She would have to dry out at the sailing club for a couple of hours till we had enough water to bring her up to the jetty again. That was when members of Loch Broom Sailing Club invited us to take the new boat out for a spin. As the focus of the club was on both the Flying Fifteen fleet and cruising yachts, there had not been much interest in the skiff.

Alasdair Smith, his son Pedear and myself obliged. We found a rig souped-up with low-stretch Dyneema and low-friction ball-bearing blocks. Bonnie enough, but a lugsail is a lugsail. This was a 'balanced lug' with a light boom but jutting just across the mast. This meant the sail did not require dipping and a tack was a simple thing so long as you were canny in the flukey Loch Broom breeze. Most people assume a dipping lugsail will not go to windward very well, but in many cases they are wrong. I would say this balanced lug did not sail as close to the wind as a *sgoth Niseach* rig will, in flattish water, but that was a reasonable trade-off for its ease of use. You could imagine apprentice sailors hopping from a Topper to work in twos and threes on this craft. She was stable and she had acceleration. What more do you want? I'd say another of the same, or else a wee bit of a challenge. Perhaps if the active Gairloch Sailing Club were to restore a *bàta* like *Speireag,* an inter-club race could be part of a gathering. *Falmadair* Trust was only able to recruit some keen young skippers when they had come through a season of racing similar lugsail-rigged small craft. It took two boats to build a keen, regular scene. Three was better still.

The purpose of *Wee Hector,* built by Mark Stockl (then with Ullapool Boatbuilders) was not clear. A role in the encouragement of tourism was one of the funding criteria. But there seemed to be no practical plan for fulfilling this. Happily Diyanne, from Reiff, across from the Summer Isles, stepped in. Diyanne was already an approved skipper of both *Falmadair* and the then *an Sulaire* Trust. She organised the move to Old Dornie harbour (also home to the Iain Oughtred design *Grey Seal* at the time). Both boats could take the ground in a drying basin. With a metre or so of rise of tide, there is access to Ceolas Eilean Ristol. From there you can explore the sounds, channels and anchorages around the Summer Isles.

This is the area celebrated in Frank Fraser Darling's *Island Years*.[9] Many would see Darling as a father figure in ecology. First published in 1940, his seminal book includes very readable accounts of such adventures as living in a hut on Eilean a' Chleirich (Priest Island) in the company of family, goats and an adopted wild gosling chick. The adventure was combined with close scrutiny of the geology, flora and fauna of a designated area. That approach continued in later research into the storm petrels breeding on North Rona, about 40 miles north-east of the Butt of Lewis. In that book and in *Island Farm*, the essential role of small craft, for transport as well as fishing, is to the fore.

I crewed for Diyanne in the mission of sailing *Wee Hector* through the channel to clear the southern shore of Isle Ristol to the anchorage at Tanera Mor. A mutual friend, the artist Saki Satom, had also fallen under the spell of lugsailing in *an Sulaire* when we'd taken part in an international artists' residency based on Tanera Mor, maybe a year before. Diyanne had made the link with the mainland community. Artists – locals and visitors – sailed happily together in the strong breeze and intense light which often coincide on the west coast of Scotland. Saki had been asked to design a stamp for the island, as part of another tradition. She had been struck by the way spoken transits, based on landscape features observed, can cross to fix a point on sea or land. We had woven routes between the islands, kedged into bays and made landings. As skipper, I had noted the essentials in the boat's log but then passed it to the artists to combine facts, observations and comment. That seemed to merge with connotations of Stevenson's *Treasure Island* in the thinking that went into Saki's stamp design.

When we had enough water we left the mooring to sail to the

stamp-launch event. The route was mainly downwind. Diyanne helmed and I trimmed. With the wind just off a quarter, she (if you can address a boat called 'Hector' that way) settled into a steady track. I came aft enough to lift her bow a tad without reducing the keel-length in the water. She was not slow. A gybe was easy enough as long as care was taken to gather in the sail as her stern came through the wind so there was no great slamming as yard and boom were allowed to back against the short mast. Now, as we approached Tanera Mor in *Wee Hector*, Saki and all involved were happy that a boat linked to the area could be in the picture again. We took a few keen visitors out around the bay, tying one reef, then the other. All too soon, it was time to think about the beat back up to the home mooring. There would be spray. Our tacks would have to be crisp. We could not really take inexperienced sailors along on the return. Our friends would be ferried in the island's workboat. Gusts hit about Force 6. The shape of this craft proved itself. As long as one of us crouched forward to help her bow grip, we could work well to windward. In the squalls, we sneaked a bit closer. She tacked well as long as you kept the momentum till the tiller went down.

Over a pint afterwards, in a warm snug, we both thought that was about as good as sailing gets. Even with these reefs in, we still had to move our weight fast as we short-tacked back up the sound. There might be a few hi-tech fibres aboard but this was still sailing by string, stick and cloth. (As it happens, my elder son, Sean, is both sailor and educator in outdoor activities in sometimes very challenging situations. At present he leads a project in Cornwall. When it comes to sailing, the terminology he uses is still 'string, stick, cloth'.)

The Loch Broom area might ring a bell for followers of the type of small craft which can be easily towed and launched, place to place. 'Character Boats' are moulded in GRP to a plug that might be taken from a good example of a proven inshore craft. The firm had used an example known as the Loch Broom Post Boat as the basis for one model. With a cover to protect varnished spars and tan sails of terylene but of traditional appearance, running costs are a fraction of those involved in keeping a seagoing yacht. (The hue came to a cotton or flax sail from the 'cutch' solution of oak bark which preserved the cloth.) I'd first come across the Loch Broom Post Boat during a short artist's residency at the museum in Irvine. Recently, James McLean, current assistant curator, sent me some photographs along with this summary: 'It was donated to the West of Scotland Boat Museum from a man named Mr W. Baillif from a company called "Character Boats" in 1983. From there it was transferred to the Scottish Maritime Heritage Association in 1985 and finally came to the Scottish Maritime Museum in 1987. Unfortunately, it arrived at the museum in very poor condition and it has not improved since then. As a result, we are currently reappraising it's suitability for display.'

Approximate dimensions are given as '14' x 6' x 18". The given story is that the clinker-built dinghy was lug rigged and used by at least two generations of postmen. The images remind me that the craft has a fairly high interior volume for its size as her fairly wide beam only gradually turns in to her raked transom stern. Her rounded bow is gradual, so leaves a reasonable length of timber keel. I can see why her shape was chosen to create a new class of dinghy. She would sit on a trailer well. Other examples of proven shapes are taken from boats from different parts of the UK coast to compose a range of different sizes and so different likely safe range.

The 'post boat' is given a gaff sloop rig with a furling jib set out on a bowsprit to make a length of 18 feet overall. The shape is still recognisable from the form returned to the museum. Rather than any type of drop-keel (centreboard), her mould includes the depth of an additional external timber keel-member seen in the museum photographs. Quite deep bilge keels, either side, would further resist leeway and also help her to sit comfortably in a drying berth. It's possible that the original had these too, but that can't be seen in the images. It's a pretty good story and it seems to be a pretty good wee boat, but like most tales, there are other versions.

Alex Eaton, retired curator/manager of Ullapool Museum, holidayed as a youngster on the Lochside (south side of Loch Broom). Alex kindly looked up notes and messages from past correspondence and winged an email across the Minch. She remembers the Lochside crofter who owned the old post boat, and the interest and publicity generated by the copy boat built by Character Boats. Unsurprisingly there would appear to have been more than one post boat used on the Lochside. Alex relates:

> Another twist to the story – in around 1970 my father purchased what purported to be a 'Loch Broom Post Boat' from a local Lochside family. She was a larger boat than the one in Irvine. She was still in good enough 'nick' for us kids to run around and have fun with (as long as we remembered to take empty tin cans for frequent bailing operations!). Being a double-ender, with a high stern, Dad rigged up a metal frame which he fixed amid ships, with our wee Seagull Forty Plus's prop getting just enough depth to operate. Sadly there are no photos of her.[10]
>
> We were friendly with the late Alexander Munro, an elderly chap who had been one of the Lochside Posties. He was a fine chap and great friend to us kids. He was born in 1880, the year of the last significant Clearance event – at Leckmelm, just across the loch from his home, and infamous in its day as a particularly heartless act. He told us tales of sailing the boat to the Post/Telegraph Office at Inverlael to collect the Lochside mails. Also of droving the sheep and cattle across the hills to the east-coast marts. Alex Munro passed away in 1975, aged 95.[11]

This is similar to the way another firm (Drascombe, though the trading name is now Devon) uses the name 'scaffie' for a GRP craft built from 1978 at about 14 feet 8 inches (4.5 metres). The design is credited to John L. Watkinson, and there is a nod to the curved bow and raked and rounded stern of the traditional type. A long central keel with pronounced bilge keels is also used to counter leeway rather than a centreboard. Rudder and tiller are a nod to Scandinavian craft and the single standing lug looks appropriate. A similar method could be used to reproduce the actual form of a small craft, proven over generations. A mould could be taken from a proven *bàta Gheàrrloch* or west-coast skiff. This would mirror the way both dinghy and keelboat designs have been kept in use by making the transition from timber or plywood to GRP. Scantlings and weights are measured to keep the playing field as level as water can be.

On the other hand, the exemplary Plockton boat project has furthered transference of a different set of skills to complement the benefits of participating in the sport of sailing. A recent project on Westray has also combined passing of boatbuilding skills with mentoring in boat-handling, rowing and sailing. If waterline length and sail areas were limited, the characteristics of regional vessels could be maintained while the boatbuilding students could go on to cruise and race with the revived craft of other areas of Scotland. Copper fastenings are expensive but recyclable. Larch of sufficient quality is getting scarce as it is used more and more for house-cladding, but well-managed forestry can still supply the small amounts of timber selected for this purpose. We can always keep planting some European larch as well as faster-growing species. Some of the hybrid larch I planted as a teenager will be house-cladding now.

NOTES

(1) *Edward Mason (ed.)*, Ardnamurchan to Cape Wrath *(St Ives, Cambridgeshire, by Imray, Laurie, Norie & Wilson Ltd, and Clyde Cruising Club, 2013), p. 128.*
(2) *'Club History', on the Loch Broom Sailing Club website: https://lochbroomsailingclub.blogspot.com/p/blog-page.html.*

(3) *Email to author from Malcolm Henry, 2021.*

(4) *Eric McKee,* Working Boats of Britain: Their Shape and Purpose *(London, Conway Maritime Press, 1983), pp. 64–5.*

(5) *Email to author from Topher Dawson, 2022.*

(6) *Email to author from Diyanne Ross, 2022.*

(7) *Ship Hector Passenger Descendants Facebook page: https://www.facebook.com/ shiphectordescendants/.*

(8) *Donald Macdonald,* A History of Lewis *(Edinburgh, Gordon Wright Publishing, 1978).*

(9) *Frank Fraser Darling,* Island Years *(first published London, G. Bell and Sons Ltd, 1946; reissued with Island Farm, West Dorset, Little Toller Books).*

(10) *Alex has now found and shared images of the vessel she describes (sent to author, 2022). These suggest a form very similar to that of Wee Hector and are the basis of the illustration used in this chapter.*

(11) *Email to author from Alex Eaton, 2021.*

32
COIGACH – AN IDEAL
INSHORE BOAT?

THE COASTLINE BETWEEN ULLAPOOL AND Cape Wrath is dramatic at every twist, height and indent. The roads will only take you to a small number of vistas. The way to see it is by boat, though it is challenging, like many of the most rewarding cruising territories. We could diversify and discuss mountains, because the scale of the great Sutherland heights is something you will never take for granted, even if you study these, from seaward, often. A small craft is probably the best way to explore the detail of the sea-lochs but it will need to be seaworthy because the North Minch will find its way in to all but a few sheltered pools. Apart from cruising by yacht and exploring by dayboat, these coastal waters have bays and jetties used by small craft setting creels. But the domain from Coigach to Cape Wrath also contains two of the most significant commercial ports in Scotland. Lochinver and Kinlochbervie are strategically placed to reach fishing grounds to the north or work out west of the Hebrides. It is also not an enormous distance, by road or by sea, to reach the east coast. Pentland Firth is not always a nightmare but its overfalls and rips can never be taken for granted.

The links between boatbuilding on the east coast and fishermen working on the west have been there for centuries, and they continue. The subject is huge and needs a book in itself, but here there is space simply to look at a few particular examples of both small craft and larger commercial ones. These may give some sense of a much larger picture. First we'll linger by the shorelines which are partly shielded by the Summer Isles. I met Ali 'Beag' Macleod when our team had *an Sulaire* moored at Tanera Mor. A self-taught accordion player, his personality would light up any ceilidh. He encouraged many a young musician, but he also had a deep passion for boats. He wanted to see and compare every detail of a *sgoth Niseach* as he had his own labour of love in saving one of the few Fifie-type craft of the area which still carried her lugsail. Remembering him, it occurs that there is much in common with handing down a tune or verses of song and keeping a line of boats of a shape proven by work in an area.

There were salmon cobles here too, but there also seems to me a recognisable variant of Fifie-type vessels. To me, they are worthy of study because they reveal how a favoured example of a known craft is adopted a good distance from where it was built, even when there has been local boatbuilding. Another example, across the Minch, is how generations of the Buchanan family in the Uig district of Lewis have ordered a beamy yole from Orkney. Working out from the exposed coast of Islibhig, they provide space and seaworthiness ideal for transporting sheep to island grazing and inshore lobster fishing. As late as the 1990s, Ian Richardson of Stromness supplied the last one.

Let's take a look at two boats of A' Chòigeach (Coigach) but focus on one as a boat which has many admirers. Both have fairly plumb ends. Both are painted in a traditional black but with meticulous yellow cove-lines and fishing numbers renewed to a style. The 26-foot *White Heather* is a workhorse. She has had generations of small deckhouses to give some protection as she worked under motor for nearly all her life. Her build was stout, with sawn frames, to take these strains. She has survived the pounding that comes from setting and hauling nets and creels and the need to recover them before a blast will destroy them. But it's her smaller neighbour, Jim Muir's *Katie*

(UL97), which is most celebrated in film, photo, drawing and yarn.

According to the owner's son, Iain, this smaller craft of 21 feet or so was very different in character because she was:

> . . . built for sailing rather than to be engined, so light and graceful, much more so than my father's 26ft *White Heather*, built for my grandfather with a Kelvin engine for bag-net anchor work, and lobsters in winter . . . Jim kept the *Katie* going through rot and rust with plenty tar and a good bilge pump, but when Jim was no longer fit to care for her she was hauled into a noost at Old Dornie, where she began to settle into the landscape. She would have gently melted into the beach like many before her (in stark contrast to the hard-edged broken glass-fibre hulks that litter the shoreline now). However, she was rescued and taken to Gardenstown – her departure and crowded send-off recorded on Kevin's video – to be restored as a project by a boatbuilding trust . . .[1]

This prompted me to look for a precedent. Ullapool Museum shows a model of *Bounty* (UL217). She has a striking but simple colour scheme of a black hull with no 'boot-top' or contrasting anti-fouling below her waterline. Her top strake is green and the white fishing numbers are also in a simple script. She has a high mast, quite steeply raked aft. Thus she carries a good amount of sailcloth as a dipping lug but that is quite high-aspect and the yard set fairly high-peaked. That yard is significantly shorter than that of the dipping lugsail as carried, across the Minch, on a *sgoth Niseach*. At the foot, the sail extends not much more than half her length but the yard is long enough to set a greater area of cloth towards the head (top edge) of the lugsail. Your eye just tells you this is perfectly suited to the craft. Everything about this vessel reveals hard-won simplicity. Her bow is not plumb but slightly raked and very slightly curved into the keel. Her stern is similar, but the curve seems to be more noticeable at the

Bounty (*dipping lug but nb yard much shorter than* sgoth Niseach)

top of the sternpost, quietly rounding into the 'breasthook' which will hold her together.

She was noticed in her day, 1933, at Old Dornie, by Francis Tudor Wayne along with a craft of very similar shape and rig but smaller in scale, *Flower of Polbain*. Wayne seems to have lived between the wonderful anchorage of Eisg Brachaidh in Sutherland and Stansted in Essex. Kevin Macleod, from an Achiltibuie family, shared Wayne's drawings and notes. Kevin researches such icons of local history when he is not picking out tunes in sessions or with The Occasionals dance band. His research led him to the Science Museum Library in South Kensington. He was able to buy copies of Wayne's meticulous record, measurements, line drawings and notes on distinguishing details.

These record *Bounty* as 22 feet in the keel and 23 feet 9 inches (7.2 metres) overall. *Flower of Polbain* was 15 feet in the keel at 17 feet 4 inches (5.3 metres) overall. The larger boat was built at Gamrie Bay and the smaller along the coast, towards Fraserburgh, at Rosehearty. Sail areas are estimated at 225 square feet and 115. Notes also describe the action of dipping the lugsail to tack the boat. The craft are very similar in line and rig, though of different dimensions. Perhaps that's a bit like a 'half *sgoth*' and a 'three-quarter *sgoth*'. Details represented include a clever wooden cleat for securing the fall of the tackle halyard without the risk of any locking turns which would jam it and so risk losing the ability to de-power the boat or tack in a hurry. I've also seen a similar feature on boats built on the west coast, including some by John MacAulay on Harris. There are three alternative mast-step positions on the larger boat and the 'steering thaft' (seat) is moveable in the smaller one. Wayne's comments also judge the shapes, build and rigs amounting to something near the ideal for a working inshore craft. He says: 'This type is probably the fastest type of sailing fishing-boat of the size in great Britain. Speeds of 8 knots through the water have been authenticated.' That would seem likely on the larger craft, but more difficult to imagine for the smaller one.

And yet, at both these scales, the shape seems to be just about the ideal development of the form in every way. The rig would give power while leaving space to work gear and tack efficiently. These subtle rakes and curves would help her tack and gybe and yet give very good directional stability. Beam and freeboard are enough to resist heeling too far and shipping water. The sheer is noticeable but not pronounced. Here is another strong candidate for a boat to link communities in cruising and in competition, the way the Drontheims, taken from the mould, can do.

The original coigach boats carried stone ballast. They ranged far, whether they were west-coast skiffs or east-coast Fifies. Kevin Macleod directed me to recordings made by Calum Maclean of the School of Scottish Studies. Among reminiscence and tales there is evidence of just how important the boat was to these coastal communities, as illustrated by Murdo John Maclean:

There was at that time a shop, long ago, och! It was before my father was born or when he was very young it was, there was a shop in Back in Lewis, far better known than any shop in Stornoway, for keeping the things that pertained to the sea, and fishermen from here, they would go across to Back to get the twine for making the nets in preparation for the summer fishing, and two of my grandmother's brothers went, Murdo and Iain, they went across with a boat they had, a sturdy Gairloch boat, two sails on her, and, to get the messages they needed, and did they not get word when they were over there, that potatoes were very cheap in Lewis, something that was very, very unusual, it was never heard of, cheap potatoes in Lewis . . . and that the potatoes were for sale, and so the men took with them as much as they could, in the boat, and they thought that when they returned home, with the demand among the people, and that there was a shortage of potatoes here, that they would go for another load and that they would put sixpence or a shilling on each bag, the weather was better than in my memory that they should go with a boat of sixteen or seventeen feet, perhaps eighteen feet across the Minch . . .

These men with the open boats, they were going up to any place where they could get herring, up to the Cape there, with open boats. And they took the boats, taking them ashore at night, and turning them upside down . . . I myself saw men who were at that work, I did see, men at that work, and going to the Loch of Skye and Loch Duart, with open boats, yes, was it not out of the sea that they took their livelihood.[2]

Vernacular sources thus confirm the impression gained from Wayne's knowledgeable eye and careful records, though they also indicate that various forms of craft were favoured. Turning to *Flower of Polbain*, Kevin shared information on the boat and her history from his father, Roddie Macleod:

[She] was owned by Murdo (the Lump) MacLeod, who lived at No. 5 Achiltibuie, where the Patersons now live. He was the father of Seordag, Mrs Murray of Lochinver, the lovely singer referred to by and recorded by Calum Maclean [see the Murdo John MacLean archive at the School of Scottish Studies]. He went all round the coasts in the *Flower*, after the herring, and claimed, according to Jim Muir, to have had a good season when he made £10. In a poem by Neil MacLeod, the Polbain bard, called '*Am Bata Uaine*', the Green Boat, he has a couple of lines, '*Feach thu ris a'Bhossom Mhor, Bata an Fhidhleir 's a Scaffag*', 'Have a go at the *Bossom Mor*, the Fiddler's boat and the scaffie'. Now, I think the *Bossom Mor* was owned by Big Angus Macleod, Polbain, who lived in the house recently renovated by Bill Drake called Castlehill, the *Bounty* was owned by the Fiddler, either the grandfather or father of Johnny Ali, and the scaffie was owned by the Bard himself. I always thought that these boats were Gairloch boats but Wayne refers to them as Fifies, so there's a puzzle. Perhaps Jim can help. They were fast, open, and fished for herring wherever the herring shoals came (MJM talks about this and their daring and excellent seamanship).[3]

That's why old boats matter. Ways of life, the personalities of great souls and the music and verse they made are evoked. I often wonder if we could catch 'jumbo' haddocks and whitings in Loch Broom and Broad Bay again if the fishing were done by handline from recreations of these craft. After all, the oyster fisheries have survived at Fowey because the craft that pursue it must work under sail. Trying to be realistic, there will always be a few livings to be made from sensitive tourism and fishing with low overheads and low impact. But of course, these do not amount to the value generated by a powerful modern fleet and the engineers, processors and retailers who are fed by it. The counter-argument is that the efficiency of fish-catchers now means that only a handful of vessels will be built and licensed, whether the rules are drawn up in Brussels, Westminster or Holyrood. You have to wonder if fishermen knew the writing was on the wall when the big landings were being made in Lochinver and Kinlochbervie in the 1990s.

NOTES

(1) Email from Ian Muir to author, 2021.

(2) Murdo John Maclean, recorded by Calum Iain Maclean, 1995 (SA1955.161). School of Scottish Studies Archives, University of Edinburgh. Transcribed from Gaelic by Roderick F. Macleod.

(3) Email from Kevin Macleod to author, 2021.

33
NORTHWEST MAINLAND AND THE HARD COST OF FISH

LICENSED FRENCH AND SPANISH DEEP-WATER vessels now work out of Lochinver. Some also dock in Ullapool. The local majority verdict seems to be that the reasons are complex and the ports need the commercial value brought by their landings and servicing. In UK terms, the value of the fishing industry to the total economy has fallen so far that a government can judge that it has no need to honour promises made for a new post-Brexit international deal. 'Official statistics on economic output of the fishing industry are volatile and can be significantly revised from year to year. According to the ONS, between 2018 and 2020 the sector contributed around 0.03% of total UK economic output and around 5% of the broader agriculture, forestry and fishing sector.'[1]

But in 2019 the same report concluded that 61 per cent of the economic output of the UK's fishing and aquaculture industries was generated in Scotland. The total number of fishers in the UK was then estimated at about 11,000, as opposed to about 20,000 in the mid 1990s. Despite the huge differences in populations, Scotland and England had very close to the same percentage of fishers in the UK's total tally (43 per cent in England, 42 per cent in Scotland). No wonder feelings run so high. Then there is the factor which can never be quantified – the real cost of fish.

From Land's End to Muckle Flugga, the subject of the fishing industry is so emotive because, like mining, many lives were lost in the attempt to make a living. Well-found offshore vessels, bristling with navigation aids, are still vulnerable. The character of the port of Kinlochbervie, at Loch Inchard, has long been set by its strong links to east-coast boatbuilding and ownership of vessels. The subject of the current state of the Scottish fishing industry and the boatbuilding and engineering that serve it is too complex for any attempt at a proper discussion here. Instead, I feel we cannot look to Kinlochbervie without remembering one particular craft and one tragedy out of many.

A name is often transferred through generations of boats. *Bon Ami* was a Hopeman-based steam drifter requisitioned by the Royal Navy in 1917. The same name was given to a multipurpose MFV built by Jones of Buckie, also for a Hopeman family. She was yard no. 88, launched in 1958. Her history is unusually intact as she is featured in a historical project. The quality of her build as well as her long, lean lines can be seen even in an image of her lying abandoned near Poole.[2] A current search, linking to the electronic reporting system, AIS, reveals that the same name is carried by a vessel registered in Ballantrae and now working out of Troon. But it was a Banff-registered *Bon Ami* (BF323) that was to embody how tragedy is still a part of the fishing industry.

Bon Ami often worked in contact with a sister ship, *Bon Accord*, under the same ownership. On 20 December 1985 she was making her way back to her normal working base at Kinlochbervie. The crew of six included a 16-year-old deckhand, Christopher Hunt. He had 'got a start' on the sister ship but then been transferred to the *Bon Ami*. Bonding with the new team had not gone so well and he had been undecided about rejoining a few days before: 'He obviously respected my point of view: I was his big brother after all. I convinced him to go back to the sea once more. He picked up his bag and I drove him down to the harbour and dropped him off. As he headed off, little did I know that this was the last time I would see him and within a couple of weeks our lives would be absolutely shattered.'[3]

The heartbreaking account is given by Roger Hunt in a memoir which is based on his thoughts as he is held hostage during terrorist attacks in Mumbai. On the night when everything changed, the wind was building up but conditions were probably not exceptionally bad for the time of year in that area. The vessels were making their way back to a harbour on the route they had followed as part of their normal working life. I was a watch officer at Stornoway Coastguard (Maritime Rescue Sub-Centre) at the time. The red 999 button lit and my Senior Watch Officer nodded for me to take the call. The harbour master at Kinlochbervie had a VHF set at home, tuned to the working channel normally used by the boats working out of the port. He told me he had copied the *Bon Ami* calling *Bon Accord*. They had grounded on a reef at Rubh na Leacaig in the approach and needed help. The harbour master asked us to call out the shore-based Coastguard Rescue Team. We had no direct radio link to the *Bon Ami* but could relay questions which could be communicated on the VHF. Normally we would shift to the international distress frequency (16) in an emergency but it was judged too risky to change. That line of communication was all we had. I was to stay on that line.

My colleague made the call-out and I listened as he also made an official request for the launch of Lochinver Lifeboat. At that time this was of a class of RNLI vessel which could make only 8 or 9 knots but could do that in just about any conditions. But this meant the lifeboat would take a matter of hours to reach the stranded boat. *Bon Accord* was close, but we could not know if they could work near enough to help without risking their own vessel. With an incoming heavy swell, one cable (0.1 of a nautical mile) could be as distant as the width of an ocean.

Our shore team was equipped with a Land Rover and trailer

A typical composite MFV, 1980s (three-quarter shelter-deck)

to transport heavy rocket-firing equipment. A light line could be fired out over a stranded vessel, if a team could get close enough. If the crew on the wreck could get hold of that they could pull out a hawser, which would then be tensioned so a 'breeches buoy' could be suspended from that line. It would then be pulled on an endless loop back and forth to take crew off, one by one. The method has saved many lives in the past but was discontinued in the 1990s. The largest ever number rescued by breeches buoy (66) was when the *Clan MacQuarry* grounded on the west coast of North Lewis on 30 January 1953. In other circumstances, as when the *Iolaire* grounded on Holm Point, the equipment could not be transported over rough terrain in time to be of use.

When it became clear that the *Bon Ami* could not be reached by *Bon Accord*, my Senior Watch Officer requested the scramble of an RAF rescue helicopter, but the nearest was stationed at Lossiemouth, over on the east coast. The temperature that night was another cruel twist. When there is a danger of icing, the helicopter must take a low-level route rather than fly the more direct way over mountains. That would also make the transit time a matter of hours rather than minutes.

There are precedents for taking crew off ships in heavy swell conditions. A report from Stornoway Lifeboat Station records a silver medal and two bronze ones, awarded to the cox and mechanics, when they went to the assistance of a small fishing vessel grounded on Sgeir Mhor in the approaches to Stornoway. In storm conditions on 30 January 1962, they floated a life raft downwind to the casualty but finally they had to use that to board the craft and carry the survivors off to the lifeboat.

One of my coastguard mentors told me how he had used a similar tactic, from the shore, to help survivors of a grounded ship at the Braigh, also just outside Stornoway. They could not rig a tripod to tension a hawser, in shingle, so they had the crew inflate a life raft to send back and fore through surf. Many a night I've asked myself if something similar could have been done for the *Bon Ami* crew. Why did I not think of these instances and propose them? Hindsight suggests a clarity which we just did not have, that night. The harbour master asked more than once for an ETA for the helicopter which was now fighting its way 'round the top' in deteriorating conditions but my colleague judged it would not help to let them know it would be a further two hours or so. This situation had occurred before and each time a report was sent, highlighting the gap in helicopter coverage, especially in winter conditions. Casualty reports also showed it was usually safer to stay with the ship. Another Stornoway Lifeboat rescue strengthened this argument.

On 29 September 1981, one of the large, new-generation trawlers grounded on Eilean Trodday off northern Skye. The hull, registered *Junella*, was also in contact with her sister ship. There was also a very heavy sea running and she could not get close enough to be of assistance. Another silver medal to the lifeboat cox Malcolm MacDonald acknowledges the seamanship involved in coming in close enough to take all 29 crew off.

But in December 1985 the *Bon Ami* was rolled off the reef into deep water before any assistance could reach her. None of the crew survived. It was the report of that terrible night that drove political pressure to result in the first contracts for civilian search and rescue helicopters stationed in Shetland and in the Solent as well as Stornoway. A bill put through Parliament by the MP for the Banff and Buchan area, home to the lost crew, also made the carrying of an electronic distress beacon mandatory. Out of that loss, many lives have certainly been saved.

We can't know the hell families went through, though Roger Hunt's frank narrative shares some of it. My colleague, the Senior Watch Officer that night, had to go through the ordeal of a Fatal Accident Inquiry. It was found that all that could have been done was done, but other colleagues concur that the pain of that night left another scar. That officer had his own problems, but the aftermath of that night might have been a factor in his taking his own life within a few years of the event.

The development of the Marine Accident Investigation Branch (MAIB), which scrutinises marine accidents along the same lines as its sister governmental organisation looks into aircraft accidents, has also led to frank reporting of lessons to be learned. In my 15 years in the coastguard service I was involved in countless incidents where a fishing vessel grounded close to a home harbour, on a route navigated countless times. When there are no survivors it's often not possible to be sure of what happened. From comparable accidents, fatigue is often a major factor. Fishermen work through hours which few in other occupations would tolerate. It's all too easy to drop your guard when you're nearly home. Often that is where the skipper or mate will judge they can take a break and see to tidying up or making the call home or to owner or buyer.

That's sometimes the time when a less experienced hand is trusted on the wheel. Even a trawler can be lifted and shoved across a narrow channel by confused seas. It's often worse when a high groundswell runs contrary to new strong breeze. Still, on a dirty night with high swell, it's sometimes incredibly difficult to make out marks or even navigation lights. I came across a frank admission of this in a yachtsman's blog on entering Kinlochbervie:

> From our waypoint it is just a matter of motoring in . . . avoiding the NCM [north cardinal mark] on the reef, and waiting until the harbour opens on the port bow. Be careful not to cut the corner but wait until you can see right in to the harbour before shaping a course between the channel markers. That sounds simple, and it is, apart from the fact that if you are coming up from the South West or across from Stornoway you cannot identify the entrance to Loch Inchard until you are almost upon it.[4]

NOTES

(1) House of Commons library report 'UK Fisheries Statistics', 16/11/2021: https:// researchbriefings.files.parliament.uk/documents/SN02788/SN02788.pdf.

(2) 'Bon Ami', on The SHIPS Project website: http://www.shipsproject.org/Wrecks/ Wk_BonAmi.html.

(3) Roger Hunt, Be Silent or Be Killed – A Scottish Banker under Siege in Mumbai's Terrorist Attacks *(Edinburgh, Luath, 2011). See chapter 3, 'Losing a Brother at Sea'.*

(4) Visit My Harbour website: www.visitmyharbour.com.

34
THE YOLES OF THE
NORTH COAST AND
SOUTH ISLES

IN 1981 A BOAT I'D always admired came up for sale. *Broad Bay* was 18 feet (nearly 5.5 metres) overall. She had quite a high mast and carried a high-peaked standing lug with a small jib tacked at her bow. This was a traditional hull but rigged so you could sail her single-handed. I had an idea of setting pots under sail and maybe just having the usual Seagull engine on a quarter-bracket, for getting out of trouble. It came as a shock to find she had been built in 1912, and had worked out of the bays of Harris, then Lewis, since the 1940s. The Fishery Office records showed that SY594 had first been Kirkwall registered. I read the handwritten entry of the place of build as 'Durness'. At that time I was an auxiliary coastguard, mainly watchkeeping. The coast-rescue network led to a phone conversation with a George Mackay, in the Durness team at that time. He was on the case and sent me a note before long: 'Your boat was built by Anson Mackay, "Arnarkie", Loch Eriboll. He and his father Angus were the only boatbuilders in Durness at that time. I was informed that they did build boats for Lewis customers, who sailed them from Loch Eriboll to Lewis.'

The *sgoth Niseach Jubilee* had just been renovated and there was a sweet 17-footer, *Bluebird*, also moored at the Port of Ness. You could have easily mistaken *Broad Bay* for a *sgoth*. So if these boats of the north coast, Orkney and Lewis are so similar, why is it worth spending time to observe variations? I would argue the reasons are similar as to why it is worth distinguishing between Fergusson, Peploe and Cadell. All three of these Colourists had studied at the Académie Julian in Paris. Their personalities and passions brought a distinct focus to their works. Peploe, for example, seems to be looking anew at the Iona landscape, his vision filtered by familiarity with Cézanne's landscapes. In the case of inshore fishing craft, features become favoured in a locality. And thus you can plot subtle shifts of shape in the yoles built all along the north coast for very similar but always challenging conditions, whoever was cutting the planks.

When it comes to Orkney and Shetland, these variations have prompted more than one doctoral study. The diversity is explored and celebrated perhaps because the innovations and departures from a Norwegian template say much about ways of life and island conditions. Because the boat is revered in these locations, there is a wealth of published material as well as curated displays and revived forms, now afloat. For that reason, I can't give as much space to the variations of north coast, Orcadian and Shetland craft as they deserve, but I'll try to outline some examples and direct the reader to existing resources.

Whenever I've driven the north coast, I've stopped off to look at any yoles, ashore or dried-out between tides. *Broad Bay* seemed a bit less deep in the keel, aft, than those I could see at about the same length. All of them were beamy and all of them carried that beam far astern. The builder had to steam and twist his larch to achieve a complex tucking-in to the sternpost but leaving a fullness until the last of that turn. That is in common with the *sgoth* but if anything, it might be even more pronounced in the north-coast yole.

I returned to photograph an example at Portskerra – one of many barely viable harbours and one which has sadly also seen its disasters. I was viewing the boat ashore but I'd also seen her moored with fore and aft anchors, ready to get out to the fish in good summer

'Southern Isles' yole (twin spritsails and jib)

conditions. Without the tape measure, I'd put this one at 18 feet, though I've seen some a bit shorter and some longer in neighbouring villages. This variation reflects boat building on Lewis too, where the Macleod family notebooks reveal every possible variation in a half or three-quarter *sgoth*, mainly according to the purse of the customer and the place where it would be kept. What didn't change much was the shape.

I would say the north-coast yole was a little bit deeper at the stern than her Lewis cousin. That would give additional grip. The sternpost might also rise higher to give a bit more height to the sheer-line there. In contrast, there is often a slight reverse sheer on a *sgoth*, at the stern, probably to let the fresh water run off when the boat is lying idle. There might well be a bit more freeboard, all round, in the north-coast yole. That would make rowing a bit less efficient but at that size, the boat would row fairly easily anyway. The method of a single iron pin for a corresponding eye fastened on the oar was also widely used across the Minch. Neighbouring boats might simply have a pair of timber 'thole pins', inserted in holes left for them in reinforced gunnels. From historic photos, it seems that different rigs were favoured for the north-coast yoles along the coast. There is nothing close to the North Lewis, lateen-like dipping lug, but a more conventional dipping lug (longer in the luff and shorter at the head) had its following.

It's when we look out to Stroma Island that we see what many would consider the ultimate development of a Norse-based inshore craft, adapted to suit conditions and purpose. There is a famous photo of the Stroma shore when the island had a strong population, around the turn from the nineteenth to twentieth centuries. The fleet of similar craft reflected that. The peak of the island's recorded population was 375 in 1901, but it was only 12 by 1961 and all had departed by the following year. Willy Bremner was among the last to be born on the island. Before he boarded *an Sulaire*, en route to the flotilla gathering at Wick, he took us up the road to his garden at Burray. We camped there and admired his Stroma yole. We could see she was iron-fastened and that this was a major renovation project. Once these fastenings bleed rust they tend to eat into the area around the nail so that large areas of planking will need replacement. We'd had a similar issue in renovation of older parts of 1935 *sgoth Jubilee*, which had not been refastened in copper during a 1970s renovation.

I had already studied examples of the Stroma yole in the courtyard of the Wick Heritage Museum. Willy's boat would have been about 22 feet overall, but with a big volume for that length. In beam she was mighty and yet fine at the bow with the lay of her planks falling near-vertical to form a distinct keel shape. Fullness, depth and freeboard were all much greater than that of *Broad Bay* or other South Isles yoles I'd admired in Stromness. As you'd expect, she was closer to the mainland boats, such as the one I'd admired in Portskerra. But this was on a different scale. You'd want every bit of that shape under you here, looking out to the rips of Pentland Firth. Several standing waves form off Stroma. I'd sailed through the Merry Men of Mey one night in *El Vigo*, to make best use of the west-setting stream. Even in a yacht designed to enter the Fastnet Race, this was a rodeo. Like the Swilkie to the north of the island, these tidal features are predictable to an extent. Still, a boat working in the area should have a decent chance of survival if caught out.

This is another craft which you might think could survive as a class by being moulded in modern materials. Then I thought back to Malcolm Henry's proposal. Better to see a local builder like Ian Richardson of Stromness or Peter Matheson, a Caithnessian now building boats in Govan, build a new one in the traditional way. A community boat, under oar and sail, could then meet the comparable craft of Lewis, Shetland and mainland Scotland for what would then in effect be a restricted class of racing and cruising under sail and oar. Maintenance of such a craft is a major issue and use of covers and access to a community boatshed are essential. The individual variations would work to advantage in different conditions, making for great interest in a gathering. Malcolm learned his own craft from Peter and also considers the Stroma yole as the ultimate development of the open inshore boat.

It is possible that this form, come a long way from Norwegian precedents, may have been a fairly recent development. According to the excellent website of the Orkney Historical Boats Society, most examples of this generation of full Stroma yoles were built between 1845 and 1913.[1] One Donald Smith is said to have learned boatbuilding from a South Ronaldsay builder, John Duncan. He also incorporated elements learned from wreckage of a Norwegian boat. This was applied to the local requirements, with load-carrying being a major factor, and the ability to survive in confused seas being the most vital. Records show building of boats up to 18 feet in the keel. That would correspond to the scale of the boat I'd seen in Willy's garden.

When it came to rig, photographs reveal variations. A dipping lug was favoured in smaller examples. Most of the larger class, over 18 feet or so, overall, carried twin masts. Like the South Isles yoles of Orkney, these could carry standing lugsails which did not have to be dipped or spritsails which were also handy and had the advantage of being easy to de-power (as I'd learned in Rathlin). In the larger sizes, sailing ability was certainly favoured over rowing. You could expect that, in an area which consistently experiences some of the most frequent and sustained strong breezes in the UK. You could also understand why a large sail area was shared between jib and two smaller sails rather than one larger main. This made things more manageable in a blow when the area of cloth would have to be reduced fast.

I now knew that *Broad Bay* was not built in Durness after all. She did not have either the depth or the freeboard. I was to come across a Deerness (South Orkney) yole of 18 feet and she could have been a twin. Looking back at a photocopy of her registration in Stornoway, the handwritten word seemed closer to that name. But it was in Stromness where I got a strong sense of a revival in the building and sailing of the South Isles yole.

Twice, I've made the passage from Lewis to Orkney in an open Lewis boat, powered by a lugsail, first in the full *sgoth an Sulaire* and then in the three-quarter *sgoth Jubilee*. Each time, the arrival brought me into the most welcoming of communities. Even those who didn't sail would come by the pontoon to see and compare the lines. Maurice Davison, skipper of the southern isles yole *Gremsa*, asked this stray Lewisman to join the crew for a voyage he'd been plotting for some time. The idea was a non-stop circumnavigation of an island which juts high from the sea. In an archipelago composed of green pastures bobbing about between the North Sea and the Atlantic, Hoy stands out, brown and bold. Several tideways collide around it. Sadly I had other work to do.

The sway from the ocean, in and out of Hoy Sound, and the outrun from Pentland Firth, present an immense challenge to a sailing vessel of any kind. From what I knew of these beamy yoles, they might be up to that adventure. Most would be about 18 feet (5.5 metres), but would also carry a short bowsprit. They had the characteristic beamy stern and sweet twist and tuck into the sternpost. Freeboard, fullness and draught aft all seemed to my eye a bit less than on the Stroma yole. It looked to me like there were two main types. Ian had worked on existing regatta traditions by building yoles tweaked to carry a very powerful though manageable sail. A high-peaked gunter on a stayed mast gave the advantages of a Bermudan rig but also retained a hint of the lugsail tradition. But you don't have to 'dip' the yard round the mast when you tack.

The power of this main would throw the boat off balance if only a small jib were run to the stem. It would have pronounced 'weather-helm'. A little tendency to pull towards the wind is not so bad, but too much of that and you're braking the boat with the rudder. Thus a downcurving bowsprit was developed to set a foresail with sufficient power to pull the bow back on track. The planking was brought up higher than would be ideal for a rowing boat. A foredeck and side decks of sheathed plywood or timber strips, according to the customer's taste and purse, also helped shed water when you drove her hard.

Then there was the ballast. No random stones here, but a neat, bolted-on addition to the keel. That would put counter-weight down where it mattered. These would be fast boats, but stable in the right hands and able to carry the canvas. But this more extreme rig was not for all. Maurice favoured the handiness of sharing the power between two near-equal spritsails, as line drawings and images, over the ages, depict. This would be seen as the 'traditional' rig though some examples, past and present, would use two standing-lugs. *Gremsa* also carried a smaller foresail. That lot amounted to a decent amount of power, but shared out along the length of the boat.

We rowed our own Lewis *sgoth* along to anchor within sight of The Pier Arts Centre that day, to nod to the new works inside the gallery which commented on her shape and materials. I removed the tiller to place in the room we'd been given in the gallery. It was made from a previous work I'd shown there some years before. Now the larch from the reclaimed work was laminated into this form. In effect an artwork had been recommissioned to get us to the gallery.

The permanent collection at The Pier still shows the founding benefactor's strong links with the St Ives artists, and there is a maritime emphasis. A painting by Orcadian artist and writer Stanley Cursiter celebrates a group of open original South Isles yoles in the geo at Yesnaby.[2] In our visiting exhibition, Colin Myers contributed a screenprint which imagined the planking of a particular Orcadian boat. My own previous work (in collaboration with Ian Richardson and Topher Dawson) had been based on a set of actual full-sized planks. After the tour of 'Green Waters' was complete, some of these planks were incorporated into the rebuild of *Broad Bay*, now donated to *Falmadair*. Colin had based his imagining of the shapes on a simple half-model he'd constructed out of scrap materials. We kept an eye out for *Gremsa* once our job was done. We were not the only ones ready to catch the ropes for Maurice and his crew. They were all quiet, allowing their faces to tell the story. Talk about low-key. Aye, they'd made it round Hoy, but not exactly non-stop. They'd had to wait a wee while for the turn of a tide. They'd got to that point just a bit too fast. So the thing to do was put a line over the side to pass the time. And they held up a decent ling to prove the point.

Back home, the Sail Hebrides committee, which organised a local boat festival, instituted an annual award named after Ed Anker, lost during his attempt at a solo circumnavigation. Ed had become a valued member of our community over a winter or two. Cruising logs and nominations could be submitted. I nominated Maurice and the crew of *Gremsa*. They had proved, once more, that both the hull and the rig of a traditional craft, in the right hands, could take on a weighty challenge. The judges, old friends of Ed from Scouting days, considered a good number of entries. Some had covered many more miles, but they reckoned the feat of *Gremsa* was closest to the spirit of our lost friend.

Maurice describes the range of factors that make a yole the shape it is. He also hints of another lost class of offshore craft:

> Major influences on local boats may be surprising to marina pleasure craft, having to haul them by hand up beaches every night, curved so they don't catch the rocks, light to lift over shingle and sea, wider beam to haul creels without swamping, and then how to stow 20 heavy creels. Creels still are our cash crop, to pay the rent.
>
> And then there is the tide, to sail at 10 knots is easy for slim or fat yoles, but to sail across another matter. The sea doesn't judge us, we just misjudge the sea.
>
> Saw an old photo of some huge *sgoth Niseach*, way over thirty feet long? We called these deep-sea boats gretboats.[3]

NOTES

(1) 'The Ness Yole and The Orkney Yawl – Two types of northern boat', Orkney Historic Boat Society website: https://www.ohbs.net/orkney-boats/.

(2) Stanley Cursiter, 'Geo at Yesnaby and Brough of Bigging' (Stromness, The Pier Arts Centre: https://artuk.org/discover/artworks/geo-at-yesnaby-and-brough-of-bigging-166948.

(3) Email to author from Maurice Davidson, 2021.

35
THE WESTRAY SKIFF AND THE FAIR ISLE YOLE

ALL THE FORECASTS HAD PROMISED light airs then change, following the fresh southerly which had taken us out clear of Tiumpan Head, Lewis. We drove the cutter-rigged *Spirit of Rema*, keeping well out from Cape Wrath but picking up a fair flood tide. The tactics brought us to a position abeam Papa Sound which leads into the shelter of Pierowall harbour. We'd had to milk light airs as the wind shifted and also await a turn of the tide to negotiate an entrance. That was when I realised Ed really did mean he carried an outboard 'for emergencies only'.

He'd bought it to get his small, liveaboard yacht, a Herreshoff 28, through the Patagonian channels. He'd resume his solo circumnavigation in the GRP shell fitted out by himself, the following year. For now, he was enjoying having the 'Hebridean autohelm' aboard. I could help him reach more of the landscape and of course the boats, of Hebrides, Orkney and Shetland. 'But,' I asked, 'doesn't any engine need a run now and again?' Ed's reply had its own logic, as did his approach to using transits and compass bearings rather than a GPS. 'Don't take all the fun out of it.'

I could run with that. It was also a way to kinship with the crews of the yoles gone before us, when oars were the only alternative propulsion. Ed did carry two great 'sweeps' and he wasn't afraid to use them in calms. At last we negotiated the turn into the pontoons, to sight the spruce pole of another small yacht, already esconced. We'd wondered if we might meet our young friends on their return from Norway. Soon our boat, like their 26-foot South Coast One Design (SCOD) *Dunderave*, had its solid-fuel hotpot stove going and the oilies were steaming.

John 'Dunderave' MacBeth and James Morrison had needed rest after surfing the last part of their North Sea passage in over 30 knots of breeze. Being young, they hadn't spent all their recovery time in their bunks. John and his team took part in the local sport, which is keen racing of the fleet of Westray yoles. The friendly harbourmaster had steered them in that direction, the way you might expect to be pointed towards galleries and sculptures in Florence. Now, our young friends took us to take a look at the craft which had enticed them onto the water again after all these hours in big seas.

James was my housemate as well as sailing companion for some years. He let the shape of these vessels speak for itself before sharing how their taste of racing, Westray-style, had gone. I already knew the scene was keen. My boatbuilder friend, Topher, told me he'd listened on the VHF to rescue boats at a regatta. Not one but three yoles were sailed under, to be picked up without much fuss.

The Westray skiff illustrates how a local development of form has been preserved, not by a museum but by being adapted for serious leisure. From James's description of a close race and from what I could observe, the fleet was also not 'one-design'. In that respect there are similarities with the Plockton scene, though the boats themselves are very different. Craft of working-boat origins tend to have variations, and maybe all boats do unless there are strictly applied measuring rules for one-design racing. The shape of each member of the fleet of skiffs was very similar, though one might have an inch or two over another. The type was originally another open boat, but partial decking has been added to these racers so they can be driven that bit harder. The shape itself is radically different from trends common to the whole family of Shetland craft, although Pierowall, Westray, is within a day's sail of Fair Isle or Foula. There is slight rake and rounding from the bow to the keel, but a pronounced rake at the stern. The beam is only one clue as to the much fuller shape. The keel also slopes back so the draught below the waterline increases aft (as with the Loch Fyne skiff). This will give more bite on the sea, at the stern. These features will decrease leeway and help her steer well. There is a large area in the rudder for a 15- to 16-foot craft. When the boat carries ballast – traditionally, selected rounded boulders packed at the interior of her keel – it also means she can carry that bit more cloth. Two or three keen crew, with little but their toes gripping the boat as they lean out, can also balance a big rig. And these were high sticks for a boat of under 16 feet, nose to tail.

The tapered masts may also have been borrowed from the Flying Fifteen design. Mainsails were nearly all Bermudan, with a very few showing an older, high-peaked gunter. I found it difficult to imagine anyone setting creels from these yoles. But of course a sensible fisherman would now have a GRP boat ready and just bristling with aerials and sensors for fish-finders. This fleet was for the purpose of having fun. But that means that this most elegant of shapes is maintained and made new. I'd already studied the shape as one, the 1912 *Emily*, had found its way to Stornoway. Dried out, you had to get behind her to see how there was a twist as well as a bend in her planking to tuck the wide beam in to the sternpost at the last moment. She also had sweet sheer – fairly high at the bow, like a McGruer racer-cruiser in fact, but the sheer on the skiff was even more pronounced at the stern.[1] A dip in freeboard, midships, would help her, under oars, but even there she would have more freeboard than the Fair Isle yoles. *Emily* had been wrecked, but parts of her wreckage were recycled into an exploration of plank shapes in the 'Green Waters' exhibition, originated at The Piers Arts Centre. In short, the skiffs of Northern

Early Fair Isle yole, with squaresail

Orkney were clearly a separate development of shape, though based on the same construction method as Norwegian and Shetland craft. They were wide and deep, and their original dipping or standing lug rigs must have been handier to tack than the Shetland squaresail. The rig and the shape of the vessel would lend themselves more to working under sail than oar, and not only when you found the breeze aft of the beam. That great beam would also lend itself to carrying a weight when it had to – stock or peat or provisions from island to island. Maybe a multipurpose Westray skiff has become a specialised racer, with a change of rig or tackle, but the shape under that rig was probably established long before any organised racing.

Despite the side decks, the rig, tackles and extravagant sails, the essential boat seemed to me to have more in common with the larger Stroma yole than it had with any of the craft from further up the island chain. Ed was keen to cruise Shetland, and I was keen to meet more boats and the folk who sailed them and those who built them. We should have stayed another night at hospitable Pierowall rather than try to catch another brief weather window to work to the north-east.

From the forecasts, it looked like we would have time to find shelter before the rising northerly really kicked in. We departed from Westray in good time and swung a wide arc at the turn, in the hope of keeping clear of the tide-rips or rost which can boil off the southern approach to Fair Isle. Yet it erupted around us as variable, curling whitecaps. The South Lighthouse seemed to be plunging and oscillating in turn. In a sturdy boat of 28 feet (8.5 metres), decked but not all that beamy, it was exhilarating. That was when I brought to mind the slim lines which are a distinguishing feature of the Fair Isle yole. As a Lewisman, I'd been taught that wide beam was good for riding out a sea. Aye, but these were not 'seas' or long waves, they were a snatching, grabbing, punching and foaming mass of white and turquoise waters. We were stopped for a brief period before tide and wind swayed to give us a bare few knots, enough to inch towards a south-facing bay and a north-facing harbour.

Winds seemed to be sweeping over an isthmus and raking across the bay, which had a fair few rocks to dodge. We would not be anchoring there. Ed considered we could not safely negotiate the transit which leads between more rocks into North Harbour, under staysail alone. He really meant it, the motor was only for emergencies. That long night, we came a few more degrees off the wind but still beating to the north. We left Sumburgh Head a good way to port. With over 30 knots of wind to face, I was happy not to experience the rost that develops off to our west and closer inshore. I had to wait another season or two before I would set foot on Fair Isle.

Unlike the larger examples of Orkney and Lewis boats, the long Fair Isle skiffs (mostly well over 20 feet) are at least as handy under oars as sail. When longlining, some boats would work further offshore and thus risk meeting the Sumburgh rost. I'd suggest that the Fair Isle skiff, though based originally on an imported Norwegian form, has been developed to be quick under oars, sail – when that is feasible –

and to use either method to get out of trouble. The Fair Isle skiff had to be substantial, but no heavier than it needed to be, for strength. Like the south-mainland boats (or Ness yole), she also had to carry a load, whether coalfish or peats.

She does not seem very deep below the waterline, but that keel is carried over much of a long length so it amounts to enough area to resist leeway (sideways drift). In that respect she is completely different from the skin boats built with no keel that are so dependent on great skill with oars to hold a course. The Fair Isle yole (or yoal) is also not very high above the waterline. That low 'sheer-line' makes for easier rowing. Her handy, small squaresail was enough for the easily driven hull form. Boat designs like this have remained so constant because experience has proved they work for the likely conditions.

A similar solution was achieved along the coasts of the southern mainland of Shetland, as described by Adrian G. Osler in *The Shetland Boat – South Mainland and Fair Isle*.[2] The mainland Ness yole is drawn out sharper at both ends to be more of a rowing craft which will cut through sea. But, like the Fair Isle boats, a squaresail was also carried to use when you safely could. Opinion seems to be a bit divided on whether the design has evolved much from its basis in imported kit boats. Thomas C. Gillmer covers a vast subject in *A History of Working Watercraft of the Western World*, so arguably there is not so much room for subtle distinctions: 'The Shetland Ness yole was simply an enlarged version of the Norway skiff. The component parts were often imported from Norway prefabricated.'[3]

Osler's more detailed study of the yoles of South Mainland and Fair Isle outlines history, seascape, detail of shape, build and rig. From the mid to late nineteenth century there were two main builders of the Ness 'yoal'. John Eunson was succeeded by a son, Geordie. George Johnson (1859–1941) did his apprenticeship with Scalloway boatbuilders before a spell in America. On return he began to build boats in the open before establishing a shed at Boddam by Voe. As always, the experience of the users was fed to the builders and an established form adapted. Locals would also know who built a yole from the look of it, so the builder's eye would also have its role.

Now I must hand over to Brian Wishart, a leading light in the current Shetland traditional boat scene. Brian recalls restoring the Ness yole *Kate* in 1986. Once again, I'm indebted to the generosity of a person from the area, taking the time to write to me to share knowledge and research:

> I have never been aboard a Fair Isle yoal, so need to be a little cautious in my comparison, but aided by the meticulous lines plans of both types in Adrian's book, we came to conclude that the Ness yoal, at least among those still in existence, is a slightly fuller boat in the forward sections than the Fair Isle yoal, which has virtually symmetrical water planes both fore and aft. Also the waterline beam of the Fair Isle yoal tends to be less than the Ness boats, so altogether they give the impression of being more tender. The longer waterline because of steeper stems on the Fair Isle boat might make the two similar in weight-carrying ability. It is possible, maybe likely, however that a century earlier there was less difference between the two types, since the Ness yoals we see now are largely the build of George Johnson, who in turn was apprenticed to Maykie Laurenson at Scalloway, in his youth, so may have adopted the fuller fore section being influenced from there.
>
> Talking about weight-carrying, these old fellows consistently said they would load their yoals until there was a handspan of freeboard amidships. This was when fishing in the 'Roost', up to 7 miles off the South end. They also said (to me intent on tacking the reluctant yoal without resorting to oars), that the handed-down rule was you were allowed up to three strokes of an oar to take her through the wind. This to me really

underlines the gradual transition between rowing as a principle means of propulsion, and having sail fill a new role, introduced gradually and cautiously over decades; perhaps generations.[4]

On Fair Isle or the mainland, vessels needed that natural buoyancy to take her crews out deeper than the saithe (coalfish) grounds and on to line-fish for haddock or ling or even halibut, in earlier days. There might be some trade-off in rowing speed for that load-carrying capacity. There were losses, as there were in every fleet of every type of craft around the world's coasts, but the designs are still built. Like all too many contemporary boatbuilders, Ian Best of Fair Isle has to run another job too, but he does continue to build the long and light but strong and full yoles. I'd not be the first to argue that the shape has greatly influenced the most successful of contemporary boats. The Scottish Coastal Rowing Association has flourished in its project of equipping coastal communities with competitive rowing craft and the skills to go with them. Iain Oughtred drew sweet lines and details for a new craft to be built from plywood, fastened and proofed with the contemporary material of epoxy resin. We've come a long way from ling-liver oil, but the wonder material needs stable and dry conditions.

Like the first imported Norwegian boats, a St Ayles skiff is built from a kit of pre-cut parts. There is licence for the trim as we saw at the first Skiff Worlds in Ullapool. Images of a fleet of skiffs launching in the surf hitting Portobello beach or Atlantic-rowing on the wild west side of Lewis seem to prove that lightness is a good quality, and shape is nearly everything.

I was to meet Ian Best at last when our *El Vigo* was alongside, in the north haven. My wife, Christine, and I gained a glimpse of the solidarity of a community that holds on, even with the risk of the isolation enforced by cancelled sailings and flights. New islanders have taken up the challenge as new sailors and rowers have attempted to keep the culture of our various vessels alive. It was not the time for technical questions. Ian and his daughter were mourning the early loss of a wife and mother. Lise Sinclair had already revisited Scandinavian kinship in her contemporary music and songwriting. We had all got together when Lise's song-suite, inspired by George Mackay Brown's great collection of stories, *A Time to Keep*, had its Edinburgh premiere. It is still available online and in CD form.[5] The work continues the shape and spirit of our maritime culture in the same way as these mysterious qualities are in the grain of the vessels built by Ian.

NOTES

(1) The shape is seen in restoration and new build, documented stage by stage in 'The Westray Skiff Project 2002', compiled by Daren Drever and Sam Harcus: http://www.globalislands.net/userfiles/scotland_6.pdf.

(2) Adrian G. Osler, The Shetland Boat – South Mainland and Fair Isle *(Lerwick and London, Shetland Amenity Trust/National Maritime Museum, 1983).*

(3) Thomas C. Gillmer, A History of Working Watercraft of the Western World *(Maine, International Marine, 1994). See p. 92 and cf. Peter F. Anson,* Fishing Boats and Fisher Folk on the East Coast of Scotland *(Boston, MA: E.P. Dutton & Co., 1930; reprinted J. M. Dent, 1971), pp. 24–5.*

(4) Email to author from Brian Wishart, 2021.

(5) A Time to Keep, *songs by Lise Sinclair based on the short stories of George Mackay Brown: background, samples and details on how to purchase can be found online at http://fair-isle.blogspot.com/2012/02/time-to-keep-songs-by-lise-sinclair.html.*

36
FROM THE NESS
YOLE TO THE
SIXAREEN

LIKE MANY BEFORE US, WE had nosed our way into the shelter of
Baltasound after departing from a snug anchorage at Ootskerries.
On that crossing, you are conscious you are at the north-eastern
extremities of something we usually call Scotland. Up here, you are
also conscious the name is a loose term only and the country is itself
composed of territories with their own histories. There seems more
sea than land, with deep-cut voes and sounds between the individual
islands. You meet vessels which await the weather window for the
transit to Norway. Ed would be following these in *Spirit of Rema*, the
boat he'd completed in a shed in New Zealand. That detour would
help my friend and skipper get used to sailing long periods on his own
again. He would also get a stamp in his passport and ship's papers so
he could show a break in his time of residency in the UK.

The North Sea crossing, solo, would be his prep for his attempt
to complete his solo circumnavigation via South Africa. But, for
now, we were sightseeing, as detours from his planned route. We had
ourselves been sighted. Our ropes were taken by a solid-looking fellow
who didn't have a Shetland voice.

'You're a bit of a way from home,' I said.

'Aye, I'm from Hoy.' Many years up top had not blunted the
twang of southern Orkney.

After the nods and the knots, Ed said he'd get the kettle on.

'Thanks, but I'll need to be heading home. You'll be wanting to see the Boat Haven?'

Ed did say we'd been figuring out tides for anchoring as close as we could get. 'Not tomorrow you won't and you're a bit late to go today. I'll be down for you at 10, if that would suit.'

It was taken as read that voyagers would be keen to visit the unique resource that has resulted from the passion of one boatbuilder. The next day, we did manage to make tea for our host before he drove us to the museum. Some might see painted boats of varying sizes with gear and tackle. Others would see subtle variations in the lines of a family of craft. To us, they were elegant solutions to one hell of a set of problems. Just how did folk gain a living, subsistence or cash economy, before the oil industry changed everything, for a time? Unlike Orkney, fertile slopes are scarce in the Shetland Isles. The vessel then becomes the main means of putting food on the board. There seems to be more keen interest in the variations of local craft in Shetland than anywhere else I've been. Will Maclean's title for an exhibition and book, *Symbols of Survival*, comes to mind. Now that the wind was blasting, we could see what a challenge that might be. Our host drove us to a vantage point where we could look to Muckle Flugga. The cod were running again and small craft were taking their picking when they could. Not today. Ed and I looked to each other. We were struggling to equate the slim, open craft we'd been studying with the waters which were building up and crashing into the bay where the lighthouse keeper's dwellings had been built. The long swells we had been able to ride the day before were now compressed into rocky channels. A rebound from skerries and cliffs added to their complexity. And then there was evidence of tidal velocity. Against the wind, that would get them standing, like the hairs on the back of your own neck.

My good friend Lawrence Tulloch had lived in these lightkeepers' cottages with his family when he was not 'on the rock'. Many of

Ness yole (contrast sixern for offshore work under sail)

his stories were passed on from his father, who was revered and recorded as 'a tradition bearer'. You could see why Shetlanders needed stories more than most. But how did they have such a sailing, rowing and boatbuilding tradition when they didn't have trees? Vessels were first imported from Norway, usually in kit form, a precursor of the Scandinavian flatpack approach. The clinker method provides strength and so planks can be lighter. Usually these were broad enough, to save time and make best use of the boards sawn from wide, slow-grown trees. They were joined with rivets, first in iron, but more recently in copper. A few 'frames' or ribs (known as 'bands' up this way) were joggled in later, at strategic stations, to provide stiffening. These would often be of oak, whereas the planks would be of a 'softwood' species, perhaps resinous pine or ideally larch.

The majority of Shetland-style craft are combination rowing and sailing vessels. The museum demonstrated the range. Narrower craft with lower sides lent themselves to propulsion by a number of oars. Rowing has become a serious leisure activity in latter-day Shetland.

Craft geared to this purpose are sufficiently close to those of the Faroe Islands that the neighbours can meet for inter-island regattas. A recent example was ashore at Baltasound harbour, race-ready.

The multipurpose and mid-sized 'fourern' showed a different emphasis. These had slightly deeper and longer keels – and a bit more beam. Both factors would help them resist drift and allow for a decent area of cloth to drive the vessel through heavy seas. We could see how a sporting or competitive drive had shaped examples of the craft into the 'Shetland model'. These had completely altered in character. The racing boats had tapered timbers where weight could be shaved off. They had planks which fell close to the vertical to form a deeper keel that would allow her to be driven to windward without sliding sideways. Masts were higher and the area of sail extravagant. These would be twitchy.

The hull form in the Shetland racing skiff had come further from its workboat origin than the Westray skiff. Duncan Sandison, founder of the Unst Boat Haven, was the person who created *Maid of Thule*. Brian Wishart remembers how the boatbuilder brought this unballasted craft to the inter-club regatta in 1956, and racing was never the same again. Subsequent photographs show a 'Maid class' of very like boats. Each has a turned-down short sprit to take the slightly overlapping foresail out. The crisp mains are again borrowed from the Flying Fifteen design. Timber masts have rake and pre-bend. The shells themselves are light but the cloth is carried by having all three crew hiking out. This is clearly seen in a photograph of four like 'Maids' starting at Scalloway regatta, on the west Mainland.

The museum was methodical in displaying examples of many variants of Shetland craft, not only in scale. Some had to carry loads – a ton of fish, for example – and others were shaped for an inshore fishing where you could hope to dart out and back in an opportunist way, between big blows. A turn of speed was an advantage in both. But outside the Unst Boat Haven we saw the culmination of a working craft built to work offshore under both oars and sail. In 1988 Duncan Sandison recreated a powerful vessel with its own strong tradition in *Far Haaf.* As with the *sgoth Niseach,* the time came when there were no intact examples of the big class of boat built for an offshore fishery. The sixern (or 'sixareen') developed into a powerful load carrier, to engage in the 'haaf-fishing'. This became a commercial rather than subsistence fishery in the 1800s. Cod and ling were cured and dried, racked out along the coast before being exported, as on Lewis. Statistical accounts reveal a significant tonnage. Some say the lairds who financed much of the boatbuilding put pressure on their tenants to risk their lives to pay their rents. For others, the earnings opened up new horizons. In July of 1881 a terrible price was exacted when 17 vessels carrying 105 men were lost in a sudden gale. Risk continues. The first *Far Haaf* was broken up by a storm, but the determined builder made her anew.

For the boatbuilders, the offshore fishery was a good time. Timber was still imported, of course, but vessels were shaped by the Shetland artisans. There have been several detailed studies of both the Norwegian origins of Shetland craft and the development of distinctive forms for local conditions such as the sixern.[1] Scholarship has combined with seamanship and racing experience to produce works which combine analysis with description. Charles Sandison's study, *The Sixareen and Her Racing Descendants,* was first published in Lerwick in 1954 (by T. and J. Manson). This is the strongest evidence that the process of refining a working craft was not so different from that in developing a successful racing yacht. In fact, the evidence reveals that the passage times of the sixareen (or sixern) in relation to their theoretical maximum speed for waterline length stand comparison with the work of any yacht designer. Yet there was very little difference between measurements taken from examples by different builders in different areas of Shetland.

Ed and I lingered by the example now on show ashore on Unst. We put our fingers to the features which showed how strength could be given without adding weight. In that respect, racing boats and workboats were alike. The sixern would run to over 30 feet (about 9.2 metres) overall. Her beam (about a third her length) and freeboard would be substantial, as would her strengthening frames and thwarts (tafts). Names of parts still show Norse origins, such as the term 'rakki' for a shaped timber traveller to slide the yard up the mast. Her rig developed from the Viking squaresail to an asymmetric form which could be 'dipped' round the mast to help her beat to windward. Work and racing boats with the modified squaresail would add sophisticated controls such as tackles which improved the forward sail shape by tensioning an area of the luff to the bow. She'd have been heavy enough to handle, but the power from six long oars or that expanse of flax or cotton would help her drive through ocean conditions with crew, catch and all. She couldn't have been built heavier because she had to be hauled up and down a boulder-beach. Most had short working lives, though sometimes precious planking was salvaged to contribute to a smaller inshore craft.

After we'd meandered a seaway back to Lerwick, Ed and I entered the arresting architecture of the maritime museum, whose shape evokes the sails of former fleets. Marc Chivers is preparing to publish his PhD thesis to add to the literature of these craft. A previously published paper of his summarises the relationship between imported craft and local development: 'What is now apparent is that boatbuilding was taking place in the eighteenth century on Shetland, and it is clear that Shetland boatbuilders were skilled and able to build boats from scratch but that the convenience of the boat trade with Norway suited the needs of the fishing industry at that time, and it was only when the needs of the fishing industry changed that Shetlanders began to build boats to their own specifications.'[2]

We also noted that the long-established engineering firm, Malakoff, was building in steel. The Promote Shetland website quotes a young manager, Ryan Stevenson, who is steeped in Shetland rowing and sailing culture, and the music scene too. It's not all about harking back to old ways, it does seem to be about carrying something forward: '"We want to create a sustainable boat-building business that means jobs like this stay in Shetland," says Ryan. "We want to keep work here, and bring in more from outside. Local is best, because the clients that are using these boats can come and meet us, and make alterations with us."'[3]

Moored alongside the museum was another example of the sixern, *Vaila Mae*.[4] She is based on lines taken from the only surviving original sixern hull, now on display in the museum. Surely this sets a precedent for preserving a valuable historic craft while giving new generations the experience of rowing and sailing the type? From the cockpit of *Spirit of Rema* we later watched local experts show some visitors the ropes. The distinctive shape of the dipping squaresail is a practical thing but also a symbol of continuation. The craft went at speed across the harbour. I was to meet Brian Wishart later. He is a committed activist in maintaining traditions of small-craft sailing in Shetland.

We found much shared ground in the approach taken by *Falmadair* on Lewis and the recently formed Shetland Maritime Heritage Society. Brian shared detailed operating guidelines and a summary of the large number of individual tasks which must be combined to sail a sixern safely. These are similar to the issues in tacking and gybing *an Sulaire*. One significant difference is that the sixern has tensioned rope stays in place, so the yard has to be placed carefully so as not to snag these. The single combined halyard and stay of the *sgoth Niseach* is simpler but leaves the rig completely unstayed if the wind is taken on the wrong side. An accidental gybe is dangerous on any boat but a potential disaster on a powerful *sgoth*.

Whether participating in sailing or observing from the shore, a vessel like the sixern instils a sense of pride, maybe not that different from that evoked by the timber Grand Prix yachts of their day on the Clyde. Maybe more, because sixern and fourern played a part in keeping forebears of present Shetlanders on their home ground. I was reminded of a public interview with John Murdo Macleod on Lewis. I put to him the question raised by so many passers-by when a team was working on a half *sgoth*, a three quarter *sgoth* and a full-sized craft. The finesse of their shapes would be discussed for ever.

'As one who built examples of all of these, which one really is the most beautiful of all?'

'The one best suited for the purpose it was built for,' he said.

Stories and boats go together. You might lose one if you lose the other. Here's a tale of the longline fishing, but in a much smaller craft than the sixern. It is set in Fetlar, a geography I can picture, as Ed and I found good holding in its sandy bay. In the same way as a wide range of various types of vernacular craft compose a whole library of Shetland craft, tales of selkie-folk, male and female, amount to a mythology.[5]

They say the Fetlar men were very proud when it came to the fishing. You could say that of the whole of Shetland. It's said of Orcadians and Hebrideans too. But the Fetlar men were even more keen. One winter, in the north of Shetland, it was very difficult to get a boat out. Hardly a lull between the gales. That's when the bet was made.

A stranger they thought must be a stormbound sailor made the wager with a Fetlar man. 'You'll not taste fresh fish till Yule.' That's all he said. He was a tall, dark fellow. He was very neat about his dress, as if his clothes were new, but he had no more to say for himself. And it looked like he was going to win. There was storm after storm. You couldn't get a boat into the sea in these conditions, far less survive it if you got out.

Then, just coming up to Tammasmas Eve – that would be about the 20th of December – there was a sudden calm. So the fisherman took his chance. There was nothing to use for bait. The rocks were well scoured by then, and any bit of salted fish had been eaten. But there was a bet on and that man was not going to be stuck.

So he took a bit of white rag to wrap round a hook. He needed something more, to entice the fish. So then he took his knife to his own foot, just enough to bleed it. He couldn't risk hurting a hand he'd need for the fishing. The white rag was smeared with his own blood – that was his bait.

He pulled the boat out himself but didn't risk going too far in case there was another change in the weather. Then he let his white and red lure into the green water. He was feeling for the lead hitting the bottom and jigging his line to lure the fish. Sure enough there was a tug and then a wriggling on the line. You could see the light colour of its long belly coming up over the maroon kelp. A small ling. What they call an *olik* up that way. That would do him. He'd win if he could get it home. Just then the sea rose very quickly and threatened to swamp his boat.

But he wasn't ready to give up yet. He'd brought along a *hjulk* of oil – a sealed small keg. And all the livers he'd kept from when they'd been able to get out – they were all boiled down into this good oil. You used it to oil the thwarts of the boat. He let go a fair bit, streaming the stuff, when he saw the first big wave building up behind him. Sure enough it dulled the crash and power of it.

But then he looked out over the sharp stern and saw a second huge wave building up. Again he spilled some oil, more still. Again it did the trick.

The third time, he looked astern to see a wave like no other. He knew it was more than the boat could take so he had nothing to lose. He threw the open keg of oil, the whole thing, over the stern of the boat as she started to rise. And sure enough the spilled mass of oil spread out. It was enough to dull the power of that big wave.

His boat took it, only just, surfing along, after the sea broke.

And that was him near enough back to the very geo he'd sailed out of. Willing hands came down to give him a lift pulling her up. Soon they were all sitting down to a good feed. It's a fine eating fish, an *olik*. So they had it, head and liver and all.

Some days after that, the fisherman met up with the dark one who'd made the wager. He didn't look in great shape. He had a deep scar right on his forehead where you couldn't hide it and a mouth full of broken teeth.

'What about our wager then?' the Fetlar man asked.

'I'm paid dear eneuch fir dat olik,' he said. 'Doo didna only smore me wi da oil but da soved me wi da oli hjulk an all.' ('I've paid plenty for that ling already. It wasn't enough to smother me in oil. You had to go and throw the cask in my face too.')

NOTES

(1) Charles Sandison, The Sixareen and Her Racing Decendants *(Lerwick, The Shetland Times, 2005).*

(2) Marc Chivers, 'Timber, boats & Shetland boatbuilding in the 1700's', The Shetland Boat: History, Folklore and Construction *illustrated blog including summaries of his own research: https://shetlandboat.wordpress.com/author/marcsboatsshetland/page/3/.*

(3) 'Meet the Boat Builder' blog, on Shetland, Islands of Opportunity website: https://www.shetland.org/blog/the-boat-builder.

(4) The website of the Shetland Times *quotes Brian Wishart on the use of the 'squaring reef' and has a video of the* Vaila Mae *charging along in a fair bit of sea: https://www.shetlandtimes.co.uk/2021/10/05/sixern-utilises-century-old-technology.*

(5) Email to author from the late Lawrence Tulloch, November 2009: 'In regard to the story of the Fetlar Fin-man I think that was a tale from Brusie Henderson. I think it was collected by the School of Scottish Studies. There are not that many stories of Fin-men in Shetland folklore. If it did not come from Brusie it would have come from Jeemsie Laurenson who was a native of Fetlar.'

According to Dr Andrew Jennings in a talk given at the Shetland Museum (25 March 2010), the Fetlar tale of the wager with the Finn was published with the quoted punchline in the Shetland Folk Book 2 *(1951). The* Shetland Folk Book *was published between 1947 and 1995 in nine volumes by the Shetland Folk Society, which was founded in 1945. The text of the lectures contains several other Finn traditions and is available online: https://www.uhi.ac.uk/en/research-enterprise/cultural/institute-for-northern-studies/research/conferences/previous-conferences-/the-finnfolk (link to UHI resource checked Oct. 2022).*

37
A BALLAD OF BOATS?

I'LL SIGN OFF NOW, BUT with another question rather than a conclusion. It was back home I met one more example of a Shetland boat. *Reevik*, built in Vidlin (north Mainland) joined the half *sgoth Callicvol*, as the only crafts of 'traditional' clenched clinker construction, larch on oak, in a fleet of nearly matching St Ayles skiffs (all epoxy fastened and coated plywood). Chris Mitchell, skipper of *Reevik*, showed me the mast-step and chainplates which showed she had been built, like so many Shetland craft, to carry sail, though her bias was clearly towards working under oars, as her performance among lighter skiffs proved.

From the position of the step, near midships, that was almost certainly a squaresail, in one of its variants. Our craft were beached in soft sand as the fleet was island-hopping in West Loch Roag. I got down low so I could enjoy the run of her planking. It seemed to me that she was something different again. She had not quite the fineness of the South Isles yole, but you could see how she would have a bit more resistance to leeway. This hull form had a touch more depth at the sternpost and a rising sheer at her stern. I thought of these features as a much narrower version of the Westray or even the Stroma way. So did the late Kenny Johnson, builder of *Reevik*, make a bit of a hop, skip and jump from tradition, or was it a more gradual variation that didn't spring from one person's brain? Do other boats built in that area show similar characteristics? As a comparison, there will usually be variants of an inherited narrative, say the Border ballad 'The Twa Corbies'. From my memory of a competitive rowing yole, ashore at Baltasound, I'm wondering if bonnie *Reevik* of Vidlin (now rowing on the Forth) is a close cousin to her. She is a balance of a shape that is relatively easily driven with one which will have excellent seakeeping.

One last question, but one I think I might be able to answer. Could the model for the new generation of epoxy-ply craft just as easily have been this example, rather than the Fair Isle yole (or yoal)? Maybe not, because her shape is a bit more complex. Even when the plywood strakes are pre-cut, there is still a bit of an art in coaxing them to lie down together. The concept of the rowing revival was that a community could easily invest in it, without a need to rely on the most specialist of skills. There are plenty of skills required in maintenance, in training, in rowing and most of all in keeping alive a culture that is as safe as it is friendly.

The racing yoles, like Reevik and the Faroese cousins, also carry six oars. That, of course, involves more members of the community than a four-oared boat like the St Ayles skiff. You could see that as an advantage in cultures where recreational rowing has remained strong or its revival is more advanced. At times, in other places, Lewis for example, it's been a struggle to find enough teams to keep the four-oared craft in regular use. But in the same way as successful working craft influenced others, all round Scotland, a new generation of rowers can learn from groups which have involved the widest sections of their home communities. This was brought home to me in a recent visit to Barra. Waiting at the slip for the Vatersay ferry, here was a near-pair of long, slim craft, both painted up in typical white with green highlights. The forms of Zulus and Fifies were once adopted by Castlebay fishers. Now the St Ayles skiff has taken on local accents.

Looking southwards from Unst and also looking back in time,

there are countless Scottish craft to study. The skills of boatbuilders, engineers, sailors, navigators and rowers, past and present, are all there, in the boatlines.

FURTHER READING

Addison, John M. and John Crawford, *BF Motor Fishing Boats*, vols 1–3 (Buckie and District Fishing Heritage Centre Ltd, 2014).

Addison, John M., John Crawford, Jim Farquhar, Ron Stewart, *Herd and Mackenzie – The Story of a Shipyard* (Buckie and District Fishing Heritage Centre Ltd, 2007).

— *Jones Buckie – The Story of a Shipyard* (Buckie and District Fishing Heritage Centre Ltd, 2008).

Anson, Peter, *Fishing Boats and Fisherfolks on the East Coast of Scotland* (New York, E.P. Dutton and Co, 1930; reprinted London, J.M. Dent, 1971). This artist and author turned his attention from the cathedrals of Europe (1929–36) to the fishing communties of Scotland. His works are now out of print but available in some libraries and sometimes second-hand.

Bathurst, Bella, *The Lighthouse Stevensons* (London, HarperCollins, 1999). Combines family history with history of engineering projects.

Christian, Jessica, *Iona Portrayed* (Strathpeffer, New Iona Press, 2000). See sections on Scottish Colourists for Scottish art relating to the Clyde, Iona and Ross of Mull.

Cursiter, Stanley, *Peploe; an intimate memoire of an Artist and of His Work* (London, Thomas Nelson, 1947). For a close study of Peploe by a fellow artist (compare Cursiter's Orcadian seascapes).

Fenton, Alexander, *The Northern Isles: Orkney and Shetland* (East Linton, Tuckwell Press, 1987).

Garner, John, *Modern Deep Sea Trawling Gear* (Oxford, Fishing News Books, 1967).

— *Modern Inshore Fishing Gear* (Oxford, Fishing News Books, 1973).

— *Deep Sea Trawling and Wing Trawling* (Port Glasgow, Gourock Ropework, 1985). On rigging gear.

Greenhill, Basil and Julian Mannering (eds), *Inshore Craft, Traditional Working Vessels of the British Isles* (Barnsley, Seaforth Publishing, 2013).

Halcrow, A. (ed.), *The Sail Fishermen of Shetland*, re-publication of earlier study focusing on larger herring drifters like the Swan, available online at https://www.shetlandfishermen.com/fleet.

Henderson, Sam and Peter Drummond, *The Purse Seiners* (Hexham, Maritime Info UK Ltd, republished Larvik, Norway by Krohn Johansen Forlag, 2004).

— *Fishing Boats of Campbeltown Shipyard* (Stroud, The History Press, 2009).

— *Sputniks and Spinningdales – a History of Pocket Trawlers* (Stroud, The History Press, 2011).

Henderson, Tom; Charles Johnson; James J. Laurenson; William Nicolson; *Shetland – Open Boat Days*, Charlie Simpson (ed.), (Lerwick, The Shetland Times, 2017).

Holdsworth, E.W.H., *Deep Sea Fishing and Fishing Boats* (reproduced on Kindle from publication circa 1874).

Love, John, *A Natural History of Lighthouses* (Dunbeath, Whittles Publishing, 2015).

Low, A. D. Morrison, *Northern Lights: The Age of Scottish Lighthouses* (Edinburgh, National Museums of Scotland and Royal Society of Arts, 2010). Strong on instruments and links to NMS collection and NLS records.

Macdonald, Murdo, *Scottish Art* (World of Art) (London, Thames and Hudson, 2000; new edition, 2021). See sections on Scottish Colourists for Scottish art relating to the Clyde, Iona and Ross of Mull.

Macleod, George (Seòras Chaluim Sheòrais), *Muir is Tìr* (Acair, Stornoway, 2005). Vessels, gear and sea-lore of the Isle of Lewis with reproductions of author's detailed drawings.

Macmillan, Duncan, *Scottish Art in the 20th Century, 1890–2001* (London, Transworld, 2001). See sections on Scottish Colourists for Scottish art relating to the Clyde, Iona and Ross of Mull.

Mair, Craig, *A Star for Seamen* (London, John Murray, 1978). Emphasis on Stevenson family history.

March, Edgar J., *Sailing Drifters: The Story of the Herring Luggers of England, Scotland and the Isle of Man* (London, Percival Marshall & Co, 1952).

— *Inshore Craft of Britain in the Days of Sail and Oar*, Volume One (Newton Abbot, David and Charles, 1970).

Marshall, Michael, *Fishing, the Coastal Tradition* (London, Batsford, 1987).

McQuarrie, Donald A., 'An Sgoth Niseach', in *Model Shipwright* No. 99, 1997.

Murray, Donald S., *For the Safety of All – A Story of Scotland's Lighthouses* (Edinburgh, Historic Environment Scotland and Northern Lighthouse Board 2021). A commissioned book combining a historical summary and retelling of written and oral history.

Nicolson, James R., *The Swan – Shetland's Legacy of Sail* (Lerwick, The Shetland Times, 1999).

Orkney Yole Association, *The Orkney Yole* (Stromness, 2021; available from The Secretary, OYA, 5 Manse Lane, Stromness, Orkney, KW16 3AP).

Osler, Adrian, *The Shetland Boat – South Mainland and Fair Isle* (Lerwick and London, Shetland Amenity Trust/National Maritime Museum, 1983, reprinted 2016). Comprehensive bibliography.

Pearson, Gavin, 'Gaelic Bards and Norwegian Rigs', in *Journal of the North Atlantic*, Special Volume 2013, pp. 26–34. Builds on earlier studies into medieval clinker boat building around the North Sea.

Pottinger, James A., *Fishing Boats of Scotland* (Stroud, The History Press, 2005).

— *Scottish Fishing Boats – A New Look* (Stroud, The History Press, 2010).

— *Wooden Fishing Boats of Scotland* (Stroud, The History Press, 2013).

— *Scotland's Fishing Boats – Old and New* (Stroud, The History Press, 2018).

Ross, Euan, *The Piper Calls the Tune* (Create Space Independent Publishing Platform, 2016). On the Scottish yachting scene.

Simpson, Charlie, *Shetland's Heritage of Sail* (Lerwick, The Shetland Times, 2011). Wide-ranging in history and in scale of craft.

Smylie, Michael, *Traditional Fishing Boats of Great Britain and Ireland – design history and evolution* (Shrewsbury, Waterline Books, 1999), pp. 50–1.

— *Herring – a History of the Silver Darlings* (Stroud, Tempus, 2004).

— *Thomas Summers and Co.* (Stroud, The History Press, 2020).

Stephen, Ian, 'Versed in Vessels: an Appreciation of Ian Hamilton Finlay's Fleet', in Alec Finlay (ed.), *Wood Notes Wild – Essays on the Poetry and Art of Ian Hamilton Finlay* (Birlinn, Edinburgh, 2001). On the boat works of Ian Hamilton Finlay.

Tanner, Matthew, *Scottish Fishing Boats* (Oxford, The Shire Library, 2009).

Wilson, Gloria, *Scottish Fishing Boats* (Cherry Burton, Hutton Press Ltd, 1995).

— *An Eye on the Coast – The Fishing Industry from Wick to Whitby* (Marlow, NPI Media Group, 2006).

— *Kindly Folk and Bonny Boats* (Stroud, The History Press, 2009).

— *Steadfast Boats and Fisher People* (Stroud, The History Press, 2011).

— *Forthright and Steadfast – The Wooden Fishing Boats of Richard Irvin and Sons* (London, Lodestar Books, 2017).

WEBSITES AND WEB PAGES
All websites last accessed in February 2022, unless otherwise noted.

www.castingthenet.scot/video/ring-netters-of-the-clyde/. List of ring-netters working in the Clyde.

www.clydeships.co.uk

www.dalmadan.com/?p=963. This site makes thorough research on Scotland's maritime history, and archived photographs freely available online. It is particularly strong on steamships and shipbuilding outwith the scope of this book.

fishingnews.co.uk/featured/swans-fishing-history-remembered/.

fishingnews.co.uk/news/ports-in-the-past-aberdeen/.

forum.woodenboat.com/showthread.php?226918-Scottish-Birlinn-(Galley)-Aileach. Comparisons between Aileach and the GalGael's 32-foot (9.75-metre) Orcuan.

www.gracesguide.co.uk/Mirrlees,_Bickerton_and_Day.

www.nationalgalleries.org/art-and-artists/776/iona-landscape-rocks. For image and discussion on Iona Landscape: Rocks, by Samuel John Peploe.

www.nationalhistoricships.org.uk/page/shipshape/scottish-fisheries-museum-anstruther.

www.nationalhistoricships.org.uk/register/1856/lively-hope. History of Lively Hope.

www.shetlandfishermen.com/fleet. As a contrast, this site reveals the range of contemporary fishing vessels working out of Shetland.

INDEX

315

BOATBUILDERS AND MODEL-MAKERS

PLACES

TRADITIONS RETOLD

ILLUSTRATIONS

The following sources are acknowledged by Christine Morrison.

p9: https://www.flickr.com/photos/tourscotland/5065112820/; p15: After a model by Macleod, George. National Maritime Museum, Greenwich. https://emuseum. aberdeencity.gov.uk/objects/64566/plan-showing-a-steam-drifter#; p21: After a model by Macleod, George. National Maritime Museum, Greenwich. https://www.rmg.co.uk/ collections/objects/rmgc-object-66795; p29: After a 3D model. https://www.wessexarch. co.uk/news/modelling-reaper; p37: After a model by Macleod, George. National Maritime Museum, Greenwich. https://www.rmg.co.uk/collections/objects/rmgc-object-65970; p46: https://fishingnews.co.uk/features/the-last-of-the-dual-purpose-herring-drifters-seine-netters-in-the-1960s/; p54: https://www.shipsnostalgia.com/media/glenugie-iii-pd347.264340/; p62: https://www.flickr.com/photos/david_christie/20705973049/ in/photostream/; p70: https://seaboardhistory.com/boats-and-disasters/; p78: https://sailboatdata.com/sailboat/victoria-30-paine; p88: https://en.wikipedia.org/ wiki/File:St_Ayles_Skiff_off_Anstruther.jpg; p96: https://www.scotfishmuseum.org/ white-wing-me-113.php; p100: https://lancegreenfield.wordpress.com/2019/02/03/ the-eyemouth-disaster-misty-return/; p112: https://www.dalmadan.com/?p=8226; p120: https://www.nationalhistoricships.org.uk/register/67/sir-walter-scott; p128: *Valkyrie. Classic Boat* magazine, #200, February 2005; p136: http://shaolinmonk.net/smeacock/ clyde19-24/pdfs/McGruer-A century of boatbuilding-Woodenboat1996.pdf; p146: After a model by Cresswell, J. https://www.shemaron.co.uk/fishing-communities-ribhinn-donn-ii/; p158: After line drawings by Oke, P.J. Royal Museums, Greenwich; p162: https://ccka.co.uk/newsite/traditional-sailing/; p170: https://www.ouririshheritage. org/content/new-contributions/donal-mac-polin-artwork-donated-to-national-museum-of-ireland-country-life; p176: Smylie, Michael. *Traditional Fishing Boats of Britain and Ireland*. 1999. Waterline Books; p182: https://www.apolloduck.com/boat/sailing-yachts-classic-yacht-for-sale/698659 from an original photo by Pat Law; p190: https:// www.wbta.co.uk/wbta/wbta-gallery; p198: https://www.shipsnostalgia.com/media/ jacobite-and-dawn-treader.306725/; p206: From original photo by Ian Stephen; p214: http://www.grantonhistory.org/ships_and_boats/nlb_vessels_pictures.htm; p226: https://www.grimsay.org/heritage/boats/find; p234: From an original photo by Kevin Whitworth. https://www.flickr.com/photos/jacurutu/; p244: From original photo, with kind permission from Peter McAlister; p253: Frame from cine film (1971) recorded by Margaret Stockall (deceased), with kind permission from Alex Eaton (Ullapool); p267: From original photo, with kind permission from Kevin Macleod (Coigach family); p275: Pottinger, James. *Wooden Fishing Boats of Scotland*. 2013. History Press; p281: https:// www.flickr.com/photos/29913197@N08/3107440135/in/album-72157611256243436/; p291: Ostler, Adrian. *The Shetland Boat, South Mainland and Fair Isle*. 1983. Photograph of model boat. Shetland Amenity Trust and National Maritime Museum; p299: https:// shetlandboat.wordpress.com/page/4/.